# Better Value Health Checks

## A PRACTICAL GUIDE

Nick Summerton

CRC Press is an imprint of the
Taylor & Francis Group, an **informa** business

CRC Press
Taylor & Francis Group
6000 Broken Sound Parkway NW, Suite 300
Boca Raton, FL 33487-2742



International Standard Book Number-13: 978-1-138-08800-9 (Paperback)
978-1-138-08803-0 (Hardback)



**Visit the Taylor & Francis Web site at**
**http://www.taylorandfrancis.com**

**and the CRC Press Web site at**
**http://www.crcpress.com**

Printed and bound in Great Britain by
TJ International Ltd, Padstow, Cornwall

# Better Value Health Checks

## A PRACTICAL GUIDE

# Contents

# Preface

Health checks are here to stay. However, many of the existing packages may offer little benefit to individuals, employers and, also, to the overall healthcare budget – some might even cause harm.

Having worked as a National Health Service (NHS) general practitioner for 30 years in addition to enjoying parallel existences in public health, clinical epidemiology and senior positions within three private screening organisations, I have acquired a broad perspective on health checks. For example, when addressing the earlier recognition of ovarian cancer my focus is not simply confined to the research evidence or the epidemiology but also considers the daily difficulties I face as a clinician when confronted by yet another individual with vague or non-specific abdominal symptoms.

In my experience those purchasing, procuring, designing or delivering health checks are all looking for some sensible advice in order to do things differently and better. Developing such recommendations would, undoubtedly, also be welcomed by those responsible for broader healthcare provision in appreciation of the potential impacts of ill-considered testing on hospitals. However, at present, such guidance is largely absent and, although I have lobbied for action in the United Kingdom with NHS public health colleagues and others, there seems little appetite to become involved.

I hope this text helps to fill the gap. Although I would not claim to have provided all the answers I have set out a new approach to health checks based on value.

# Author

**Dr. Nick Summerton** is an experienced general practitioner and public health physician with specific interests in diagnostics and screening. He is also a member of the Royal College of General Practitioners, a fellow of the Faculty of Public Health and has been awarded a doctorate from the University of Oxford for original work on primary care diagnostics and clinical epidemiology.

In addition to working as a general practitioner since 1988, he has occupied a variety of parallel positions as a public health consultant, medical director (National Health Service [NHS] and Bluecrest), clinical lead (BUPA and body mass index [BMI]), senior lecturer/reader and as a clinical advisor to NICE, the DH, Royal Colleges, print media and various commercial organisations.

Dr. Summerton has an extensive publication record in both research and education journals. His other books are *Diagnosing Cancer in Primary Care* (1999), *Medicine and Health Care in Roman Britain* (2007) and *Primary Care Diagnostics* (2011).

# Acknowledgements

In developing the ideas contained in this book I have been assisted by numerous individuals over many years. However, I am especially grateful to Professor Sir Muir Gray, Professor David Smith, Professor David Mant, Dr Wolfgang Seidl and Mrs Rita Courtier.

I should also like to thank the staff at CRC Press/Taylor & Francis for their encouragement and hard work in getting this book to press – in particular Alice Oven, Gabriel Schenk, Linda Leggio and Annie Lubinsky.

Finally, I should like to thank my family, Ailie, Katrina, Sian and Emily, for their constant support and encouragement.

# List of abbreviations

| | |
|---|---|
| AAA | Abdominal aortic aneurysm |
| AAT | Alpha-1 antitrypsin |
| ABPI | Ankle-brachial pressure index |
| ACCF | American College of Cardiology Foundation |
| ACR | Albumin-to-creatinine ratio |
| ACVD | Atherosclerotic cardiovascular disease |
| AF | Atrial fibrillation |
| AFP | Alpha-fetoprotein |
| AHA | American Heart Association |
| AIDS | Acquired immune deficiency syndrome |
| ALP | Alkaline phosphatase |
| ALT | Alanine aminotransferase |
| AMD | Age-related macular degeneration |
| Anti-CCP | Anti-cyclic citrullinated peptide |
| AST | Aspartate aminotransferase |
| AUDIT | Alcohol Use Disorders Identification Test |
| BCC | Basal cell carcinoma |
| BCG | Bacile Calmette-Guérin |
| BMD | Bone mineral density |
| BMI | Body mass index |
| BP | Blood pressure |
| BPH | Benign prostatic hyperplasia |
| CA-125 | Cancer antigen 125 |
| CBT | Cognitive behavioural therapy |
| CDC | Centers for Disease Control and Prevention |
| CDT | Carbohydrate deficient transferrin |
| CHD | Coronary heart disease |
| CIN | Cervical intraepithelial neoplasia |
| COPD | Chronic obstructive pulmonary disease |
| CRP | C-reactive protein |
| CT | Computed tomography |
| CVD | Cardiovascular disease |
| DH | Department of Health (United Kingdom) |
| DRE | Digital rectal examination |

| | |
|---|---|
| DXA | Dual-energy X-ray absorptiometry |
| ECG | Electrocardiogram |
| eGFR | Estimated glomerular filtration rate |
| ESR | Erythrocyte sedimentation rate |
| FAP | Familial adenomatosis polyposis |
| FDA | U.S. Food and Drug Administration |
| FEV1 | Forced expiratory volume in 1 second |
| FEV6 | Forced expiratory volume in 6 seconds |
| FH | Familial hypercholesterolaemia |
| FIT | Faecal immunochemical testing |
| FOBT | Faecal occult blood testing (using guaiac-based assays) |
| FRA-BOC | Familial Risk Assessment – Breast and Ovarian Cancer tool |
| FRAT | Falls Risk Assessment Tool |
| FRAX | Fracture Risk Assessment Tool |
| FVC | Forced vital capacity |
| GAD | Generalised anxiety disorder |
| GAD-7 | Generalised Anxiety Disorder Seven-Item Scale |
| GGT | Gamma-glutamyl transferase |
| GI | Gastrointestinal |
| GOLD | Global Initiative for Chronic Obstructive Lung Disease |
| GP | General practitioner |
| GPCOG | General Practitioner Assessment of Cognition |
| *H. pylori* | *Helicobacter pylori* |
| HbA1c | Glycated haemoglobin |
| HDL | High-density lipoprotein |
| HIV | Human immunodeficiency virus |
| HNPCC | Hereditary non-polyposis colorectal cancer (Lynch syndrome) |
| HPV | Human papillomavirus |
| HRT | Hormone replacement therapy |
| IGRA | Interferon-gamma release assay |
| LDL | Low-density lipoprotein |
| Lp-PLA2 | Lipoprotein-associated phospholipase A2 |
| LR | Likelihood ratio |
| LUTS | Lower urinary tract symptoms |
| MCV | Mean cell volume |
| MI | Myocardial infarction |
| MMS | Multimodal screening |
| MRI | Magnetic resonance imaging |
| NAFLD | Non-alcoholic fatty liver disease |
| NASH | Non-alcoholic steatohepatitis |
| NHS | National Health Service (United Kingdom) |
| NICE | National Institute for Health and Care Excellence |
| NSCLC | Non-small cell lung cancer |
| PAM | Patient activation measure |
| Pap | Papanicolaou cervical cytology smear |
| PD | Panic disorder |

| | |
|---|---|
| PHP | Personalised health plan |
| PHQ-9 | Patient Health Questionnaire |
| PoCT | Point-of-care testing |
| PROM | Patient Reported Outcome Measure |
| PSA | Prostate-specific antigen |
| RCT | Randomised controlled trial |
| ROC | Receiver operator characteristic |
| ROCA | Risk of Ovarian Cancer Algorithm |
| SAD | Social anxiety disorder |
| SCC | Squamous cell carcinoma |
| SCLC | Small cell lung cancer |
| SHIM | Sexual Health Inventory for Men |
| SIGN | Scottish Intercollegiate Guidelines Network |
| TB | Tuberculosis |
| TIA | Transient ischaemic attack |
| TPOAb | Thyroid peroxidase antibody |
| TSH | Thyroid-stimulating hormone |
| TVUS | Transvaginal ultrasound |
| USPSTF | U.S. Preventive Services Task Force |
| UVA/UVB | Ultraviolet A/B radiation |
| VC | Vital capacity |
| VOMIT | Victims of Medical Imaging Technology |
| WHO | World Health Organization |

# 1

# Introduction

Individual health checks – incorporating multiple components – have proved to be much more popular with the general public than with healthcare professionals or those responsible for government-funded national screening programmes. Many employers and organisations also struggled to decide if they are a good benefit to offer to workers and members.

In the private sector the emphasis seems to have been on providing packages incorporating as many tests as possible, with only minimal consideration being given to the impacts of such testing on health. As a GP I have often been faced with an anxious patient grasping a sheet of mildly abnormal blood results derived from such a health check. Even more concerning some private tests being offered are of doubtful validity, reliability or utility with the potential for significant harm.

Public-sector initiatives – such as the National Health Service (NHS) Health Check Programme focusing on cardiovascular disease prevention – have been equally disappointing. Here the testing being promoted has been determined primarily by considerations of cost. Having been personally involved in some of the preliminary discussions during the planning of the NHS Health Check Programme, I am aware of at least two key omissions from the portfolio: a screening electrocardiogram (ECG) for atrial fibrillation and ankle-brachial blood pressure index measurement to refine cardiovascular risk. Subsequent evaluations have found only minimal evidence for any beneficial effects of the programme.

However, there is a wealth of good research supporting the impacts of a range of preventative and earlier disease recognition initiatives on health. But it often seems that those designing or developing health checks cast only a cursory glance at such evidence before continuing with their search for new gimmicks or cheaper options. There is an urgent requirement for a fresh approach.

Within many health systems there is now a growing interest in 'value' as a more appropriate mechanism to design and deliver care. Value is defined as health outcomes achieved relative to the costs of care. Therefore, value increases when better outcomes are achieved at comparable (or lower) cost, or when equivalent outcomes are achieved at lower cost.

Carefully designed health checks – incorporating preventative activities, risk stratification, screening, early diagnosis and the mitigation of health problems due to ongoing heath conditions – ought to represent high-value care with improved outcomes and reductions in costs. For example, detecting early stage bowel cancer is associated with improvements in survival plus reduced levels of subsequent physical and psychological disability. Direct healthcare costs are also lower (because of less complex/invasive treatments), with less financial burden on individuals, families and employers due to faster recovery and less time off work.

By focusing on better value health checks, the emphasis moves away from cost-oriented or operational discussions about the process of health checks to the actual health benefits – or outcomes – achieved. Designing a better value health check should be about thinking backwards from the desired outcomes as opposed to just focusing on tests and dubious assessments of 'customer satisfaction'. For example, in relation to ovarian cancer, investing in annual CA-125 monitoring is a much better value option than having a face-to-face consultation with a private doctor to discuss symptoms and undertake an internal examination. It is always 'nice' to have some time off work to chat for an hour with a doctor, but is this really delivering the value that individuals, employers and insurance companies are seeking?

Various public health data sets certainly highlight that there is a considerable burden of premature death and disability that better value health checks could potentially help to address. Only around 15% of individuals with atrial fibrillation or alcohol problems are currently detected as well as less than 50% of individuals at raised cardiovascular risk due to increased blood pressure, lipid disorders or impaired glucose regulation.

Focusing on value might also highlight some less positive effects from ill-considered testing. For example, investigations such as 'total body imaging' can easily lead on to adverse outcomes due to the identification of incidental findings that, although of no pathological significance, generate considerable anxiety and, not infrequently, require some exploratory surgery to put an individual's mind at ease. Some low-cost imaging tests – such as the chest X-ray – are used inappropriately to reassure individuals that they have been 'screened' for lung cancer. They have not.

Taking time off work to see an NHS GP after a health check to run over results that have been inadequately explained is also not good value for money. A focus on value therefore ensures that we do not ignore the possible adverse consequences of health checks and that we design packages to ensure that the likely benefits outweigh any potential harms.

Above all, health checks need to be viewed as just one step in a process of care and might produce a variety of outputs. Outcomes are therefore about much more than what happens at the health check. For some individuals, the health check identifies nothing of significance, and they may just need a further checkup in the future. For others it highlights specific risk factors and they will need research-based guidance and support as to how to lower these risks with a view to preventing subsequent problems such as diabetes or cardiovascular disease. Another group will have an abnormal result that requires further investigations, and a few individuals might need some specific treatment or a surgical intervention.

This book focuses on the issues to be considered by organisations or individuals wishing to design and deliver better value health checks for adults in addition to those wanting to purchase or procure a package that will actually make a difference to health and wellbeing. The target audience is anyone with an interest in health checks within both the developed and the developing world.

Chapter 2 builds on this introduction and examines, in detail, some of the key challenges that need to be taken into account as well as highlighting the opportunities. Chapter 3 sets out a definition of a better value health check plus the six key architectural features in addition to some of the detailed operational issues that must be considered in seeking to enhance value.

Based on a careful review of good quality primary research evidence, systematic reviews and guidelines, Chapters 4–15 cover some specific diseases or disorders that might be considered for a better value health check focused on adults and appropriate for particular population groups. However, these chapters are offered up as a basis for an informed discussion between designers and developers and those undergoing, purchasing or procuring health checks as opposed to a proscriptive list.

Finally, there is a growing recognition that employers have both an interest in better value health checks (e.g. in relation to organisational outcomes such as productivity) as well as a key role in facilitating health improvements after a health check. Therefore, Chapter 16 specifically focuses on delivering better value for organisations.

# 2

# Health checks: Challenges and opportunities

## 2.1 WHAT ARE THE ISSUES WITH HEALTH CHECKS?

Health checks – also termed *multiphasic screenings, health assessments, periodic health examinations or evaluations* and *preventative health reviews* – have a long pedigree.

As far back as 1861 the British physician Horace Dobell put forward an argument for the regular assessment of apparently well individuals in order to identify developing health problems. Subsequently, in the United States, Gould suggested that everyone should undergo a regular – or periodic – health examination. The rationale behind both of these initiatives was that spotting diseases and disorders in their earliest stages would improve the effectiveness of treatment and, therefore, survival (1).

During the first half of the twentieth century health checks were enthusiastically embraced by the medical profession, life insurance organisations and companies. The annual comprehensive physical examination was endorsed by the American Medical Association in the 1920s and rapidly became a standard element of primary care in the United States. Those selling life insurance also began using health checks as a mechanism to assess the financial risk posed by applicants, with gradually increasing comprehensiveness and complexity over time. In addition, private industries and organisations viewed health checks as a way to comply with legislation in addition to enhancing productivity and efficiency. Moreover, within some companies, this interest evolved into a particular focus on senior executives as it was felt that the wellbeing of such individuals was especially important for the success of a company. For example, by the 1950s, the Greenbrier Clinic in the United States was running 3-day health checks for key clients and, in Japan, top executives were admitted to hospital for 5 days of health checks, known as the 'Human Dry Dock' (2).

Both Dobell and Gould advocated health checks for everyone but, for a time, their ideas were largely ignored. The first health checks were actually targeted at specific groups such as schoolchildren, military recruits and immigrants.

Some were also directed at the prevention or the earlier recognition of discrete conditions including dental problems, tuberculosis or cancers.

Nowadays it is simple to use any Internet search engine to find a myriad of distinct types of health checks. Across the developed world all adult age groups and both genders are well represented. It is also easy to unearth checks that focus on particular conditions such as heart disease, cancer, diabetes, liver or kidney problems, digestive disorders, hormonal issues, allergies, lifestyle choices (e.g. smoking, alcohol, diet and exercise), sexual health and joint and bone disorders. Some health checks have even been developed to prepare individuals for specific life events such as marriage, pregnancy or retirement.

Health checks also continue to be developed and delivered by a wide variety of groups: healthcare professionals, employers, health insurers, in addition to private and public/state healthcare providers.

Partly because of the various different historical influences on the evolution of the health check together with the wide variety of stakeholders with interests in health checks, it has become a portmanteau concept with considerable variation in relation to purposes, components and outputs. This raises many challenges for those seeking to design, purchase or procure health checks.

### 2.1.1 Purposes

Determining the primary purposes of a health check is about answering the question: '*Why are we doing this?*' But when I am asked to scrutinise an existing health check package or to comment on a proposed new development, I have frequently struggled to identify the health-related purposes of the individual components and, on some occasions, the package as a whole.

Not infrequently it appears as if the primary purposes of health checks developed by the private sector (including some insurance companies) are more associated with marketing, income generation and immediate customer satisfaction than with longer-term wellbeing. Linked to this there is often considerable emphasis on issues such as the use of advanced and innovative technologies, the length of time the assessment takes, the numbers of tests being offered along with the comfort and facilities of the screening environment. Politics can also play a part – for example, in January 2008 the UK prime minister Gordon Brown announced that 'everyone in England will have access to the right preventative health check-up… there will soon be check-ups on offer to monitor for heart disease, strokes, diabetes and kidney disease' (3).

The wellbeing-oriented purposes might also be hidden behind or incorporated within other secondary purposes such as the mitigation of insurance risks or enhanced employee productivity.

The other issue to consider in conjunction with the health-related purposes (i.e. *Why are we doing this?*) is the health-related outcomes (i.e. *What are we seeking to accomplish?*). Outcomes are events or happenings that occur because the health check has (more or less) achieved its health-related purposes.

In relation to purposes and outcomes, a frequent dilemma that arises for those developing health checks focused on earlier disease recognition is to decide if the check should be offered to all individuals or just to those without any symptoms. In other words, in enhancing earlier disease recognition should the purposes be 'diagnosis' and 'screening' or just 'screening'?

The Cochrane review on general health checks, for example, defined general health checks as involving 'a contact between a health professional and a person that is not motivated by symptoms and where several screening tests are performed to assess general health' (4).

Similarly, policy makers and many of my non-clinical public health colleagues often seem to see a clear-cut distinction between diagnosis and screening. In my view, this has led to some rather muddled thinking and siloed working with, for example, in England different bodies being charged with having responsibility for developing guidance on improving earlier symptomatic cancer diagnosis (the National Institute for Health and Care Excellence [NICE]) and cancer screening (the National Screening Committee). Even more worrying such a separation might actually lead to the general public ignoring some important cancer-related symptoms – such as new onset rectal bleeding discovered after being given the 'all clear' by bowel cancer screening or breast changes noticed after a normal mammogram.

If one of the primary purposes of a health check is to improve earlier disease recognition with a view to enhancing survival (outcome), the current tight division between diagnosis and screening makes no sense. There is also a requirement to appreciate that symptoms can be classified into two broad groupings: those that precipitate a consultation with a doctor (iatrotropic) and those that do not (non-iatrotropic) (5).

For those with an interest in health checks, there is a golden opportunity – and an urgent requirement – to think much more carefully about the health-related purposes of a health check and about how these purposes might contribute to delivering specific outcomes. Purposes and outcomes are considered in greater detail within Chapter 3 as they are two key elements of the architecture of a better value health check.

### 2.1.2 Components

Having personally reviewed numerous health checks developed by a variety of groups, it is clear that there is considerable variation in the selection of the individual components and also how they are assembled into a health check.

The possible elements that might be included in a health check are listed in Table 2.1.

There also seems to be an increasing tendency for private providers of health checks to select increasingly complex – or headline-catching – components such as advanced imaging or complex genetic testing. Unfortunately, the glitter of the new technology can easily divert attention from the basic requirements to ensure that there is robust research evidence concerning the accuracy of the new testing in addition to the impact of the technology on health-related outcomes.

Those designing or developing health checks also need to be aware that all of the elements of a health check – not simply the specified clinical data

Table 2.1 Health check components

| Components | Example content |
|---|---|
| Patient characteristics | Age, gender, ethnic origin<br>Lifestyle (smoking, alcohol, diet, exercise) |
| Medical history | Personal health, family health, medications, symptoms/ signs |
| Clinical examination | Specific measurements such as height, weight, waist circumference, blood pressure, pulse<br>General clinical examination |
| Risk assessment questionnaires (paper and computerised) | Generalised Anxiety Disorder Seven-Item Scale (GAD-7), Patient Health Questionnaire (PHQ-9) (depression), Fracture Risk Assessment Tool (FRAX), diabetes risk questionnaire, Alcohol Use Disorders Identification Test (AUDIT), Örebro (back problems) |
| Physiological testing | Electrocardiogram, spirometry, audiology, vision |
| Pathology | Biochemistry, haematology, immunology |
| Endoscopy | Sigmoidoscopy, colonoscopy, upper gastrointestinal endoscopy |
| Imaging | Plain X-rays, computed tomography, magnetic resonance imaging, ultrasound |
| Genetic testing | *BRCA* gene (breast cancer) |

components – may exert some influence on outcomes. As discussed in relation to the OXCHECK (6) and Ebeltoft (7) studies (see Section 2.2.2), invitation questionnaires and letters sent to the participants attending a health check might also have important impacts on wellbeing beyond the effects of the various measurements and investigations undertaken. It is therefore always best to think in terms of a package as opposed to individual elements.

Component variability is also seen in relation to the process of testing. In this context two particular aspects of variability are worth highlighting: information and eligibility.

#### 2.1.2.1 INFORMATION

Many people assume that health checks are always beneficial, but this is not always the case. Sadly, no test is 100% accurate; consequently, some 'normal' test results will be wrongly classified as 'abnormal' (false positives) and some 'abnormal' test results will be wrongly classified as 'normal' (false negatives).

Back in 1972 Rang coined the term 'Ulysses syndrome' for those individuals who are harmed as a result of a positive test that, on more detailed assessment, turns out to be a false positive finding (8). In common with Ulysses the individual sets out on a long journey – through a series of further investigations and assessments – with many adventures along the way. No positive outcomes derive from the experience but these individuals, like Ulysses, are left traumatised both physically and psychologically by their experiences.

Subsequently others have coined terms such as VOMIT (Victims of Medical Imaging Technology) to draw attention to the problems associated with ill-considered imaging (9). The possible adverse effects experienced here are not only linked to the radiation but also to the tendency to pick up incidental abnormalities that, although of no clinical significance, frequently require additional imaging and surgical procedures including biopsies to resolve matters.

The other area of concern is 'overdiagnosis' when conditions are detected that, although on the face of it might seem important, the subsequent care pathway reveals no impact of the diagnosis on outcomes (10). For example, most cancer screening programmes have been shown to enhance the recognition of conditions that are characterised as pre-cancers, dysplasia or atypical cells. By far the majority of these are harmless and will never become invasive cancers.

In seeking to balance benefits and harms the taxonomy developed by Harris and colleagues (11) is particularly helpful (Table 2.2).

Prostate-specific antigen (PSA) testing for prostate cancer serves as a particularly useful marker for some of the current challenges that need to be addressed by those with an interest in health checks.

As illustrated in Table 2.3, there are both pros and cons of PSA testing (12). Therefore, prior to testing, individuals need to be furnished with appropriate information on these issues – ideally with time to reflect on and discuss them.

However, there is much evidence that individuals are not receiving the information on this specific test that they should. For example, a questionnaire study of 219 men referred to a 'fast track' prostate cancer service in the United Kingdom with an elevated PSA result highlighted some worrying issues. Nearly two-thirds of the respondents were unaware that they had even had their PSA measured. Moreover, the information provided about the limitations of PSA testing and the consequences of a positive test result were also significantly deficient (13).

The state of pre-screening discussions about PSA testing in the United States was examined using data obtained in the 2012 and 2014 *Behavioural Risk Factor Surveillance System* surveys. Within a group of 217,053 men, 37% were told only about the advantages of PSA screening compared to 30% of men who were advised about both the advantages and the disadvantages. The trend between the two surveys was also concerning: men in 2014 were significantly more likely to have undergone PSA testing without having discussed either the advantages or the disadvantages than had been the case 2 years previously (14).

For those charged with designing, delivering or procuring health checks, I would argue that there is a particular responsibility to select components and assemble packages so that the health-related benefits outweigh any potential harms. Moreover, some would go even further proposing that the ethical standards ought to be particularly high for health checks – in comparison with, for example, a patient-initiated doctor consultation – as many individuals attending for a health check will have no pre-existing concerns.

As discussed in Chapter 3 informed, shared decision making should be a key element of any health check to ensure that the net outcomes are beneficial to the individual (i.e. where potential harms have been discussed and adequately considered before any testing takes place).

Table 2.2 Possible harms of health checks

| Possible area of harm to individuals from a health check | Explanation | Examples |
| --- | --- | --- |
| Physical harms | Physical problems such as disability, discomfort or new diagnoses resulting from initial testing, and any subsequent investigations and treatments | • Radiation exposure<br>• Adverse consequences of biopsies and other surgical procedures such as infections/bleeding<br>• Treatment-related problems |
| Psychological harms | Psychological problems such as anxiety, depression or condition-specific distress due to labelling | • The receipt of unexpected results from initial or subsequent investigations<br>• Waiting to receive results after a health check |
| Financial strain | Financial concerns (including strains on family and relationships) due to thinking about the possible consequences of the health check and being diagnosed with a disease or disorder | • Costs of missing work and other expenses due to subsequent interventions after a health check<br>• Disruption of established financial plans |
| Opportunity cost | Activities forgone because of time, effort and resources required to participate in the health check plus any subsequent investigations or referrals | • Distraction from other health-related activities (e.g. self-care, exercise, seeking help for other health problems)<br>• Less time with friends, family and other activities<br>• Hampers career progression and other interests |

Table 2.3 Pros and cons of PSA testing according to the UK Department of Health

| Pros of PSA testing | Cons of PSA testing |
| --- | --- |
| It may reassure you if the test result is normal | It can miss cancer and provide false reassurance |
| It may give you an indication of cancer before symptoms develop | It may lead to unnecessary worry and medical tests when there is no cancer |
| It may find cancer at an early stage, when treatment could prevent the cancer becoming more advanced | It cannot tell the difference between slow-growing and fast-growing cancer |
| PSA testing may reduce your risk of dying from prostate cancer by 21% | It may make you worry by finding slow-growing cancer that may never cause any symptoms or shorten your life |
| If treatment is successful, you may avoid the risks of advanced cancer | To save one life from prostate cancer, 27 men would have to be diagnosed with it |
| In cases of advanced cancer, treatment will usually extend life | |

#### 2.1.2.2 ELIGIBILITY

Currently, there seem to be two extremes when considering who should – or should not – be offered a particular health check. At one end of the spectrum entry to a health check package might be so tightly controlled that the potential impacts on health-related outcomes are significantly curtailed. At the other end, some private providers of health checks seem willing to offer unfettered access to testing governed more by an individual's ability to pay as opposed to their ability to benefit.

In the United Kingdom, the government-funded National Health Service (NHS) Health Check initiative falls into the first category. In this programme individuals can only have a check if they are aged 40–74 and have not already been diagnosed with a stroke, heart disease, type 2 diabetes or kidney problems. Also, people will be ineligible if they are being treated for high blood pressure or elevated cholesterol (15).

Unfortunately, due to the highly focused nature of this programme some important chances are being missed to improve health outcomes. For example, many individuals ineligible for an NHS Health Check remain at increased risk from cardiovascular diseases due to the inadequate control of modifiable risk factors. By excluding such individuals from health checks a golden opportunity is being lost to facilitate improvements in care and adherence to treatments with a view to reducing morbidity and mortality. Cancer screening uptake could also be enhanced by supplementing the current national programmes with opportunistic reminders (e.g. breast screening mammograms) or testing (e.g. faecal occult blood for colorectal cancer) in the context of an NHS Health Check.

Particular groups of adults are often inappropriately excluded from health checks such as older people (see Chapter 15), cancer survivors and those with physical or learning disabilities. Based on a systematic review of the available research evidence it has been concluded that health checks are cost-effective in identifying previously unrecognised health needs, including life-threatening conditions such as cancers and cardiovascular disease, amongst individuals with intellectual disabilities (16).

At the opposite extreme unregulated or uncontrolled testing might well pick up some important conditions, but such an approach is much more likely to generate a wealth of false-positive results and overdiagnoses. Furthermore, while the price of such testing might be high – suggesting, to some, 'high quality' – it is likely that these costs will be dwarfed by the subsequent resources required to address the raft of false-positive results. Such additional expenditure will not only fall on health services but also on individuals, their families and their employers.

Ideally a carefully considered balance needs to be struck between these extremes driven by value. In this context, it is also important to ensure that the systems are in place to deal with all the abnormalities identified by a health check with a view to impacting on outcomes. Part of the discordance between the research evidence for the effectiveness of individual tests and that for the effectiveness of testing combinations might relate to designing health checks that incorporate too many components (see Section 2.2).

A specific operational issue that often arises concerns the haphazard application of the exclusion criteria for specific tests linked to issues such as age, gender, medical history and physiological state. For example, according to most guidelines, PSA testing should not be undertaken in the presence of an active urinary infection, a history of ejaculation or heavy exercise in the previous 48 hours or having had a recent prostate biopsy (12). Coeliac testing (see Chapter 7) using antibody screening is unlikely to be helpful if an individual has already established themselves on a gluten-free diet. Faecal occult blood testing is also somewhat pointless if the individual has described any recent episodes of overt rectal bleeding (see Chapter 7).

It is always important to have some knowledge of an individual's current medical problems and past medical history, as assessing the relevance of a test or interpreting an abnormal result can be tricky if any findings are considered out of context. For example, the significance of an abnormal glycated haemoglobin (HbA1c) result will be different in an individual who is not already known to have diabetes than in a person who has established type 2 diabetes (see Chapter 9). In the former group it has roles in estimating the risk of developing diabetes and for the diagnosis of diabetes; in the latter it is useful in assessing diabetic control and the likelihood of developing complications.

Medications can also affect an individual's results – for example, in relation to thyroid (17), liver (18) or *Helicobacter pylori* (see Chapter 7) testing. Fasting, dehydration and excessive exercise also all need to be borne in mind when interpreting any abnormal findings.

Table 2.4 Possible effects of normal pregnancy on some common laboratory results

| Test | Possible effects of normal pregnancy on result |
| --- | --- |
| Haemoglobin | Decreased |
| White cell count | Increased |
| Thyroid | TSH: Slightly decreased during the first trimester, normal in the second trimester, slightly raised in the last trimester<br>Thyroxine: Increased over the first half of pregnancy |
| Liver | Bilirubin: Decreased<br>ALT/AST: Slightly decreased<br>ALP: Increased up to fourfold in the third trimester |
| Kidney | Sodium: Slightly decreased<br>Potassium: Slightly decreased<br>Urea: Decreased<br>Creatinine: Decreased |
| Cholesterol | Increased |
| Triglycerides | Increased |

In relation to general adult private health screening, one issue that seems to have caused me particular problems over the years is pregnancy. Changes in a woman's physiological state can mean that many 'normal' results might be categorised as 'abnormal' (19). Moreover, some tests – such as HbA1c – are not considered suitable for use in pregnancy, as reference ranges have not been firmly established (20). Some common pregnancy-related changes are detailed in Table 2.4.

### 2.1.3 Outputs

According to Boulware and colleagues, a health check consists of 'one or more visits with a healthcare provider to assess a patient's overall health and risk factors for preventable disease, and it results in the delivery of clinical preventative services that are tailored to a patient's age, sex, clinical risk factors and laboratory testing' (21). This definition is typical of many and emphasises the importance of considering the next steps after testing such as the provision of advice and, where appropriate, ongoing care.

If a health check is about improving health-related outcomes, it is not simply the initial testing that matters but also the subsequent care pathway. Therefore, if a disease or a disorder is detected as a result of a health check there are additional requirements to be confident that there is an available treatment (or surveillance plan), that the individual will benefit from the treatment and that it does not simply represent overdiagnosis.

As illustrated in Table 2.2 it is clear that harm can occur at any point in the health check process. To mitigate psychological distress, the way the findings from a health check are handled after testing is particularly important (including the results of any follow-up testing). It also needs to be recognised that the period between the health check and receiving the results can be extremely stressful.

The UK government's funded adult national screening programmes for breast cancer, bowel cancer, cervical cancer, diabetic retinopathy and abdominal aortic aneurysms have been commended for the consideration of the whole care pathway with an explicit focus on outputs and next steps (22). The following criteria derived from the UK Department of Health (DH) publication *Criteria for appraising the Viability, Effectiveness and Appropriateness of a Screening Programme* (23) (see the Appendix) highlight the issues that they feel warrant particular consideration after initial testing:

- There should be an agreed policy on the further diagnostic investigation of individuals with a positive test result and on the choices available to those individuals.
- There should be an effective intervention for patients identified through screening, with evidence that intervention at a pre-symptomatic phase leads to better outcomes for the screened individual compared with usual care.
- There should be agreed evidence-based policies covering which individuals should be offered interventions and the appropriate intervention to be offered.
- There should be evidence from high-quality randomised controlled trials that the screening programme is effective in reducing mortality or morbidity.
- There should be evidence that the complete screening programme (test, diagnostic procedures, treatment/intervention) is clinically, socially and ethically acceptable to health professionals and the public.
- The benefit gained by individuals from the screening programme should outweigh any harms, for example, from overdiagnosis, overtreatment, false positives, false reassurance, uncertain findings and complications.
- The opportunity cost of the screening programme (including testing, diagnosis and treatment, administration, training and quality assurance) should be economically balanced in relation to expenditure on medical care as a whole.
- Adequate staffing and facilities for testing, diagnosis, treatment and programme management should be available prior to the commencement of the screening programme.

Within the United Kingdom, over recent years, a lot of criticism has been levelled at those undertaking private health checks as it is often felt that there has been a lack of consideration for the outputs from any testing. Sending a previously healthy individual home from a health check with a raft of new and unaddressed worries is certainly a very poor outcome.

The DH has even compared their approach with the private sector and made the following comment: 'NHS screening programmes care for you throughout the whole process, including further treatment and care if you need it. In the case of private screening, the care and treatment you may need following screening may not be available from the provider' (24).

Having spent much of my career working within UK private health screening settings in addition to UK general practice one of the issues that I feel needs to be addressed is the information received by individuals after private testing. In my own experience there is often inadequate guidance in relation to any new problems identified and imprecise advice on mechanisms to improve health.

In a recent survey of 1170 UK GPs, 43% reported that they had seen an increase during the past 12 months in patients attending general practice after undergoing private health screening. While some of these visits may be appropriate there seems to be a growing concern amongst many of my GP colleagues that private screening companies are just taking advantage of the publicly funded service available via the NHS. Margaret McCartney, a leading commentator on health screening, was quoted as stating: 'I am concerned that there is little investigation of the impact of private health screening on the NHS. There are numerous companies whose management plan seems to consist of handing the patient a 50-page dossier and highlighting supposedly "abnormal" results which they are told to discuss with their GP' (25).

A previous survey from 2009 found similar results and, interestingly, when the findings were presented to the chief medical officer of a private screening company his response was as follows:

> My understanding of the UK healthcare system is that it treats for any condition irrespective of where it is diagnosed. The fact we found a disease does not relieve the NHS of its responsibility to the patient. A screening company cannot be responsible for a patient's treatment. It's the same as if a GP diagnoses a condition. They are not necessarily responsible for that patient, they may refer them to someone else. So, should GPs be stopped from referring to consultants? (26)

Clearly, this highlights a particular problem in health economies such as the United Kingdom where healthcare is funded through general taxation. Here there is a risk of some gaming of the system as it is quite possible to simply pass things back to the publicly funded NHS. However, even in other healthcare systems funded via social health insurance, community-based insurance or voluntary health insurance it is equally important to ensure that possible next steps are adequately covered before embarking on a health check.

In the United States, the Affordable Care Act (ACA) sought to address the issue of unnecessary or low value health checks (27). By virtue of the ACA, screening recommendations that are graded A or B according to the strength of the research evidence by the U.S. Preventive Services Task Force (USPSTF) (see Table 2.5) now must be covered by health insurance plans nationally (28). So, in terms of improving outcomes from cancer, the following areas are insured:

- Colorectal cancer screening tests for individuals aged 50–75.
- Mammograms every year or two for women over 40. Funding is also available for some other services to prevent breast cancer (e.g. consulting a

genetic counsellor or speaking with a doctor about medication to prevent breast cancer).
- Regular screening for cervical cancer and the HPV vaccine to prevent cervical cancer.

However, eluding these efforts to transform healthcare delivery and control costs is a growing direct-to-consumer medical marketplace. This enables low-value medical testing to be offered directly to the U.S. general public including, for example, genetic susceptibility testing for conditions such as Parkinson's disease. The direct-to-consumer market was valued at $15 million in 2010, $130 million in 2015 and is projected to reach $350 million by 2020. According to Lovett, public or private insurers are then left paying for any subsequent consultations or interventions even though the physician would not have initiated the testing cascade (29).

If we consider a health check as being about improving patient outcomes at comparable or lower cost than is currently the case for a specific care pathway, then this should encourage much greater scrutiny of the health checks being offered – including the outputs.

For some quite legitimate reasons relating to evidence interpretation, speed of implementation, costs and patient choice, many private health checks offer tests that might not be available routinely within publicly funded health systems such as the UK NHS or through basic health insurance schemes. For example, lung cancer screening (see Chapter 5) is not available in the United Kingdom – nor is lipoprotein-associated phospholipase A2 testing (see Chapter 4). So, it seems even more unreasonable to expect an individual's regular physician to advise on the results from tests which are quite unfamiliar to them. Moreover, such unfamiliarity is more likely to lead to onward referrals and investigations with adverse impacts on costs.

## 2.2 DO HEALTH CHECKS WORK?

Certain adult screening programmes for specific conditions have been subjected to rigorous assessment and, in the United Kingdom, the following have been recommended: breast cancer, bowel cancer, cervical cancer, diabetic retinopathy and abdominal aortic aneurysm (24).

In the United States, the USPSTF grades the topics listed in Table 2.5 as A or B recommendations for particular groups of non-pregnant adults (28).

But problems seem to arise when these individual screening tests or preventive interventions are aggregated together into a health check incorporating a variety of different components. While there is a considerable body of research evidence that many of the constituent components of health checks such as smoking advice, blood pressure management and statin prescribing are effective, the evidence for packages of tests is less clear cut. There are a number of possible reasons for this discordance:

- As discussed in Section 2.1 there seems to be tremendous variability in relation to the purposes, elements and outputs from health checks. Checks that are simply about assembling masses of clinical data from a battery of

Table 2.5 USPSTF recommendations

| Topic | Grade |
|---|---|
| Abdominal aortic aneurysm screening | B |
| Alcohol misuse: Screening and counselling | B |
| Aspirin preventive medication | B |
| Blood pressure screening | A |
| *BRCA* risk assessment and testing/counselling | B |
| Breast cancer preventive medications | B |
| Breast cancer screening | B |
| Cervical cancer screening | A |
| Chlamydia screening | B |
| Colorectal cancer screening | A |
| Depression screening | B |
| Diabetes screening | B |
| Fall prevention in older adults | B |
| Gonorrhoea screening | B |
| Healthy diet and physical activity counselling | B |
| Hepatitis B screening | B |
| Hepatitis C screening | B |
| HIV screening | A |
| Lung cancer screening | B |
| Obesity screening and counselling | B |
| Osteoporosis screening | B |
| Sexually transmitted infection counselling | B |
| Skin cancer behavioural counselling | B |
| Statin preventive medication | B |
| Tobacco use counselling and interventions | A |
| Tuberculosis screening | B |

tests with little consideration being given to the next steps are unlikely to have any significant impact on health-related outcomes.

- Tudor-Hart's inverse-care law, which states that the availability of good medical care tends to vary inversely with the needs of the population served, has been shown to apply to many areas of healthcare. In relation to health checks, there is evidence that those at highest risk for developing cardiovascular disease are least likely to attend for checkups (30). Individuals who accept an invitation for a health check have a relatively higher socioeconomic status, lower cardiovascular risk, less cardiovascular morbidity and lower mortality (31).
- Effective management of risks is less likely to occur in programmes that try to deal with too many risk factors simultaneously. For example, smoking cessation advice is considerably less effective when delivered in the context of multifactorial health checks (32).

Some research has been undertaken that has focused on the effectiveness – or ineffectiveness – of health checks involving multiple components. Furthermore, three systematic reviews have been published that have assembled and aggregated all the best-quality studies.

### 2.2.1 Reviews

In 2007 Boulware and colleagues examined 7039 articles for their systematic review; eventually selecting 50 publications based on 33 studies (10 randomised controlled trials and 23 observational studies) that satisfied their inclusion and quality criteria (21). They commented that the literature was complex and heterogeneous but, from their analysis, were able to conclude that health checks improve the delivery of some recommended preventive services such as cholesterol testing, cervical cancer screening and faecal occult blood testing and may also lessen patient worry. However, they could not find any evidence for effects on costs or mortality.

Subsequently, in 2012, Krogsbøll and his Cochrane associates obtained data from 14 good-quality randomised controlled trials with the aim of determining if general health checks reduced morbidity or mortality (4). Their results are summarised as follows:

- Nine trials reported mortality rates. Pooling these results did not identify any effect of health checks on total mortality.
- For cardiovascular mortality and cancer mortality there were no significant effects seen in the pooled results, but one study identified a reduction in cancer mortality as a result of health checks.
- No general effect of health checks on morbidity (well-defined clinical events such as heart problems, strokes, cancers, chest problems and other chronic disorders) was identified. However, one study found substantially more people in the checkup group with high blood pressure and high cholesterol.
- New diagnoses were reported and found in four studies.
- Impacts on secondary care were examined in five trials and no effects were identified in relation to admission rates, numbers of people admitted more than once, or the number of days in hospital.
- Disability was studied in three trials, but no significant impact was detected.
- Two trials found no evidence that health checks caused or reduced worry.
- Two trials demonstrated benefits on self-reported health. In the 1999 Inter99 study the researchers found significantly slower deterioration of both physical and mental health components in the intervention group (33).

A third systematic review was published in 2014 and included six trials based within general practice settings. The authors concluded that health checks were associated with statistically significant, albeit small, improvements in surrogate outcome measures (i.e. cholesterol, blood pressure and body mass index [BMI]), especially among high-risk patients (34).

Based on the first two of these reviews (4,21), the Society of General Internal Medicine made the following assertion as part of their 'Choosing Wisely' initiative: 'For adults without a chronic medical condition, mental health problem or other health concern don't perform annual health checks that include a comprehensive physical examination and lab testing' (35).

But there are two particular issues that need to be taken into account in relation to this statement and the underlying aggregated evidence.

#### 2.2.1.1 DEFINITION

The 'Choosing Wisely' declaration focused on 'routine health checks in asymptomatic patients' as something of low value that physicians and patients should question. But, as pointed out earlier, their definition of a health check is too restrictive in relation to improving outcomes by excluding individuals with symptoms.

Previously, in 1979, the Canadian Task Force on the Periodic Health Examination had concluded that the annual checkup should be abandoned in favour of a more selective approach determined by a person's age and gender (36).

#### 2.2.1.2 THE NATURE OF THE EVIDENCE

A number of concerns must be raised about the appropriateness of aggregating the individual studies into systematic reviews:

*Heterogeneity*: Within all of the reviews the individual studies included were quite dissimilar in terms of settings (community, general practice and workplace), geographical locations, the use of different healthcare professionals, the outcome measures and the interventions chosen. For example in the Krogsbøll review, 7 of the 14 studies had chest radiographs as one component of the check (see Chapter 5). It also excluded trials that targeted specific diseases (e.g. colon cancer screening), evaluated specific tests or only focused on elderly populations (4).

*Publication dates*: Most of the studies included in the reviews dated from before 1990 (one from 1963). In general, health checks conducted in the 1960s concentrated solely on detection whereas in the subsequent decade they started to consider how to manage the risk factors identified. It was only from the 1980s onwards that the focus of the health checks being evaluated in these reviews shifted from testing to testing plus intervening.

*Time frames*: There were significant differences between the studies in terms of length of follow-up (ranging from 4 to 22 years). If the period of follow-up is too short it may be that not enough time has been allowed for any significant effects to be detected. In this regard a salutary lesson is provided from the experience gained in the North Karelia community-based programme on cardiovascular disease prevention. The initial evidence from North Karelia showed no significant reduction in smoking or weight and a significant lowering of cholesterol only in males but not in females (37). The programme was nevertheless rolled out to the rest of Finland and was subsequently associated with a fall in coronary death rates of 80% with changes in cardiovascular risk factors (blood pressure, smoking and cholesterol) accounting for 60% of this mortality reduction (38).

*Outcome measures*: Although little impact was found on mortality by any of the systematic reviews, it is important to point out that most of the studies included were not originally designed to assess death rates. However, given the sheer weight of general research evidence linking the surrogate outcome measures of cholesterol, smoking and blood pressure to cardiovascular mortality and morbidity I would strongly argue that changes in these modifiable cardiovascular risk factors represent reasonable proxy markers for the success of a health check. Moreover, mortality is not the only outcome that matters to individuals attending health checks.

## 2.2.2 Individual evaluations

### 2.2.2.1 OXCHECK

The OXCHECK randomised controlled trial (6) was an attempt to assess the impact of health checks designed to reduce heart disease risk amongst individuals aged 35–64. Based within five urban general practices in Bedfordshire, United Kingdom, 2205 men and women who attended a health check in 1989–1990 and a re-examination in 1992–1993 (intervention group) were compared to 1916 controls who had an initial check in 1992–1993.

The study was nurse led with data being collected on blood pressure, cholesterol level, smoking status, weight, height and alcohol consumption. The OXCHECK was also a pragmatic – and real-world – approach to health checks with the follow-up intervention being negotiated between the nurse and the participant on an individual basis governed by a protocol for each risk factor.

The details of the various interventions included in OXCHECK are best summarised as presented in Table 2.6.

The screening update in the first round was 80% and, after 3 years, the following outcomes were reported as a result of the intervention:

- Mean serum cholesterol was significantly reduced by 3.1%.
- Self-reported saturated fat intake was significantly lowered.
- Small reductions in blood pressure were seen.
- But no effect was demonstrated on smoking rates or excessive alcohol use.

### 2.2.2.2 NHS HEALTH CHECK

Internationally, the UK's NHS Health Check Programme is a unique initiative, aiming to provide a routine structured clinical assessment and management for adults aged 40–74 years without a number of pre-existing conditions such as stroke, heart disease, type 2 diabetes or kidney problems. Also, as mentioned earlier, individuals are excluded if they are already being treated for high blood pressure or elevated cholesterol.

The NHS Health Check is made up of three key components: risk assessment, risk awareness and risk management. It was originally designed to be undertaken in GP surgeries and local pharmacies but in order to enhance accessibility checks were subsequently made available in other settings such as mobile units and leisure/sports centres.

Table 2.6 OXCHECK interventions

| Interventions | Details |
|---|---|
| Baseline questionnaire | • All potential participants were sent, prior to randomisation, a baseline questionnaire concerning smoking status, social status, attitudes to health together with the WHO chest pain symptoms questionnaire (39) |
| Nurses | • Nurses were trained in the identification and the modification of risk factors in addition to the use of a specific communication model. This model emphasised the importance of identifying and responding to a patients' concerns about their health, negotiating change according to an individual's priorities and reinforcing change through supportive follow-up<br>• The nurses attended a 2-day induction course, an annual study day and a monthly evening training session with medical and nursing coordinators |
| Health checks | • Health checks took around 45 minutes and were conducted by nurses according to a strict protocol<br>• Information was obtained on the patient's personal and family medical history (ischaemic heart disease, cancer, stroke, hypertension and diabetes), dietary intake (using a food frequency chart), smoking, alcohol intake and physical activity<br>• Blood pressure, height and weight were measured, and blood was taken for cholesterol estimation<br>• Patients deemed to be at 'high risk' were invited to attend for a 10- to 20-minute follow-up visit with a nurse and were counselled about risk factors |

The risk assessment entails collecting information on age, gender, smoking status, family history, ethnicity, physical activity and alcohol use in addition to measuring height, weight, blood pressure and blood cholesterol. A BMI and a cardiovascular risk score are also calculated.

Following an NHS Health Check, individuals can be referred on directly to publicly funded stop smoking programmes, alcohol misuse counselling, physical activity interventions and weight management services. However, people with raised blood pressure, elevated blood sugar or increased cardiovascular risk are simply passed back to their usual physician (i.e. an NHS GP).

Three evaluations have been undertaken of the impact of the NHS Health Check programme:

- Robson and colleagues looked at the data on the 214,295 individuals who had attended health checks in the first four years of the programme. They found that uptake was greater in people aged 60–74 (19.6%) compared to those aged

40–59 (9%). Interestingly, attendance was also higher in the more socially disadvantaged compared to the more affluent (14.9% versus 12.3%). In this descriptive study, they noted that 7844 new cases of hypertension, 1934 new cases of type 2 diabetes and 807 new cases of chronic kidney disease were identified. Moreover, of the 27,624 individuals referred to their GP as being at highest cardiovascular risk, 19.3% were started on statins and 8.8% were commenced on anti-hypertensive therapy (40).

- In an attempt to discover if the new cases of hypertension, coronary heart disease, chronic kidney disease, atrial fibrillation and diabetes identified could be ascribed to the programme, 38 GP practices providing heath checks were matched to a comparable group of 41 practices that did not provide health checks. There was no difference in the prevalence of all five conditions between the two groups of practices suggesting a lack of any significant impact from an NHS Health Check (41).
- Chang and colleagues examined the electronic medical records for a randomly selected sample of 138,788 patients eligible for an NHS Health Check and registered with 462 general practices. Overall, 21.4% had participated in a health check and the impact was calculated as a net reduction in the 10-year risk of cardiovascular disease of 0.21%. This is equivalent to one cardiovascular event – such as a stroke or heart attack – being avoided each year for every 4762 individuals who attend an NHS Health Check. There were also very small improvements in blood pressure, cholesterol levels and BMI but no impact on smoking rates (42).

Although the NHS Health Check programme has to be commended for improving accessibility in addition to referring or signposting individuals onto other services, any health impact appears, at best, modest. The issue in relation to the overly tight focus of the programme with many individuals being ineligible has already been highlighted. Also there is a continuing requirement to ensure that the services to which individuals are referred actually work.

The other issue about the NHS Health Check programme is that, although it relies on GPs acting on the findings, there is a growing gulf between GPs and the NHS Health Check programme. In a recent survey, only 22% of 517 GPs in England backed the approach; 90% felt that there was insufficient evidence to support the scheme, while 9% said they would pull out of offering the checks themselves in future years (43). This matters as, without GP involvement to deal with any abnormal findings, the potential impacts on outcomes will not be realised. Those designing or delivering health checks – whether private or public – always need to consider the whole pathway of care downstream from the initial assessment.

#### 2.2.2.3 EBELTOFT

Ebeltoft is a coastal town in Denmark with around 13,000 inhabitants and four general practices (with nine general practitioners). In September 1991, a random sample of 2000 individuals drawn from a list of all the men and women aged 30–49 years registered with the four practices were invited to participate in an evaluation of the effectiveness of health checks (7). The 1370 individuals agreeing to take part were then divided into three approximately equal groups – a control group and two health check groups (A and B). Stratified randomisation was used to ensure that all three divisions were comparable at the onset of the study in relation to age, gender, BMI and smoking status.

The individuals allocated to group A were given a health check which included screening for cardiovascular risk factors, lung and liver function, fitness, vision and hearing. This division also received written feedback from their GPs.

The individuals within group B were given a health check and written feedback; in addition, they were provided with an opportunity to attend their GP for a focused discussion.

As in all health checks it is important to be clear about all the components, not simply the specified tests, as every element will exert some influence on the outcomes. This detail matters to those designing health checks if there is a desire to replicate any of the positive effects identified in any evaluation. The various interventions included in Ebeltoft are summarised in Table 2.7.

After 5 years of follow-up, there were no significant differences between the findings in the two health check groups (A and B) so the data were aggregated. The combined results from the two groups were as follows:

- At initial screening a heightened cardiovascular risk was noted in 11.4%, raised cholesterol in 9.7%, high blood pressure in 9.6% and elevated liver enzymes in 12.6% (7).
- After 5 years – and in comparison with the control group – there were significant reductions in cardiovascular risk, blood pressure, and total cholesterol amongst those undergoing health checks (44). In the subgroup of individuals who were overweight there were also significant reductions in BMI and more significant reductions in blood pressure than in the whole group. Moreover, no long-term psychological effects were identified after information about increased cardiovascular risk had been shared with those undergoing health checks (45).
- In relation to healthcare costs there was no evidence for any effect on hospital admission rates or specialist referrals due to the checks nor any increase in GP visits following the checks (46–48).

The overall conclusion of the Ebeltoft research team was that preventive health checks and consultations in primary care for 30 to 49 year olds produced significantly improved cardiovascular outcomes without extra direct and total costs over a 5-year follow-up period (49).

The reasons why there were no differences between the health check groups (A and B) might be explained by some contamination in the interventions between the two groups. For example, all participants who had been advised that they had an elevated cardiovascular risk were encouraged to see their GP regardless of their randomisation group. There was also nothing to stop members of either intervention group visiting their own GPs or discussing matters with others within the Ebeltoft community.

Table 2.7 Ebeltoft interventions

| Interventions | Details |
| --- | --- |
| Invitation questionnaire | • All 2000 individuals invited to participate received an 'invitation questionnaire' containing general questions relating to age, gender, height, weight, occupation and co-habitation status.<br>• Attitudes toward health, use of tobacco, alcohol, medication and physical activity were also assessed. |
| Participant questionnaire | • The 1370 individuals agreeing to participate in the study received a more extensive baseline supplementary questionnaire covering working conditions, living conditions, health problems, healthcare behaviour, leisure time activities, quality of life, partner's occupation and important life events.<br>• Goldberg's 12-item general health questionnaire was completed. |
| GP education | • Before the study began, all nine general practitioners in the four practices participated in four meetings on the prevention of heart and lung disease, dietary advice and engaging in health discussions with patients. |
| Health checks | • These were undertaken by one of three specially trained laboratory technicians. The elements included consisted of the following:<br>• Cardiovascular risk score<br>• ECG<br>• Blood pressure<br>• Spirometry (FEV1, VC, FVC)<br>• Liver testing (GGT, AST, ALT)<br>• Creatinine<br>• Non-fasting blood glucose<br>• Serum urate<br>• Urinary dipstix (glucose, albumin, blood)<br>• BMI<br>• Waist/hip ratio<br>• Carbon monoxide concentration in expired air<br>• Physical endurance<br>• Sight (Snellen test)<br>• Hearing (screening audiometer)<br>• HIV status |

(*Continued*)

Table 2.7 (*Continued*) Ebeltoft interventions

| Interventions | Details |
| --- | --- |
| Written feedback | • Within 2–3 weeks of the health check, all those in groups A and B received personal written feedback from their GPs with an emphasis on explaining test results in easily understood terms.<br>• Where values fell outside the normal range, the feedback incorporated advice primarily relating to lifestyle changes.<br>• All participants were also sent leaflets on healthy lifestyles from the Danish Heart Foundation.<br>• If signs of disease or indications for further examination were present, the communication also included suggestions about seeking medical care. |
| Health discussions | • Participants in health check group B received, with their written feedback, an invitation to make an appointment with their GP to discuss their health in order to receive information and advice on lifestyle change.<br>• The following elements were included in this intervention:<br>  • 45-minute GP consultation<br>  • 15 minutes allocated to the GP to prepare for and to conclude the consultation<br>  • Prior to the meeting, the participant completed a further short questionnaire with a view to suggesting suitable discussion topics<br>  • At the end of the health discussion each participant was invited to set a maximum of three health-related lifestyle goals for the following year. In decreasing frequency, these related to weight, diet, physical activity, smoking, alcohol use and work. They were also confirmed in writing with one copy being given to the participant and another being retained by their GP<br>  • If required, a further 30-minute consultation could be booked with their general practitioner 3 months later |
| Follow-up | • Follow-up involving questionnaires and health checks took place 1 and 5 years after the start of the study.<br>• Participants in health check group B were offered annual GP consultations. |

There is a question about how special the intervention was, as it seemed to involve only a minimal amount of training by the nine GPs involved in this study. With this in mind, it is interesting to note that the percentage of participants in discussion group B who agreed to the follow-up consultants was 97.1% in 1992 but rapidly fell to 35.7% (1993), 16.9% (1994), 15.1% (1995), 8.6% (1996) and 7% (1997).

Given the design of Ebeltoft (i.e. with little GP input until after the data had been collected by laboratory technicians) the findings are particularly interesting from a value perspective. Moreover, it can be argued that the magnitude of the effects on the surrogate outcome measures might have been even greater if

- Account had been taken of the health-promoting effects of the initial questionnaires.
- Individuals aged greater than 49 years had also been invited to participate.
- More pharmacotherapy such as statins had been used. As a GP practising in the same period as the Ebeltoft (as well as more recently) I am aware how the approach to cardiovascular risk reduction has become much more aggressive – especially with the increased use of anti-hypertensives and statins. The positive impacts in the Ebeltoft study were largely achieved by lifestyle changes alone. Since 1994 and the publication of the landmark Scandinavian Simvastatin Survival Study, the management of cardiovascular risk has dramatically changed (50).
- The GPs had been selected differently. They were chosen geographically as opposed to having any specific interest or expertise in health checks or health screening. Although it might be suggested that such an approach may have contributed to enhancing participation, it can also be argued that enlisting the help of GPs with specialist skills in facilitating behaviour change, earlier disease recognition or prevention would have delivered greater effects.

In summary, I would suggest that there is some research evidence in support of continuing to undertake heath checks involving multiple components but things need to be done differently and better to enhance their value. Moreover, echoing the view of the Canadian Task Force (36) I would argue for the adoption of a more tailored approach that takes into account the research evidence, individual concerns and a person's risk profile.

### 2.2.3 The clinical examination

In appreciation of the costs of seeing a clinician (and also the opportunity costs if they have other areas of patient responsibility), the routine clinical examination as a component of a health check is one specific area that warrants careful scrutiny.

According to Mehrotra and colleagues (51), from 2002 to 2004, approximately 44 million U.S. adults received an annual preventive health examination and 19 million women a preventive gynaecological examination (including a pelvic assessment). Visits for these two elements exceeded the number of annual attendances for either acute respiratory infections (30 million) or hypertension (48 million) during this 2-year period. The estimated $7.8 billion spent on such examinations was comparable to the $8.1 billion spent on breast cancer care in 2004.

There is also a significant opportunity cost to consider here. Assuming that a routine clinical examination takes around 20–25 minutes, for every U.S. adult to have a preventive examination would absorb 41% of the time of primary care physicians.

In their 1979 review, the Canadian Task Force expressed concerns that the clinical examination had simply become a ritual and went on to comment that is was 'non-specific and casts a searching net far too broadly...is inefficient and, at times, potentially misleading' (36). On my part, I was recently asked to scrutinise the clinical examination requirements for an insurance company as well as for an organisation delivering preventive health checks. In both situations the specifications read more like a random list of ingredients than a carefully constructed recipe for health and wellbeing!

The continuing presence of the routine clinical examination as an element of a health check might simply reflect inertia. For example, although assessing the character of the pulse may have been helpful to Galen in the first century AD does it still have any value today? Just because an aspect of the examination is useful for an individual with specific symptoms attending hospital will it exhibit similar validity, reliability and utility amongst people without any symptoms in the context of a health check?

However, examining an individual is not simply about early disease recognition but also has therapeutic and legal elements. As a GP it often seems to me that if a patient perceives that they have had a thorough (and courteous) examination they are often much more likely to be comfortable with my clinical judgement. In contrast, if I rigidly adhere to those elements of the clinical examination that I consider have sufficient accuracy I sometimes find it more difficult to reassure the patient.

But before we lay hands on an individual it is important to be quite clear about purposes. For example, if I listen to a person's chest, is it to assist me with the earlier recognition of conditions such as chronic obstructive pulmonary disease (COPD) or lung cancer (in which case am I confident about reliability and validity)? Is it to help with reassurance (in which case am I being honest with the individual and their family?)? Is it for other doctor-centred reasons such as defensive medical practice or to appear competent in the eyes of colleagues?

I would argue that it is especially important to be clear about both the purpose and the accuracy if the patient is going to be subjected to something particularly unpleasant or embarrassing such as a rectal or a vaginal examination. In 1990 Hennigan and colleagues criticised GPs for their reluctance to perform rectal examinations (52). However, although there is some evidence that the rectal examination may have a role in the assessment of men with urinary problems, there is nothing to recommend the procedure as part of the routine gynaecological assessment in women (53). Moreover, a case-control study showed no benefit of routine digital rectal examination in reducing mortality from cancer of the distal rectum (54). A survey of internal medicine residents in Minneapolis,

Minnesota, also revealed that most doctors had received little formal instruction in undertaking a rectal examination and ensuring patient comfort (55). Patients were frequently uncertain why the examination had been performed and lacked any understanding of the results of the examination.

In my view, some simple elements of the clinical examination remain important in the context of a heath check such as measuring blood pressure, assessing body composition and BMI in addition to the waist circumference. However, in discussions with those purchasing or procuring health checks I now always recommend that the unfocused head-to-toe physical examination is abandoned for asymptomatic individuals in favour of clinical data components that actually deliver value.

## 2.3 IS THERE A DEMAND FOR HEALTH CHECKS?

One of the particularly intriguing aspects of general health checks is that, despite the well-publicised reservations by bodies such as the Canadian Task Force on the Periodic Health Examination (36), the Society of General Internal Medicine (35), the U.S. Preventive Services Task Force (28) and the UK Department of Health (24), there remains a considerable and growing demand. This seems to be driven by the public, healthcare professionals, companies, insurers, the media and even politicians and civil servants in the case of the NHS Health Check Programme. Both within the United Kingdom and the United States, many private screening organisations and health insurers continue to recommend and encourage annual check-ups.

According to Mehrotra and Prochazka (56),

- One-third of U.S. adults receive a health check in any given year – something that has remained relatively stable from 2002 to 2010.
- Around 10% of all visits to U.S. primary care physicians are for health checks.
- The content of the health check in the United States is poorly defined – components can be variable, and some have been included because of billing regulations established by health plans and Medicare.
- Many private health plans in the United States have created a financial incentive for physicians to provide annual health checks by reimbursing them at a higher rate than for other office visits.

Across the world, the preventive healthcare technologies and services market size is also increasing. It was valued at $139.1 billion in 2015 and is projected to rise by over 12% during the next 5 years. This growth is attributed to the increasing prevalence of lifestyle-associated and other chronic diseases together with aging populations (57).

Undoubtedly, some physicians will have been taught during their training that the routine annual checkup is a valuable procedure and will continue to adhere to this view. In a postal survey of 1679 primary care providers within the United States, 65% of respondents agreed that an annual health check was necessary and 88% admitted to performing routine physical examinations (58). The reasons given were as follows:

- It provides time to counsel patients about preventive health services (94%).
- It improves patient-physician relationships (94%).
- It is desired by most patients (78%).
- It improves detection of subclinical illness (74%).
- It is of proven value (63%).

Many of the respondents also believed that the following core tests should be included as part of the annual review: mammography (44%), lipid panel (48%), urinalysis (44%), blood glucose estimation (46%) and haematology profile (39%).

In a study in Canada, a number of family physicians received unannounced visits from a group of 62 standardised (or simulated) patients. In comparison with the preventive care recommendations of the Canadian Task Force on the Periodic Health Examination (36), there was evidence of the underuse of interventions that were recommended in addition to the overuse of some tests that were not recommended. The family physicians surveyed provided, on average, 41% of recommended manoeuvres for which, according to the Task Force, there is good or fair evidence for inclusion in a periodic health check but 17% of manoeuvres for which there is good or fair evidence for exclusion from a periodic health assessment (59).

Research from Portugal also highlighted some mismatches between the U.S. Preventive Services Task Force recommendations and the practices of 255 Portuguese family physicians. In direct opposition to the published evidence, 66% of the surveyed family physicians considered it appropriate to undertake a screening digital rectal examination and 32% to arrange a screening chest radiograph (60).

As a GP in England I have frequently encountered individuals who come in seeking a health check. Moreover, during my 30-year GP career, I have participated in a number of local or national health check initiatives such as 'new patient checks' for those who join a general practice, 'over 70 health checks' and opportunistic checks for specific conditions, for example, pulse assessment for atrial fibrillation.

The general public in the United Kingdom are certainly enthusiastic about check-ups – and politicians know this. In a recent survey of 2024 individuals concerning their attitudes to cancer screening, almost 90% believed that it is 'almost always a good idea' and, intriguingly, 49% said that they would like to be tested for cancer even if it was untreatable (61).

Elsewhere in Europe there are equally high public expectations for health checks. For example, in Portugal the importance of the periodic health check appears to be culturally rooted in the population with a regular consultation request being 'doctor, I want to do a general analysis'. In a telephone survey of 1000 Portuguese adults in 2013, 99.2% believed that they should undergo routine blood and urine testing every 12 months (62).

Brotons and colleagues have collected some interesting data on the attitudes toward preventive services amongst patients visiting primary care practices within

22 European countries. They concluded that a high proportion of individuals with unhealthy lifestyles (especially risky drinkers) do not perceive the need to change their habits, and about half of patients reported not having had any discussion about healthy lifestyles with their GPs. Many people also seem to overestimate their need to be screened for cardiovascular risk factors and for cancer (63).

In 2002, Oboler surveyed members of the public in Denver, Boston and San Diego concerning health checks (64). Of the 1203 respondents, 66% believed that, in addition to regular care, an annual health check is necessary. More than 90% of respondents also thought that their physician should address diet, exercise, tobacco use and alcohol during the annual assessment, and about 60% believed sexual history and seat belts should be discussed. Around 90% of participants considered that blood pressure, heart, lungs, abdomen, reflexes and prostate (men) and breast (women) ought to be examined. In relation to the specific components of a health check, their expectations were as listed in Table 2.8.

In the United States, the public is also enthusiastic about cancer screening. Moreover, this commitment is not dampened by false-positive results or the possibility that testing could lead to unnecessary treatment. Schwartz has warned that such attitudes create an environment ripe for the premature diffusion of technologies such as total-body computed tomography (CT) scanning placing individuals at risk of overtesting and overtreatment (65).

These and other surveys have repeatedly demonstrated the public's unwavering enthusiasm for regular check-ups, but for those with an interest in health checks some specific issues need to be borne in mind:

- In the Portuguese survey, it was also clear that patients tend to overestimate the importance of investigations as opposed to lifestyle counselling. For example, having routine blood testing (including cholesterol and glucose) was ranked much higher than advice on weight, alcohol or smoking (66).
- In general, there is poor understanding of the purposes of health checks and the accuracy of testing – including the risks of false positives and false negatives (67). Also, people inflate the benefits and underestimate the harms

Table 2.8 Public expectations of specific health check components

| Component | Percentage of respondents feeling that the component should be included in a health check (%) |
|---|---|
| Urinalysis | 50 |
| Cholesterol screening | 63 |
| Blood glucose testing | 43 |
| PSA testing (men) | 67 |
| Faecal occult blood testing | 44 |
| Chest X-ray | 32 |
| Mammography (women) | 71 |
| Cervical smear | 75 |

they might gain from screening and prevention including the risk reduction achieved. In a questionnaire survey in New Zealand over 90% of respondents overestimated the benefits of breast and bowel cancer screening and 82% and 69% overestimated the benefits of preventive medication to reduce the chances of hip fractures or cardiovascular diseases, respectively (68).

- Doctors are not discriminating between tests according to the strength of the evidence (59). To help individuals understand benefits and harms a physician must first appreciate the risks themselves and then communicate this information effectively.

In 1979, the Canadian Task Force Stated: 'the public will have to understand why the annual check up should be discarded and why different procedures should be introduced for different age groups' (36). While this seems a reasonable statement based on the evidence, the tone and approach are probably more appropriate for the twentieth century than the twenty-first where patient empowerment and informed shared decision making have gained much greater prominence.

We certainly need to enhance public knowledge about health checks but, equally importantly, those developing or designing health checks must aquire a better appreciation of the values, attitudes and expectations of both individuals and organisations. As discussed in Chapter 3, one of the fundamental architectural elements of a better value health check is to understand and clarify needs.

## 2.4 HOW MIGHT THE QUALITY OF HEALTH CHECKS BE IMPROVED?

Since Wilson and Jungner published their original screening criteria back in 1968 (69) a number of additional checklists and frameworks have been developed (23,70–72) (see the Appendix). In addition, many governments have written quality assurance guidelines for their national screening programmes (e.g. for breast cancer, cervical cancer and colorectal cancer).

However, although having access to such criteria and guidance is invaluable for those with an interest in health checks, it is all too easy to miss the wood for the trees. For the private sector, there will obviously be additional requirements to consider including profitability and customer satisfaction. There might also be conflicting goals for those focused primarily on health checks in comparison with those concerned with overall healthcare.

As outlined in this chapter there is little doubt that the current situation in relation to health checks is confused and messy with worries about the underlying research evidence in respect of certain components. In this context some might suggest seeking to reduce the apparently inappropriate practice by, for example, deterring individuals from using the service (e.g. by increasing costs or levying premiums if further healthcare is required after a private health check) or attempting to dissuade individuals from attending health checks by promoting strong information on the adverse consequences of private health checks.

But this text is about developing a different approach and an overarching vision – based on value – in order to unite the interests and activities of all those with a stake in health checks – whether developers, procurers or purchasers. I believe that well-designed health checks can deliver value in terms of health outcomes per dollar or pound spent – their value increasing when better outcomes are achieved at comparable (or lower) cost, or when equivalent outcomes are achieved at lower cost (73).

A better value health check is one in which each element of a health check, from the choice of the components and the way they are delivered, to the pathway after the clinical data collection has been undertaken, has been carefully scrutinised with outcomes and costs in mind.

Moreover, the outcomes need to encompass not just what seems important to doctors and nurses but, in addition, consider what matters to those having a health check. According to Korenstein (74), high-value care is also about achieving maximal benefit and minimal harm (physical, psychological and financial) in the context of a particular person's values and priorities.

So, for individuals I am not suggesting denying, dissuading or deterring them from having a health check – but finding ways to divert them to a new model. Defining and outlining the nature of this model – better value health checks – is the purpose of this text.

## REFERENCES


1. Han PKJ. Historical changes in the objectives of the periodic health examination. *Ann Intern Med* 1997;127:910–917.
2. Raffle AE, Muir Gray JA. *Screening: Evidence and Practice*. Oxford: Oxford University Press, 2007.
3. Gordon Brown speech on NHS. *BBC News* 2008 January 7. http://news.bbc.co.uk/1/hi/uk_politics/7175083.stm
4. Krogsbøll LT, Jørgensen KJ, Grønhøj Larsen C, Gøtzsche PC. General health checks in adults for reducing morbidity and mortality from disease. *Cochrane Database of Systematic Reviews* 2012;(10). Art. No.: CD009009. doi: 10.1002/14651858.CD009009.pub2
5. Summerton N. *Primary Care Diagnostics: The Patient-Centred Approach in the New Commissioning Environment*. Abingdon: Radcliffe Medical Press, 2011.
6. Imperial Cancer Research Fund OXCHECK Study Group. Effectiveness of health checks conducted by nurses in primary care: Final results of the OXCHECK study. *BMJ* 1995;310:1099–1104.
7. Lauritzen T, Leboeuf-Yde C, Lunde IM, Nielsen KD. Ebeltoft project: Baseline data from a five-year randomized, controlled, prospective health promotion study in a Danish population. *Br J Gen Pract* 1995;45:542–547.
8. Rang M. The Ulysses syndrome. *CMAJ* 1972;106:122–123.
9. Hayward R. VOMIT (victims of modern imaging technology): An acronym for our times. *BMJ* 2003;326:1273.
10. Welch HG, Schwartz LM, Woloshin S. *Overdiagnosed. Making People Sick in the Pursuit of Health*. Boston, MA: Beacon Press, 2011.

11. Harris RP, Sheridan SL, Lewis CL et al. The harms of screening: A proposed taxonomy and application to lung cancer screening. *JAMA Intern Med* 2014;174:281–285.
12. Should I have a PSA test? http://www.nhs.uk/livewell/prostatehealth/pages/psa-test.aspx
13. Lamplugh M, Gilmore P, Quinlan T, Cornford P. PSA testing: Are patients aware of what lies ahead? *Ann R Coll Surg Engl* 2006;88:284–288.
14. Turini GA, Gjelsvik A, Renzulli JF. The state of prescreening discussions about prostate-specific antigen testing following implementation of the 2012 United States Preventive Services Task Force statement. *Urology* 2017;104:122–130.
15. What is an NHS Health Check? http://www.nhs.uk/conditions/nhs-health-check/pages/what-is-an-nhs-health-check-new.aspx
16. Robertson J, Hatton C, Emerson E, Baines S. The impact of health checks for people with intellectual disabilities: An updated systematic review of the evidence. *Res Dev Disabil* 2014;35:2450–2462.
17. Dong BJ. How medications affect thyroid function. *West J Med* 2000;172:102–106.
18. Oh RC, Hustead TR. Causes and evaluation of mildly elevated liver transaminase levels. *Am Fam Physician* 2011;84:1003–1008.
19. Soma-Pillay P, Nelson-Piercy C, Tolppanen H et al. Physiological changes in pregnancy. *Cardiovasc J Afr* 2016;27:89–94.
20. Hughes RC, Rowan J, Florkowski CM. Is there a role for HbA1c in pregnancy? *Curr Diab Rep* 2016;16:5. doi: 10.1007/s11892-015-0698-y
21. Boulware LE, Marinopoulos S, Phillips KA et al. Systematic review: The value of the periodic health evaluation. *Ann Intern Med* 2007;146:289–300.
22. Seedat F, Cooper J, Cameron L et al. *International Comparisons of Screening Policy-Making: A Systematic Review.* Warwick: University of Warwick, 2014.
23. Criteria for appraising the viability, effectiveness and appropriateness of a screening programme. October 2015. https://www.gov.uk/government/publications/evidence-review-criteria-national-screening-programmes
24. Private screening for health conditions: NHS recommendations. January 2014. https://www.gov.uk/guidance/private-screening-for-health-conditions-nhs-recommendations; https://www.gov.uk/government/publications/leaflet-thinking-of-having-a-private-screening-test
25. Just what the doctor didn't order: The rise of private screening. *Pulse Magazine* 6 March 2017. http://www.pulsetoday.co.uk/clinical/just-what-the-doctor-didnt-order-the-rise-of-private-screening/20033987.article
26. Investigation: GPs cope with fallout from private screening explosion, *Pulse Magazine* 24 June 2009. http://www.pulsetoday.co.uk/investigation-gps-cope-with-fallout-from-private-screening-explosion/11008350.article
27. About the Affordable Care Act. Preventive Care. https://www.hhs.gov/healthcare/about-the-aca/preventive-care/index.html

28. U.S. Preventive Services Task Force Recommendations. https://www.uspreventiveservicestaskforce.org/BrowseRec/Index
29. Lovett K. Direct-to-consumer medical testing in the era of value-based care. *JAMA* 2017;317:2485–2486.
30. Waller D, Agass M, Mant D et al. Health checks in general practice: Another example of inverse care? *BMJ* 1990;300:1115–1118.
31. Gøtzsche PC. General health checks don't work. *BMJ* 2014;348:g3680.
32. Meader N, King K, Wright K et al. Multiple risk behavior interventions: Meta-analyses of RCTs. *Am J Prev Med* 2017;53:19–30.
33. Jorgensen T, Jacobsen RK, Toft U, Aadahl M, Glumer C, Pisinger C. Effect of screening and lifestyle counselling on incidence of ischaemic heart disease in general population: Inter99 randomised trial. *BMJ* 2014;348:g3617.
34. Si S, Moss JR, Sullivan TR, Newton SS, Stocks NP. Effectiveness of general practice-based health checks: A systematic review and meta-analysis. *Br J Gen Pract* 2014;64:e47–53. doi: 10.3399/bjgp14X676456
35. Choosing Wisely. General Health Checks for Asymptomatic Adults. February 2017. http://www.choosingwisely.org/clinician-lists/society-general-internal-medicine-general-health-checks-for-asymptomatic-adults/
36. Canadian Task Force on the Periodic Health Examination. The periodic health examination. *Can Med Assoc J* 1979;121:1193–1254.
37. Puska P, Tuomilehto J, Salonen JT et al. Changes in coronary risk factors during comprehensive five-year community programme to control cardiovascular diseases (North Karelia project). *BMJ* 1979;ii:1173–1178.
38. Vartiainen E, Laatikainen T, Peltonen M et al. Thirty-five-year trends in cardiovascular risk factors in Finland. *Int J Epidemiol* 2010;39:504–518.
39. Imperial Cancer Research Fund OXCHECK Study Group. Prevalence of risk factors for heart disease in OXCHECK trial: Implications for screening in primary care. *BMJ* 1991;302:1057–1060.
40. Robson J, Dostal I, Sheikh A et al. The NHS Health Check in England: An evaluation of the first 4 years. *BMJ Open* 2016;6:e008840. doi: 10.1136/bmjopen-2015-008840
41. Caley M, Chohan P, Hooper J, Wright N. The impact of NHS Health Checks on the prevalence of disease in general practices: A controlled study. *Br J Gen Pract* 2014;64:e516–e521.
42. Chang KC, Lee JT, Vamos EP et al. Impact of the National Health Service Health Check on cardiovascular disease risk: A difference-in-differences matching analysis. *CMAJ* 2016. doi: 10.1503/cmaj.151201
43. GPs shun NHS health checks, GP Online. 14 August 2013. http://www.gponline.com/exclusive-gps-shun-nhs-health-checks/article/1207087
44. Engberg M, Christensen B, Karlsmose B, Lous J, Lauritzen T. General health screenings to improve cardiovascular risk profiles: A randomized controlled trial in general practice with 5-year follow-up. *J Fam Pract* 2002;51:546–552.
45. Christensen B, Engberg M, Lauritzen T. No long-term psychological reaction to information about increased risk of coronary heart disease in general practice. *Eur J Cardiovasc Prev Rehabil* 2004;11:239–243.

46. Lauritzen T, Jensen MS, Thomsen JL, Christensen B, Engberg M. Health tests and health consultations reduced cardiovascular risk without psychological strain, increased healthcare utilization or increased costs. An overview of the results from a 5-year randomized trial in primary care. The Ebeltoft Health Promotion Project (EHPP). *Scand J Public Health* 2008;36:650–661.
47. Thomsen JL, Parner ET, Karlsmose B, Thulstrup AM, Lauritzen T, Engberg M. Effect of preventive health screening on long-term primary health care utilization. A randomized controlled trial. *Fam Pract* 2005;22:242–248.
48. Thomsen JL, Karlsmose B, Parner ET, Thulstrup AM, Lauritzen T, Engberg M. Secondary healthcare contacts after multiphasic preventive health screening: A randomized trial. *Scand J Public Health* 2006;34:254–261.
49. Rasmussen SR, Thomsen JL, Kilsmark J, Hvenegaard A, Engberg M, Lauritzen T, Søgaard J. Preventive health screenings and health consultations in primary care increase life expectancy without increasing costs. *Scand J Public Health* 2007;35:365–372.
50. Scandinavian Simvastatin Survival Study Group. Randomised trial of cholesterol lowering in 4444 patients with coronary heart disease: The Scandinavian Simvastatin Survival Study (4S). *Lancet* 1994;344:1383–1389.
51. Mehrotra A, Zaslavsky AM, Ayanian J. Preventive health examinations and preventive gynaecological examinations in the United States. *Arch Intern Med* 2007;167:1876–1883.
52. Hennigan TW, Franks PJ, Hocken DB, Allen-Mersh TG. Rectal examination in general practice. *BMJ* 1990;301:478–480.
53. Campbell KA, Shaughnessy AF. Diagnostic utility of the digital rectal examination as part of the routine pelvic examination. *J Fam Pract* 1998;46:165–167.
54. Herrinton LJ, Selby JV, Friedman GD et al. Case-control study of digital-rectal screening in relation to mortality from cancer of the distal rectum. *Am J Epidemiol* 1995;142:961–964.
55. Wilt TJ, Cutler AF. Physician performance and patient perceptions during the rectal examination. *J Gen Intern Med* 1991;6:514–517.
56. Mehrotra A, Prochazka A. Improving value in health care – Against the annual physical. *N Engl J Med* 2015;373:1485–1487.
57. Grand View Research. *Preventive Healthcare Technologies and Services Market Size and Forecast by Technology (Early Detection and Screening, Vaccines, Chronic Disease Management, Advanced Technologies to Reduce Errors), and Trend Analysis from 2013–2024*. San Francisco, CA: Grand View Research, 2016.
58. Prochazka AV, Lundahl K, Pearson W et al. Support of evidence-based guidelines for the annual physical examination. A survey of primary care providers. *Arch Intern Med* 2005;165:1347–1352.
59. Hutchison B, Woodward CA, Norman GR et al. Provision of preventive care to unannounced standardised patients. *Can Med Assoc J* 1998;158:185–193.

60. Martins C, Azevedo LF, Santos C et al. Preventive health services implemented by family physicians in Portugal – A cross sectional study based on two clinical scenarios. *BMJ Open* 2014;4:e005162. doi: 10.1136/bmjopen-2014-005162
61. Waller J, Osborne K, Wardle J. Enthusiasm for cancer screening in Great Britain: A general population survey. *Br J Cancer* 2015;112:562–566.
62. Martins C, Azevedo LF, Ribeiro O et al. A population-based nationwide cross-sectional study on preventative health services utilization in Portugal – What services (and frequencies) are deemed necessary by patients? *PLoS ONE* 2013;8:e81256. doi: 10.1371/journal.pone.0081256
63. Brotons C, Bulc M, Sammut MR et al. Attitudes toward preventive services and lifestyle: The views of primary care patients in Europe. The EUROPREVIEW patient study. *Fam Pract* 2012;29:i168–i176.
64. Oboler SK, Prochazka AV, Gonzales R et al. Public expectations and attitudes for annual physical examinations and testing. *Ann Intern Med* 2002;136:652–659.
65. Schwartz LM, Woloshin S, Fowler FJ, Welch HG. Enthusiasm for cancer screening in the United States. *JAMA* 2004;291:71–78.
66. Sa L, Ribeiro O, Azevedo LF et al. Patients' estimations of the importance of preventive health services: A nationwide, population-based cross-sectional study in Portugal. *BMJ Open* 2016;6:e011755. doi: 10.1136/bmjopen-2016-011755
67. Cockburn J, Redman S, Hill D, Henry E. Public understanding of medical screening. *J Med Screening* 1995;2:224–227.
68. Hudson B, Zarifeh A, Young L, Wells JE. Patients' expectations of screening and preventive treatments. *Ann Fam Med* 2012;10:495–502.
69. Wilson JMG, Jungner G. *Principles and Practice of Screening for Disease.* Geneva: World Health Organization, 1968.
70. Bijlsma M, Rendering A, Chin-On N et al. Quality criteria for health checks: Development of a European consensus agreement. *Prev Med* 2014;67:238–241.
71. Andermann A, Blancquaert I, Beauchamp S et al. Revisiting Wilson and Jungner in the genomic age: A review of screening criteria over the past 40 years. *Bull World Health Org* 2008;86:317–319.
72. Harris R, Sawaya GF, Moyer VA, Calonge N. Reconsidering the criteria for evaluating proposed screening programs: Reflections from four current and former members of the U.S. Preventive Services Task Force. *Epidemiol Rev* 2011;33:20–35.
73. Porter ME, Teisberg EO. *Redefining Health Care. Creating Value-Based Competition on Results.* Boston, MA: Harvard Business School Press, 2006.
74. Korenstein D. Patient perception of benefits and harms. The Achilles heel of high-value care. *JAMA Intern Med* 2015;175:287–288.

# 3

# Better value health checks: Key elements

Better value healthcare is about enhancing patient outcomes while also seeking to control total care costs. On the face of it a health check ought to represent high-value healthcare. For example, spotting colorectal cancer earlier should lead to the use of less aggressive and extensive treatments but with improved survival. Care processes might also be more timely with faster recovery times and fewer complications. Furthermore, improvements in the long-term management of diseases and disorders can result in a reduction in the requirements for subsequent care (1).

However, as discussed in Chapter 2, there is considerable variation in relation to the purposes, components and outputs of currently available health checks. Therefore, to ensure that the enhanced value desired from a health check is actually achieved, there is a need for much greater clarity about the definition, the architecture and the operational elements of a health check.

It is also important to identify and apply the findings from good-quality research to ensure that both the elements included within a health check in addition to the optimal care pathways to be followed after a health check are evidence based. Moreover, such research evidence needs to be applicable to the individuals or the population being subjected to a health check.

## 3.1 DEFINITION OF A BETTER VALUE HEALTH CHECK

In this text a better value health check is defined as the comprehensive assessment of an adult focused primarily on prevention and earlier disease/disorder recognition with a view to enhancing health outcomes. Moreover, such outcome improvements need to be achieved at comparable (or lower) total care costs than is currently the case for a specific disease or disorder care pathway.

A better value health check includes a number of elements derived from the following:

a. An assessment of patient characteristics, lifestyle, symptoms/signs, medications, and personal/family medical history (including specific risk assessment questionnaires/tools)

b. A clinical examination and clinical measurements
c. Physiological, pathology and genetic testing
d. Endoscopic and imaging investigations

However, although the health check might include questions about symptoms/signs and a review of ongoing medical problems, it needs to be distinguished from the following:

- Clinical interactions where the primary purpose is a focused medical review of an individual with a specific chronic medical disorder (e.g. diabetes, chronic obstructive pulmonary disease [COPD] or heart failure)
- Clinical interactions initiated by individuals primarily concerned about a particular symptom or sign such as a breast lump or coughing up blood (iatrotropic features) (2)

Obviously, nothing in medicine is absolutely clear-cut and, for example, some people may seek an appointment with a healthcare professional because they have experienced rectal bleeding (iatrotropic symptom) whereas others might only acknowledge the symptom on direct questioning during the course of a health check (non-iatrotropic symptom). Similarly, an individual with diabetes attending for a health check may be noted to have excellent control (based on their HbA1c result) but also be discovered to have a low blood glucose, perhaps reflecting overtreatment.

In the context of a time-pressured healthcare service – such as the UK National Health Service (NHS) – a health check might provide individuals with an opportunity – and the implied permission – to raise other health-related concerns (especially those of a sensitive or embarrassing nature). For the clinician delivering a health check it may also be possible to inform individuals about health risks, emerging health information and the appropriate utilisation of healthcare. The more generalist and holistic approach within a health check should complement the increasingly specialist and siloed nature of modern healthcare.

Although it is always important to view a health check as a key component of an individual's ongoing healthcare, the number of interactions should be fixed. In my view, a single health check episode will generally involve no more than two or three separate dealings between an individual undergoing a health check and those delivering the service. For example, based on the four elements listed above:

Basic health check:

Interaction 1: Obtaining clinical data (a), (b) and/or (c)
Interaction 2: Discussion of findings and next steps

Advanced health check:

Interaction 1: Obtaining clinical data (a), (b) and/or (c)
Interaction 2: Obtaining clinical data (d)
Interaction 3: Discussion of findings and next steps

Clearly, on some occasions, such as the identification of an urgent result, further conversations might be required but this should be the exception rather than the rule.

## 3.2 ARCHITECTURE OF A BETTER VALUE HEALTH CHECK

To design a better value health check, it is useful to focus on six fundamental issues: needs, purposes, outcomes, costs, measurements and risk.

### 3.2.1 Assessing needs

Demand is about what people want from a health check and can be influenced by a variety of factors including an individual's health beliefs in addition to media stories and campaigns. Supply is what services are available linked to, perhaps, the interests of those individuals developing health check packages and/or the availability of specific tests. Supply can, in itself, also drive demand.

Need in healthcare is about the capacity to benefit. Thus, if an abnormality is detected at a health check then an effective intervention should be available to meet that need and improve an individual's overall health.

An individual's values and priorities always matter; but assessing health needs in the context of a health check is not simply about listening to what people want or relying on the experience of those with a vested interest in health checks. In my view there is a requirement for a much more systematic approach to determining priorities based on research evidence, epidemiological data and structured discussions/surveys of key stakeholders. For those designing health checks the following questions are suggested as a mechanism to encourage a greater focus on needs:

1. Within the specific population being targeted by the health check is the proposed health check addressing important diseases or disorders in terms of prevalence or incidence and/or inappropriate variations in practice or outcomes?
2. Within the specific population being targeted by the health check are there any specific health concerns for individuals, organisations or communities?
3. Within the specific population being targeted by the health check what are the adverse health-related outcomes that the health check is seeking to address and reduce?
4. Are there cost-effective treatments or solutions for the diseases or disorders targeted by the health check? Moreover, is the combination of such treatments or solutions together with a health check likely to represent enhanced value along the care pathway compared to current practice? For example, does earlier treatment (after a positive screening test result) offer better value than later treatment (after an individual visits their doctor with a specific iatrotropic symptom)?

5. What prevention and early disease recognition services or initiatives are already available to individuals (e.g. publicly funded, company paid, via private medical insurance or from voluntary or charitable sources)? Moreover, are such services accessible, acceptable, appropriate, efficient, equitable and effective? On occasion it might be that a new health check (or some elements of a health check) may be unnecessary – all that is required are improvements to the quality of existing services.

Based on a careful review of research evidence and guidelines, Chapters 4–16 highlight some specific diseases or disorders that might be considered for a better value health check focused on non-pregnant adults and appropriate for particular population groups. However, these chapters are offered up as a basis for an informed discussion with those undergoing, purchasing or procuring health checks as opposed to a proscriptive list. Some areas such as routine screening for haemoglobinopathies have also been excluded as it is suggested that this testing is more appropriately targeted at children under the age of 1 year and antenatally.

## 3.2.2 Clarifying purposes

There are two primary purposes to a better value health check: prevention and earlier disease recognition. The detailed content of these two purposes is illustrated in Table 3.1.

## 3.2.3 Determining outcomes

Outcomes are events or happenings that occur because the health check has (more or less) achieved its purposes.

Improving outcomes encompasses enhancing positive outcomes in addition to reducing negative outcomes. Thus, it is important to maintain a broad perspective and not to focus simply on the perceived advantages of a health check but also to consider the risks of physical, psychological and financial harm – both immediately and in the medium and longer term (see Chapter 2). It is worth bearing in mind that outcomes might be poor because the right test has been used badly or the wrong test has been used correctly.

To design a better value health check there is also a requirement to think backwards from the outcomes to the purposes rather than the other way around. So, as touched on earlier, many will exclude individuals with non-iatrotropic symptoms or signs from a health check, but this ignores the imperative to improve outcomes by spotting specific diseases and disorders earlier. When looked at in this way screening and diagnosis simply represent complementary paths to earlier disease recognition.

In using a screening test for earlier disease recognition it is important to keep in mind lead-time bias. The lead-time is the length of time between the detection of a condition by screening and its usual clinical presentation and diagnosis (based on traditional criteria such as symptoms). If screening has no impact on outcomes

Table 3.1 Health check purposes

| Primary purpose | Why are we doing this? | Content |
|---|---|---|
| Prevention | To reduce the likelihood of diseases or disorders first starting<br>To seek to reduce the impact of established diseases or disorders | *Knowledge, attitudes and practices*: To alter an individual's health knowledge, attitudes and practices with a view to facilitating changes in, for example, unhealthy lifestyle practices/modifiable risk factors and/or health-seeking behaviours<br>*Determining chemoprevention*: To categorise individuals without diseases or disorders into subgroups according to their likelihood of benefitting from a specific preventative treatment or approach<br>*Trending*: To follow-up individuals without diseases or disorders, and/or clinical data over time (i.e. at subsequent health checks) in order to facilitate preventative activities<br>*Mitigation*: To contribute to monitoring diseases or disorders over time with a view to mitigating any adverse outcomes (including treatment side effects)<br>*Complementary*: To ensure that the health check considers the context in relation to, for example, other relevant prevention initiatives and geographical/cultural issues |
| Earlier disease recognition | To detect diseases or disorders at an early stage | *Risk stratification*: To categorise individuals into subgroups (e.g. high, intermediate, low) according to their likelihood of developing specific diseases or disorders<br>*Screening*: To detect unrecognised diseases or disorders in the absence of any symptoms or signs within a certain broad category of adults (e.g. all those aged over 45 years, all women) |

(*Continued*)

Table 3.1 (*Continued*) Health check purposes

| Primary purpose | Why are we doing this? | Content |
|---|---|---|
| | | *Case-finding*: To detect unrecognised diseases or disorders in the absence of any symptoms or signs within a discrete group of individuals linked to their baseline risk<br>*Diagnosis*: To detect unrecognised diseases or disorders (or unrecognised recurrences of previous conditions) in an individual attending with non-iatrotropic symptoms, signs or incidental test findings<br>*Prognosis*: To predict the likely course of a disease or disorder based on the initial findings at a health check<br>*Reassurance*: To confidently advise individuals that they do not have specific diseases or disorders and/or that they are at low risk for developing specific diseases or disorders, but to also provide appropriate 'safety-netting' guidance linked to, perhaps, any new symptoms developing<br>*Trending*: To follow-up individuals and/or clinical data over time (i.e. at subsequent health checks) in order to facilitate earlier disease recognition<br>*Complementary*: To ensure that the health check considers the context in relation to, for example, other relevant screening initiatives and the ongoing investigation of symptoms, for example, it is pointless to offer a faecal occult blood test to an individual who is already being investigated for overt rectal bleeding |

compared with symptomatic diagnosis then all that will have been achieved is giving some individuals added months of anxiety rather than additional months of life.

As discussed in the previous chapter, two of the systematic reviews of the effectiveness of health checks focused on mortality as the key outcome of interest. At the other end of the spectrum many private companies delivering health checks seem to be wedded primarily to customer satisfaction.

However, neither of these approaches is sufficient. Information on death rates needs to be supplemented by data on disability, pain and discomfort and quality of life. It is also very useful to examine individuals' views concerning the effect of the health check on their general wellbeing (physical and psychological) in addition to any symptoms. What is the point of a health check if the person feels they had a wonderful experience but there have been no impacts on their longer-term health?

Members of the public and clinicians might also have differing views about what outcomes matter most. Therefore, in recent years, Patient Reported Outcome Measures (PROMs) have assumed an increasingly important role in assessing health outcomes from the user's perspective. They consist of a series of questions designed to ascertain people's views about their symptoms, their functional status and their health-related quality of life. For example, in relation to the earlier recognition of colorectal cancer by faecal occult blood testing at a health check, the following PROMs are suggested (3):

- Survival
- Disease control
- Complications of treatment such as dietary issues, faecal leakage, stool frequency, diarrhoea, gastrointestinal symptoms, erectile dysfunction, vaginal symptoms; presence of stoma (colostomy or ileostomy)
- Degree of health (i.e. physical functioning, emotional functioning, social functioning, mobility, depression, pain, fatigue, sexual functioning, bowel functioning)
- Quality of death

Traditionally, there has also been a tendency to focus on outcome measures linked to specific diseases or disorders. However, in consideration of the wider impacts that health checks might have on an individual's wellbeing - for example, in relation to false-positive findings - generic measures should always be considered alongside condition-specific measures. The EuroQol is a useful tool for this purpose that includes general questions concerning mobility, self-care, usual activities, pain and discomfort and anxiety and depression (4).

Clearly, PROMs questionnaires directed at individuals cannot provide information on changes in the levels of key risk factors for cardiovascular disease such as blood pressure or cholesterol. Therefore, although PROMs are important in assessing the effectiveness of a health check, it is necessary to maintain a broad perspective and also to consider surrogate outcome measures when there are robust research links to hard outcomes such as death and disability.

Those seeking to design better value health checks need to appreciate that outcomes are not simply about the health check but the whole care pathway including any subsequent healthcare activities taking place after the health check. Porter also suggests that, for preventive care, health outcomes should be considered in relation to defined patient populations with similar health circumstances such as healthy adults, disabled elderly people or individuals with defined sets of chronic conditions (1). In addition, he argues that outcomes should be assessed for periods long enough to capture information on any potential harms from the health check including the requirements for any additional investigations and care arising from side effects of the health check (e.g. due to false-positive findings, false-negative results or overdiagnoses).

Table 3.2 makes some suggestions for the health check outcomes for individuals that might be considered.

Those designing health checks need to think very carefully about the desired outcomes and how the effectiveness of a health check in achieving the outcomes can be assessed. This is something that is discussed further in Section 3.3.

### 3.2.4 Considering costs

In the United States, a periodic health check might appear good value for money on a per visit basis. But because it is common the overall total spending amounts to around $10 billion annually (5). Moreover, if the entire adult population had a health check each year then the costs would be three times higher ($30 billion).

On top of this there are opportunity costs to consider, for example

- Travel and waiting time to attend a health check at $9.8 billion per year (all U.S. adults)
- Lost GP appointments (taken up by health checks; see Chapter 2)

According to Prochazka and Caverly, there are also costs related to both the initial testing at the health check and any necessary additional investigations required afterwards. Of particular concern they calculated that, for the period 2002–2004 in the United States, an estimated $322 million was spent annually on laboratory tests that no guideline group had recommended (6). In terms of further investigations the costs of, for example, follow-up biopsies of normal breasts triggered by false-positive mammogram results was set at between $14 and $70 billion annually. They also considered that – more broadly – the follow-up testing from general health checks substantially contributes to the estimated $210 billion in annual spending on unnecessary medical services.

In certain circumstances the costs of some preventive and early diagnosis interventions might even exceed the costs of just treating the condition effectively later on during its course, with identical health outcomes.

There is certainly evidence that a health check leading to earlier cancer recognition can reduce care costs linked to subsequent treatment and follow-up (see Chapters 7 and 13). Moreover, the impacts may extend beyond reductions in

Table 3.2 Health check outcomes for individuals

| Outcomes | Examples/Content |
|---|---|
| Death | • Five-year *cancer* survival following testing (including follow-up investigations and treatment)<br>• Five-year *overall* survival following testing (including follow-up investigations and treatment) |
| Disability | Retaining and regaining health:<br>• Extent of return to normal activities (including work) following a health check plus any necessary aftercare<br>• Time to return to normal activities (including work) following a health check plus any necessary aftercare |
| Quality of life | • Quality of life achieved/retained following a health check plus any necessary aftercare |
| Distress<br>Discomfort<br>Destitution | Linked to effects of the health check *plus* any necessary aftercare, e.g.<br>• Pain (increased/reduced)<br>• Anxiety/depression (increased/reduced)<br>• Impacts on income |
| Surrogate/intermediate outcomes | • Reduced health risks/risk factors such as changes in lipid levels, blood pressure measurements and smoking status<br>• New diagnoses/earlier stage diagnoses<br>• Missed/delayed diagnoses |

direct health costs to effects on employers, individuals and families. Indirect costs that might fall on individuals include those associated with loss of working time, travel and parking costs plus out-of-pocket expenses such as the requirements for adjustments to diet or accommodation. In relation to the benefits of earlier cancer diagnosis, work by the National Cancer Registry in Ireland has revealed that there is a doubling of the travel costs associated with stage 3 colorectal cancer compared to stage 1 colorectal cancer (7).

One of the major challenges for those with an interest in better value health checks is to ensure that the consideration of costs extends beyond the basic price of the health check. For companies purchasing health checks for their staff they also need to focus on the broader impacts of the health check on their workforce including absenteeism, presenteeism and productivity. For insurers, having an individual on a trajectory towards improving their health after a health check will impact on longer-term insurance costs.

Undoubtedly, it is much cheaper to develop a health check that simply measures blood pressure as opposed to also advising and guiding individuals with high blood pressure about the next steps in order to reduce their cardiovascular risk. However, it is well known that labelling an individual as having high blood pressure – with no aftercare – can have adverse effects on their wellbeing. There is evidence for increased absenteeism from work after such a diagnosis as well as negative effects on an individual's perceptions of their ability to recover from unrelated acute illnesses (8,9).

Testing packages offered by private providers certainly vary in price linked to the systems, staffing, skills and structures being deployed. But, while downward pressures on all these elements might alter the cost of the testing package, they do not, on their own, guarantee better value.

Over recent years, as technology has advanced, some private health check companies have begun to sell packages containing scores of tests. In this context there is a need to bear in mind that a 'normal' result is defined in relation to the overall distribution of findings obtained from a number of individuals. For most tests this 'reference range' is designed to accommodate 95% of results for people without any disease. Thus, 1 in 20 (5%) of 'abnormal results' may not be truly abnormal but simply outside this defined range. Therefore, undertaking more and more tests makes it increasingly likely that a 'normal' individual will be falsely categorised as 'abnormal' (false positive). As a GP I am all too well aware of the consequences of such overtesting – an anxious patient and increased costs to employers for time off work and to the health service to determine the nature of the 'abnormal' result.

For those seeking to develop health check packages delivering multiple tests, they need be aware of the information presented in Table 3.3.

Rather than simply providing masses of tests those designing health checks should think extremely carefully about the costs and consequences of both the individual components and the combination. Getting this balance right is no easy task.

Following a health check and initial screening tests there are often a variety of possible pathways that might be followed in order to establish a definitive diagnosis. Ensuring the individual is on the correct pathway with sufficient support is key to improving outcomes, controlling costs and ensuring a high-value health check. For example, Halpern and colleagues examined the cost-effectiveness of four diagnostic approaches to the evaluation of asymptomatic microscopic haematuria: computed tomography (CT) only, cystoscopy only, renal ultrasound plus cystoscopy, or CT plus cystoscopy. Ultrasound plus cystoscopy

Table 3.3 Number of tests and false positives

| Number of independent tests undertaken (all with a normal reference ranges set at 95% of individuals) | Percentage of 'normal' individuals labelled as 'abnormal' by testing and requiring further assessment (false positives) (%) |
|---|---|
| 1 | 5 |
| 10 | 40 |
| 20 | 64 |
| 30 | 78 |
| 40 | 87 |

detected 245 cancers per 10,000 patients and was most cost effective with an incremental cost per cancer detected of $53,810. Replacing ultrasound with CT detected just one additional cancer with much increased incremental cost per cancer detected of $6,480,484 (10).

Unfortunately cost data can often be difficult to find and judgements might need to be made. However, such information is gradually becoming more readily available as healthcare systems focus more on value (11).

### 3.2.5 Choosing measures wisely

In seeking to deliver a better value health check very careful consideration needs to be given to the predictive validity, the reliability (reproducibility) and the utility of all the clinical data elements of a health check. Measurements also have to be practicable within the setting where the health check is being undertaken.

*Predictive validity* represents the ability to predict the outcome of interest such as survival or an earlier stage diagnosis.

The predictive validity of any element in health check can be expressed in a number of ways (i.e. sensitivity, specificity, positive predictive value, likelihood ratio and receiver operator characteristic [ROC] curve) (2) (Table 3.4).

A highly specific test means few false positives. If a clinical data component with low specificity is used in a health check many people without diseases or disorders will test positive, potentially receiving unnecessary diagnostic procedures to confirm that they are free of a specific condition. A highly sensitive test means that there are few false-negative results and thus fewer cases of disease are missed.

It is therefore desirable to choose clinical data elements that are both highly sensitive and highly specific, but this is not always possible. Therefore, in designing a health check it is necessary to think very carefully about the requirements linked to testing for a specific condition in relation to any possible trade-offs between sensitivity and specificity. Informed decision making is also about ensuring that individuals attending for health checks are aware of any such compromises and the balances set between false positives/true positives and false negatives/true negatives.

Table 3.4 Common measures of predictive validity

| Measures of predictive validity | Definitions |
|---|---|
| Sensitivity | The probability of a positive result in relation to the clinical data if the disease or disorder is present (the 'true-positive' rate). |
| Specificity | The probability of a negative result in relation to the clinical data if the disease or disorder is absent (the 'true-negative' rate). |
| Positive predictive value | The probability that the disease or disorder is present if the clinical data result is positive [present]. (The negative predictive value is the probability that the disease or disorder is absent if the clinical data result is negative [absent].) |
| Likelihood ratio | The likelihood that a given result in relation to the clinical data would be expected in an individual with the disease or disorder compared to the likelihood that the same result would be expected in an individual without the disease or disorder. Likelihood ratios indicate how many times more (or less) likely a result is in an individual with the disease or disorder compared to an individual free of the disease or disorder. |
| Receiver operator characteristic (ROC) curve | A graphic representation of the relationship between the true-positive rate of the clinical data and the false-positive rate of the same clinical data as the criterion (cutoff point) of a positive result is changed. |

The positive predictive value often makes the most intuitive sense to those with an interest in health checks. However, for those seeking to design better value health checks it is important to be aware that the predictive value is affected by the prevalence. It situations where the prevalence is low – such as those attending health checks as opposed to hospital outpatient clinics – the number of false positives tends to increase resulting in a lowering of the positive predictive value. A clinical data element with 90% sensitivity and 95% specificity has a positive predictive value of 95% if the underlying prevalence of disease is 50% but only 15% if the prevalence is 1%.

In relation to health checks, we also need to consider the false-positive paradox. The probability of a positive result is determined not only by the predictive validity of the clinical data but by the characteristics of the population undergoing the health check. When the incidence of the condition being sought is lower than the clinical data element's false-positive rate, even tests that have a high specificity (i.e. a very low chance of giving a false-positive result in an individual case) will give more false than true positives. Hence, it is very important at the outset to be aware of the prevalence or incidence of conditions in any group undergoing health checks. For example, when HIV prevalence or incidence is low due to effective HIV prevention interventions, rapid point-of-care HIV tests (see Chapter 14) result in a high number of false relative to true-positive results, although the absolute number of false results will be low (12).

In recent years, there has been an increasing interest in the use of the likelihood ratio, a ratio between the sensitivity and the specificity. The magnitude of the likelihood ratio provides a measure of the predictive ability of the clinical data. Clinical data components with likelihood ratios greater than 1 increase the chances of diseases or disorders; the larger the likelihood ratio, the more compelling is the argument for diseases or disorders. Conversely, clinical data elements that have likelihood ratios between 1 and 0 decrease the probability of diseases or disorders; the closer the likelihood ratio is to 0, the more convincing the finding argues against a specific condition. Some clinical data components, when present, have a dramatic effect on the likelihood of diseases or disorders but change the probability little when they are absent. Other features are more useful if they are absent because the negative finding practically excludes diseases or disorders.

A particular advantage of using likelihood ratios as opposed to individual sensitivity and specificity values is that the characteristics of the clinical data element can be combined into a single number. It is also possible to describe the element in a more clinically meaningful series of strata for different levels of the clinical finding. The use of likelihood ratios also avoids any major concerns about the possible impact of disease prevalence on the predictive validity. However, as in the case of all of the measures of predictive validity, likelihood ratios cannot be easily transposed from one population to another, and there is a need to ensure that they are applicable to the individuals undergoing the health check.

Another issue to consider is that individuals first presenting to a clinician at a health check will often have conditions that are at an evolutionary stage when the predictive characteristics of some clinical data components will be changing. As time passes the characteristics of the clinical data may become fixed and moreover the person will have had time to reflect on his or her story. This can often be the cause of complaints as the individual assumes that they have been given a 'clean bill of health' at the health check. In light of this it is always important to 'safety net' and to encourage individuals to be alert for any new or changed symptoms or signs that might arise after a health check. In my experience, this is particularly important in relation to colorectal cancer, prostate cancer and ovarian cancer (see Chapters 7, 12 and 13).

*Reliability* or *reproducibility* is about the variation in measurements taken by a single person or instrument on the same item, under the same conditions, and, perhaps, 2–3 weeks apart.

Securing a reproducible response from an individual at a health check answering a clinical question or completing a questionnaire matters if we are going to have confidence that a clinical data element represents a useful tool. Moreover, it is also important to seek to ensure that different clinicians conducting a health check are likely to be able to elicit similar information from the history or from the clinical examination when confronted by the same individual.

The most straightforward way to express reliability is by simply calculating the proportion of agreement but this ignores the effect of chance accounting for the findings. To assess the chance-corrected proportional agreement the kappa statistic is used and different ranges for kappa have been categorised with respect to the degree of agreement they suggest. Values greater than 0.80 may be taken to represent almost perfect agreement, values between 0.61 and 0.80 substantial agreement, values between 0.41 and 0.60 moderate agreement, values between 0.21 and 0.40 slight agreement and values of 0.20 or below represent poor agreement beyond chance.

Finally, as for predictive validity, it is important to appreciate that reliability is also influenced by the clinical context.

*Utility* is about the ability of one or more clinical data elements of the health check to bring about improvements in outcomes relative to the current best alternative – which could include not having a health check.

Considering utility is particularly important in the context of a better value health check as it is quite possible to end up with a mass of valid and reliable clinical data and even identify a range of early diseases or disorders – but such information does not, in itself, necessarily generate any health benefit (13).

Therefore, utility is about ensuring that the data outputs from the health check are able to guide downstream management in order to improve outcomes. Utility is also not simply about looking at subsequent treatment outcomes but also the impacts (positive and negative) on social relationships (e.g. stigmatisation and social isolation), an individual's healthcare values, attitudes and beliefs in addition to any effects on lifestyle (e.g. changes to diet, exercise and smoking habits).

In choosing measures for inclusion within a health check there is also a need to exercise some caution in ensuring that any research evidence or guidance being used to assist in the selection of a clinical data component is actually relevant to the situation under consideration. This issue is particularly important in seeking to make judgements concerning applicability:

1. Is the research study population sufficiently similar to the population that is undergoing a health check (in terms of, e.g. age, gender, lifestyle [e.g. smoking or alcohol use], medical history [including medications], ethnic origin)?
2. What is the exact nature of the measure being examined within the research study? It is always important to appreciate that this is often not simply about, for example, a 'test' but all the other elements that might be associated with this 'test' (see Chapter 2).

3. What outcomes are being assessed in the research study? Are these outcomes relevant and important to individuals undergoing health checks?
4. Is the comparison group in the research study appropriate?

## 3.2.6 Adopting a risk-oriented strategy

A better value health check is about seeking to exploit all the information obtained from an individual in a more efficient and rational fashion with more appropriate testing. Key to this is understanding an individual's baseline risk of diseases or disorders linked to features in their lifestyle, personal characteristics and personal or family medical history. It is also important to appreciate that everyone has a different baseline risk and that no one is at zero-baseline risk of developing, for example, some form of cardiovascular disease or cancer – even those who have undergone a health check.

Recently, I encountered a 70-year-old gentleman with iron deficiency anaemia and abdominal discomfort. During the course of the subsequent GP consultation, he stated 'well at least one thing is certain, I don't have bowel cancer as I had a health check including bowel cancer screening with occult blood testing last month'. After a lot of further discussion, he finally agreed to a referral and subsequently underwent resection for his tumour. Other individuals who are non-smokers or ex-smokers have been equally bemused that I might consider them to be at risk from lung cancer.

For those with an interest in health checks it is often useful to think in terms of a number of probability steps increasing or decreasing the likelihood of diseases or disorders occurring.

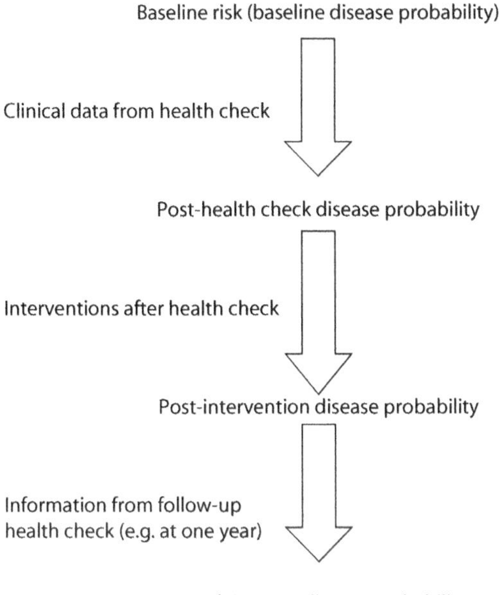

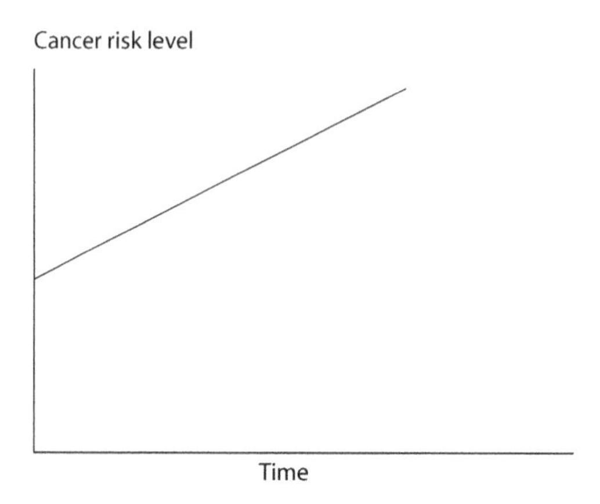


Figure 3.1 Baseline cancer risk over time.

Assessing an individual's baseline cancer risk, for example, generally relies on their age and gender. However, this risk might be further refined at the health check – or ideally before the health check – by obtaining additional information on an individual's symptoms, family history, lifestyle and past medical history. Appropriately selected clinical data elements can then be used to add precision to this baseline risk to produce a post–health check disease probability. This process is further facilitated by the application of a number of computerised risk assessment tools applicable to health checks such as the Fracture Risk Assessment Tool (FRAX), QRISK3 and also Familial Risk Assessment – Breast and Ovarian Cancer (FRA-BOC) tool (see Chapters 4, 6 and 13).

In relation to cancer, everyone can be considered to be at a certain level of individual baseline cancer risk. As illustrated in Figure 3.1 this risk will gradually increase over time as the people get older. On occasion, the whole line might shift upwards depending on additional factors that affect the baseline risk such as a new medical problem, a change in the family history or a fresh symptom.

Furthermore, addressing risk is about providing the individual with an evidence-based risk reduction plan incorporating lifestyle recommendations (e.g. diet, exercise, alcohol and smoking), specific suggestions about screening (types and frequencies) and when to seek further medical attention for, perhaps, investigation, referral or treatment. The risk reduction plan needs to be built on the risk assessment and carefully tailored to the individual as, for example, the screening suggested to a person at elevated risk due to a family history of colorectal cancer or a history of adenomatous polyps will be different to that for an asymptomatic patient whose only risk factor is being 60 years old (see Chapter 7).

Successful compliance with preventive activities such as smoking cessation, an improved diet and increased exercise should result in a move down towards a new level of risk (see Figure 3.2).

In relation to screening it is suggested that, after an initial reduction following the testing (related to the sensitivity of the screening test), there will then be a gradual drift up towards the previous risk level (depending on the natural history

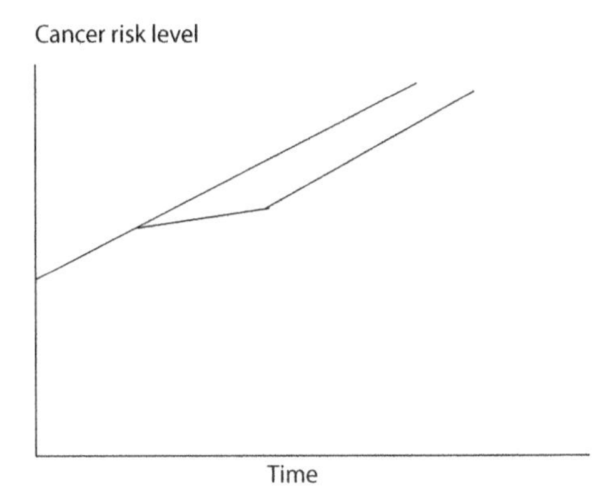


Figure 3.2 The impact of prevention activities on cancer risk.

and the incidence of the cancer). A subsequent screen will then push the risk down again resulting in a 'sawtooth'-type risk profile (see Figure 3.3).

By adopting such a risk-oriented approach, I would argue that it is easier to emphasise to an individual that, although a health check might reduce their risk, it can *never* eliminate that risk and they should remain alert for any new symptoms or signs. The benefits are a better-informed customer and a more balanced and focused discussion about what might (or might not) be done next (e.g. continuing monitoring, further testing, treatment or onward referral). Using a risk-oriented approach can also increase value by better targeting of testing.

Precision medicine – or personalised medicine – is an attempt to classify individuals into subpopulations that differ in their susceptibility to a particular disease, in the biology or prognosis of diseases they may develop, or in their response to a specific treatment. The idea is that preventative or therapeutic interventions can be concentrated on those who will benefit – sparing expense and side effects for those who will not benefit. The model suggests that health checks are customised to individuals, with testing being used to more precisely guide the next steps based on, for example, an individual's genetic make-up.

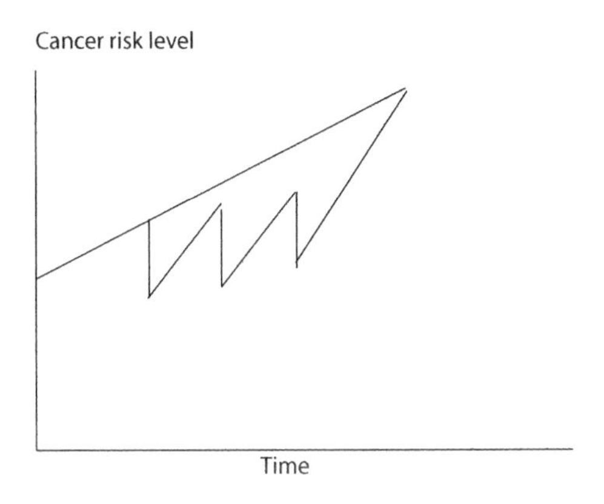


Figure 3.3 The impact of screening activities on cancer risk.

Precision medicine is an obvious development of the risk-oriented approach as technologies develop and improve. For example, if it is found that a particular genotype increases a person's risk for type 2 diabetes then, perhaps, this individual can initiate lifestyle changes or even embark on a treatment programme to lessen their chances of developing type 2 diabetes later in life.

But, for genetic tests it is important to maintain a sense of perspective and keep the following key issues in mind (14):

1. Does the genetic test accurately detect the absence or presence of a specific genetic variant such as a gene or genetic change?
2. Is the genetic test result related to the presence, absence or risk of a specific disease or disorder?
3. Does the genetic test result provide additional information that is not already available enabling the individual to make a healthcare decision that would not have been otherwise possible? If the genetic test result simply confirms something that the person already knows, then the test has not provided useful information.
4. Does the cost of the genetic test justify by its usefulness?
5. Do the expected health benefits exceed the expected negative consequences by a sufficiently wide margin that the test is worth doing exclusive of the cost?

## 3.3 OPERATIONAL ELEMENTS OF A BETTER VALUE HEALTH CHECK

Building on the six fundamental elements of a better value health check, I now examine some of the more detailed operational considerations – before the health check, during the health check and following the health check – in order to ensure that the health check actually delivers the best value. It is all too easy to set off with a sound vision and principles but to find that these become lost in the process of delivery or implementation.

### 3.3.1 Enhancing value before undertaking the health check

#### 3.3.1.1 TAKING STOCK

Building on the architecture, it is always important to commence by re-visiting the following questions:

1. What are the target diseases and disorders? Linked to this it is also important to ensure that these conditions are relevant and important to the population and the individuals undergoing health checks.
2. What are the health-related purposes of the health check and its constituent clinical data components?
3. What health-related outcomes are being addressed? Is it likely that the direct and indirect costs along the whole care pathway will be reduced by undertaking the health check?
4. What services are currently available and how might these be improved in terms of eligibility, accessibility, acceptability, equity, efficiency, effectiveness and safety?

#### 3.3.1.2 CONSIDERING THE INFORMATION REQUIREMENTS

According to Hoffman and colleagues, many discussions concerning breast, prostate and bowel cancer screening fail to provide balanced information – in a national survey involving 1134 participants most discussions (51%–67%) addressed the pros of screening but only a few (7%–14%) covered the cons (15). However, in relation to delivering better value health checks there is evidence for the positive impacts of shared decision making – incorporating decision aids– for prostate, colorectal and breast cancer screening. Trikalinos and colleagues found that cancer-related decision aids increased knowledge without generating any anxiety (16). Moreover, individuals are more likely to make informed decisions, have accurate risk perceptions and select options that best agree with their values.

It also seems that employing shared decision making in making choices concerning cancer screening results in preferences that reflect the nature of the research evidence. According to Lillie, most tools improve knowledge and reduce decisional conflict (17). Frosh and colleagues also noted that men older than 50 years provided with a written decision aid providing information about prostate-specific antigen (PSA) screening options and outcomes were significantly less likely to choose testing (18). Similarly, for women aged 38–45 years contemplating mammography screening an online decision aid led to increased knowledge and, moreover, a reduction in the desire to opt for earlier screening (19). In contrast, a web-based decision support tool for colorectal cancer screening was very effective in prompting previously unscreened individuals to select an evidence-based screening test (20).

Of course shared decision making in the context of a health check is not simply about specific tests – it also covers chemopreventative treatment decisions such as the use of aspirin, tamoxifen or statins – as well as smoking cessation options (21). In seeking to improve cardiovascular disease outcomes applying a decision aid resulted in a significant increase in patient preferences for effective risk-reducing strategies (including medication) from 42% to 63% (22).

Studies also illustrate the potential for shared decision making to reduce costs. Consistently, around 20% of people who participate in shared decision making choose less invasive surgical options and more conservative treatment than individuals who do not use decision aids (23).

The U.S. Preventive Services Task Force (USPSTF) has proposed that clinicians should inform patients about preventive services where there is clear evidence of net benefit. It is also important to ensure that balanced, evidence-based information about any testing (including the potential benefits and harms, alternatives and uncertainties) is both available and accessible in various formats prior to any testing being undertaken. For preventive services for which the balance of potential benefits and harms is a close call, or for which the evidence is insufficient to guide a decision for or against screening, it is suggested that clinicians should assist people to determine whether individual characteristics and personal preferences favour performing or not performing the testing (21).

Shared decision making as the process by which individuals are involved as active partners with the clinicians in choosing a preferred type of health check (or a specific component of a health check) involves several stages:

1. Clarifying the decision by carefully defining and explaining the problem. This should also encompass an appreciation of the uncertain nature of medical knowledge and practice.
2. Discussing the evidence base and checking understanding.
3. Acknowledging the person's role in decision making.
4. Unbiased and effective communication about the potential benefits and the possible harms of different options.
5. Exploring the individual's attitudes to the benefits and harms outlined.

In communicating risks care needs to be taken with the vocabulary used as well as the denominator chosen. One person's understanding of 'likely' may be a chance of 1 in 10 whereas another may think it means a chance of 1 in 2. If different denominators are used (i.e. 1/100 or 30/1000), some individuals might mistake which is the greater risk. Portraying options can also be difficult; for example, it is recognised that many patients find the choice 'doing nothing' unpalatable and, in this situation, the use of more positive options such as 'watchful waiting' may be more acceptable.

A sound practical model for how to accomplish shared decision making in routine practice is provided by Elwyn and colleagues and consists of three steps: introducing choice, describing options and helping people explore preferences and make decisions (24).

*Introducing choice* – or choice talk – is about ensuring that individuals know what reasonable options are available. This can be undertaken by e-mail, letter or telephone.

*Describing options* – or option talk – is about providing more detailed information about the options. To start with it is important to check existing knowledge and clarify any misunderstandings. Perhaps using a decision support tool (e.g. website, DVD or written information) the available options are then listed and described (including possible harms and benefits).

*Helping people explore preferences and make decisions* – decision talk – is the third element. A key aspect of this is about understanding an individual's preferences – i.e. what matters most to them – and helping them to move to a decision. For health checks it is also important to acknowledge that decisions do not need to be taken immediately and people might need time and decision support resources to help them to make a choice.

Decision support tools can be particularly helpful in summarising information in formats that are more accessible to patients – especially comparative data on harms and benefits.

Based on the European Consensus agreement (25) the overall information requirements prior to a health check are summarised in Table 3.5.

Table 3.5 Information requirements

| Information | Detail |
| --- | --- |
| Overview | The provider should provide information that is understandable, timely, verifiable, accurate, complete, truthful and not misleading about the health check and its potential results, in a way that enables individuals to make an informed choice about the health check.<br>The information must be presented in a way that also considers the individual's understanding, culture and language. |
| Communication and informed consent | The provider shall verify if the information requirements of the client are met, inform about the handling of residual material from the testing, inform about complaints procedures, obtain explicit informed consent, specify the findings consented and provide sufficient time and opportunity for the client to reconsider the health check. |
| Scope and purposes | The provider shall specify what is addressed by the health check including the condition, natural course and seriousness, risk factors, symptoms, available treatment and follow-up. The purpose, accuracy and implications of each component must also be clear. |

#### 3.3.1.3 OFFERING A BALANCED PACKAGE

The traditional approach to health checks has been to offer a fixed number of components. However, to enhance value it is suggested that, although retaining a core package remains useful (see Table 3.6), for the majority of individuals some elements benefit from tailoring.

In my view tailoring is a key element of delivering better value by

1. Helping to ensure that the net benefits of a specific test exceed any potential harms linked to false positives, false negatives and overdiagnoses.

Table 3.6 Suggested core components for a health check

| Core components |
| --- |
| BMI and body composition |
| Waist circumference |
| Blood pressure |
| Haematology (full blood count) |
| Biochemistry (liver, renal, bone and lipid profiles) |
| Urinalysis |
| Cardiovascular risk score (see Chapter 4) |
| Diabetes risk score (see Chapter 9) |
| Depression score (Patient Health Questionnaire [PHQ-9]) |
| Anxiety score (Generalised Anxiety Disorder Seven-Item Scale [GAD-7]) |

2. Facilitating a more explicit focus on an individual's baseline risks, values, expectations and concerns in determining who should be tested for a specific condition and, moreover, what is the most appropriate modality to use.
3. Contributing to avoiding any unnecessary duplication of tests (e.g. by liaison with a person's usual healthcare provider).
4. Encouraging individuals to comply with any necessary pre-testing requirements, for example, in relation to diet and medications.
5. Confirming that individuals satisfy a test's eligibility criteria.
6. Ensuring that sufficient consideration has been given to the potential outputs from any testing. This links into Section 3.3.1.2 on information requirements.
7. Enhancing precision beyond the core testing to help to focus the next steps in the care pathway. Table 3.7 details some examples of tests that might be harnessed to supplement the core package.
8. Examining alternatives. Any suggested test should be considered not only against similar technologies (e.g. imaging versus imaging) but also in relation to and in conjunction with other approaches (e.g. imaging versus history/examination/prediction rules or versus physiological measurement or versus endoscopy or versus testing combinations).

It is obviously not feasible or appropriate to tailor every test to every individual. Therefore, my favoured approach to design a health check is to offer a core package supplemented by up to five individually tailored elements. In addition, for some organisations, there might be a further planning stage before this individualised tailoring such that the core package is also made more appropriate to the overall demographic profile (i.e. age and gender), the geographical locations or the nature of the work undertaken (e.g. working practices/environment) within an organisation. For example, if all employees are aged over 45 then it might be useful for some cancer markers such as faecal occult blood testing to be included within the core package.

I would suggest that there are a number of possible approaches to individual tailoring:

Table 3.7 Enhancing precision

| Core component | Additional tests that might be included to enhance precision |
|---|---|
| Glucose | HbA1c (see Chapter 9) |
| Diabetes risk score | |
| Liver function | ELF score (see Chapter 8) |
| Cardiovascular risk score | Lipoprotein-associated phospholipase A2 (see Chapter 4) |

- A structured discussion between an appropriately trained physician and the individual seeking a health check. This is best undertaken by phone.
- The transmission of a list of 'tailoring questions' to individuals with the completed questions being reviewed by an appropriately trained physician who can then suggest additional tests by e-mail from a pre-agreed menu (and any supplementary questions can also be covered by e-mail correspondence).
- The development of a computerised algorithm that can be completed by the individual undergoing the screening – ideally with online links to decision support tools and other shared decision making resources.

It is clear that different models of tailoring will suit different individuals and pockets. There are also advantages and disadvantages of each approach – the structured discussion often throws up issues that might not have been foreseen and also focuses attention more on an individual's concerns and expectations. But the shared decision making occurring as a result of the computerised algorithm may be of a much better quality.

Some selected examples of focused tailoring questions are listed in Table 3.8.

With the caveat that care needs to be taken not to make the list too long, two further elements are also worth considering:

1. The inclusion of additional risk assessment questionnaires such as FRAX (Fracture Risk Assessment Tool) or Alcohol Use Disorders Identification Test (AUDIT).
2. Open questions:

    a. 'Do you suffer from any other medical condition(s) requiring regular treatments or reviews?'
    b. 'What worries you most about your health?'

#### 3.3.1.4 ENABLING ACCESSIBILITY

For health checks to be able to generate positive impacts on both individual health and the public health (including organisational health) they need to be accessible. In order to enhance accessibility a number of barriers have to be addressed as follows.

*Price*: Although considering costs along the whole care pathway is a key element of a better value health check there is no doubt that lowering the basic

Table 3.8 Examples of tailoring questions

| Domain | Example |
|---|---|
| Personal characteristics | • What is your age in years?<br>• What is your gender? |
| Lifestyle | • Do you drink alcohol every day or do you ever have more than six drinks on one occasion?<br>• Do you smoke now or have you smoked within the last 5 years?<br>• Do you work indoors most of the time? |
| Current medications | • Do you take any tablets or have any injections for diabetes?<br>• Do you take any medicines for high blood pressure?<br>• Do you take any medicines for raised cholesterol? |
| Personal medical history | • Have you ever been told by a doctor that you have heart disease or have had a stroke or mini-stroke?<br>• Have you been diagnosed with coeliac disease, colitis or Crohn disease? If 'YES' please specify which condition(s).<br>• Have you been diagnosed with thyroid problems?<br>• Have you ever been diagnosed with cancer? If 'YES' please specify which type(s) of cancer. |
| Family medical history | • Have any of your immediate family (mother, father, brothers, sisters) been diagnosed with heart disease or strokes UNDER THE AGE OF 60?<br>• Have any of your immediate family (mother, father, brothers, sisters) been diagnosed with bowel, breast, prostate, ovary or pancreatic cancer? If 'YES' please specify which type(s) of cancer.<br>• Have any of your immediate family (mother, father, brothers, sisters) been diagnosed with coeliac disease, colitis or Crohn disease? If 'YES' please specify which condition(s).<br>• Have any of your immediate family or other relatives been diagnosed with thyroid problems? |
| Symptoms | • Do you have pain or stiffness in any of your muscles or joints?<br>• Do you have irritable bowel or are you currently troubled by any of the following: constipation, diarrhoea, or stomach pain?<br>• Do you currently suffer from indigestion or heartburn? |

*(Continued)*

Table 3.8 (*Continued*) Examples of tailoring questions

| Domain | Example |
|---|---|
| | • Have you noticed that you have started passing urine more frequently and/or getting up at night to pass urine?<br>• Has your memory been poor in the last 12 months and is it affecting your life? |
| Recent investigations/ tests | • When did you last have a mammogram?<br>• Have you ever had a PSA test and when? |

price of a health check improves uptake. Costs can be reduced and efficiency enhanced by, for example,

- Negotiating prices and services with suppliers
- Establishing systems and processes to avoid any unnecessary repeating or duplication of tests
- Optimising the use of transport and information technology
- Addressing fixed costs (e.g. premises)
- Scrutinising the expensive elements of the testing package such as the use of clinical staff or the skill set required for the purposes of the testing

*Convenience*: Offering health checks at a range of times, days and locations (with easy parking and transport links) will enhance accessibility. However, another key inconvenience faced by many attending health checks is the requirement to fast for 8 hours in order to accurately assess lipid and glucose levels. But, as discussed further in Chapter 9, a fasted glucose is unnecessary (in most cases) to check for diabetes. In relation to cholesterol measurements, accurate results might now also be obtained without fasting (or with only a brief fast) provided that the triglyceride result is not above 4 mmol/L (26,27).

*Eligibility*: There are adults who should not have routine health checks. Pregnancy was discussed in Chapter 2 and, for the following, a routine health check might also not be appropriate:

- Severe mental health issues
- Inability to give consent
- Unable to stand unaided or get up onto a medical bed
- Inability to keep still (e.g. due to a severe tremor)

However, many other individuals are often inappropriately excluded from health checks such as those with symptoms, those with co-morbidities, those with physical or learning disabilities, or cancer survivors.

*Alternatives*: To enhance accessibility for some it might be that alternative (and more acceptable) approaches to testing may need to be considered such as self-testing (e.g. for HPV – see Chapter 13).

## 3.3.2 Enhancing the value of the health check

In addition to selecting components that are valid, reliable and outcome oriented, particular attention needs to be paid to the way these measures are used to collect clinical data in the context of a health check.

Broadly, there are requirements to establish, document, implement and maintain quality management systems in addition to continually improving their effectiveness. Three questions need to be addressed:

- Are robust clinical governance systems (including risk management, internal and external quality assurance, audit and training) in place?
- Have specific safety issues been considered including infection control, errors (e.g. in identification and transmission of results), adherence to standard operating procedures and the approach to abnormal results (tester and recipient)?
- Who has overall responsibility and authority for quality? Have appropriate roles been assigned and communicated?

Some specific issues to consider include the following.

### 3.3.2.1 STANDARD OPERATING PROCEDURES

Standard operating procedures should be developed for each element of the health check focused on achieving efficiency, quality outputs, safety and uniformity of performance. From a clinical perspective I have personally written a number of clinical work instructions for private screening organisations that are structured as follows:

1. *Overview* – What is the test? Why have the test? Specific issues to consider?
2. *Operation* – Purpose? Preparation? Exclusions or inclusions? Procedure?
3. *Referral criteria and next steps* – This also needs to address any immediate actions to follow should, for example, an individual be found to have a very high blood pressure or a significantly abnormal pulse rate or rhythm at the time of the assessment.

### 3.3.2.2 RESOURCE MANAGEMENT

Consideration needs to be given to a number of aspects of resource management:

- *Provision of resources* – Determining and providing the resources needed
- *Human resources* – Determining the competence of the personnel and ensuring the competencies on the basis of appropriate education, training and experience
- *Infrastructure* – Determining, providing and maintaining the infrastructure needed, such as building space and associated utilities, process equipment and supporting services
- *Work environment* – Determining and managing the work environment such as noise, temperature and lighting

#### 3.3.2.3 QUALITY ASSURANCE

For blood samples being sent to an external laboratory there is a requirement to carefully consider approaches to mitigate pre-analytical errors linked to, for example, venous sampling, handling (i.e. consider using a centrifuge) and transportation. The pre-analytical phase is the most vulnerable part of the total testing process.

The control and the regular calibration of all measuring equipment used in the context of a health check are also critical to ensure valid results. Point-of-care testing (PoCT) is a specific concern in relation to health checks as a variety of potential sources of error have been highlighted. The following list of problems is of particular relevance to lipid and glucose testing:

- Wrong sample container used for venous sampling
- Poor sampling techniques used for fingerprick testing
- Delays in sample analysis and failure to mix samples
- Failure to follow the instruction manual
- Lack of maintenance or servicing
- Failure to carry out quality control
- Failure of coding
- Failure to understand error codes or warning messages
- Lack of training

With most modern PoCT devices, there has been significant technological investment in the development of sophisticated inbuilt quality checks within the testing unit itself. Manufacturers have recognised that, in the future, the main consumers of PoCT will be health professionals from a non-laboratory background, and they have deliberately tried to make the devices as simple as possible for the operator and, at the same time, as well controlled internally as is feasible. Some have even suggested that, with such technical advances, internal and external quality assurance have become redundant.

However, according to Gill and Shepherd, there remains a role for traditional internal and external quality control as an independent check of the quality of PoCT systems (28).

Many glucose monitoring systems come with control solutions which permit the test strips and meter to be checked against a pre-calibrated blood glucose sample. Such internal quality control should always be undertaken

- Before using a new box of test strips
- When a new operator uses the meter
- If there is any suspicion that the meter or test strips are not working accurately (e.g. producing two consecutive low or high glucose results)
- If there is any suspicion that the meter might have been damaged
- After cleaning the meter (or after any maintenance or service)
- At least once a week

The term *external quality assessment* is used to describe a method that allows for benchmarking of the PoCT results against those of a laboratory. Traditionally, the comparison has been made with the performance of a reference laboratory. However, an alternative approach is split or parallel patient sample testing in which the same sample is tested by PoCT and by a local laboratory (already linked itself to the reference laboratory). Potential advantages of split sample testing for those conducting health checks are as follows:

- It is a robust external check of quality.
- The testing utilises a sample of identical matrix (e.g. whole blood) to that of routine patient samples.
- It is a more cost-effective external assessment of quality.
- With samples equivalent to routine specimens, it can also check the pre-analytical component of testing.

Overall, any approach to PoCT quality control needs to consider the manufacturer's recommendations, the device technology and the capability of the users.

## 3.3.3 Enhancing value after the health check

### 3.3.3.1 ENSURING EFFECTIVENESS

It is always important to seek to monitor outcomes following a health check. However, one of the particular challenges is to determine whether a health check (or one of the interventions included within the health check) has actually contributed to a specific health-related outcome. In parallel with a health check other things may have altered in an individual's lifestyle or within their environment that might have led to impacts on their health. It can often be quite tricky to untangle the outcomes attributable to a health check from those due to other factors such as national media campaigns, legislative changes or an individual prescribed a treatment by their regular doctors. Moreover, there is no guarantee that even apparently straightforward interventions following a relevant finding at a health check might improve outcomes. For example, on the face of it hepatitis B immunisation should lead to a reduction in liver disease and lowered mortality. But it is also possible that those individuals who feel 'liver protected' because of the immunization might continue to engage in other risky activities such as drinking more alcohol or adopting a lifestyle that increases their chances of contracting hepatitis C, thereby confounding the beneficial effects of the hepatitis B immunization.

For those interested in designing better value health checks there is also a requirement to distinguish between effectiveness and efficacy. Efficacy is the ability of the science and technology of healthcare to bring about improvements in health when used under the most favourable circumstances (such as in the context of a research study). Effectiveness, on the other hand, is the degree to which attainable improvements in health are, in fact, achieved in the real world.

Taking faecal occult blood screening (using faecal immunochemical testing [FIT] or faecal occult blood testing [FOBT], see Chapter 7) and bowel cancer mortality as an example, my approach to determining if a test is likely to be causally linked to improvements in outcomes hinges on seven questions. Clearly, some of these questions can be addressed before testing when any new test is first introduced into a health check; but with continued use of a test an organisation offering health checks ought to be able to answer all these questions for individuals procuring, purchasing or undergoing such testing (Table 3.9).

#### 3.3.3.2 REVIEWING SAFETY AND QUALITY

It is always important to regularly review and to seek to continually improve the quality of health checks including corrective and preventative actions. Publication of an annual performance and monitoring report is recommended.

More specifically there are requirements to

- Ensure any errors or incidents have been dealt with competently and sensitively
- Ensure that lessons are learnt from any errors or incidents with appropriate changes to systems being made to prevent any recurrence(s)
- Set and review agreed minimum and target standards to be achieved by a health check programme, for example,
    - Have any exclusion criteria been applied correctly?
    - Has there been adequately informed consent or choice?
    - Have results reached the correct individuals within the pre-agreed time period?

#### 3.3.3.3 BOOSTING IMPACTS ON INDIVIDUALS

Whenever I appraise a health check proposal I pose the following questions with a view to ensuring that all the findings are dealt with appropriately and without placing an unnecessary burden on the NHS (or private health insurers) or generating unwarranted anxiety amongst individuals having health checks:

1. How are urgent abnormal findings defined and communicated to individuals? Urgent abnormal findings can arise at the health check (e.g. abnormal blood pressure or pulse readings) or as a result of the subsequent detailed analysis of, for example, blood samples or electrocardiogram (ECG) recordings.
2. How are routine abnormal findings or findings of uncertain significance defined and communicated to individuals?
3. How are normal findings defined and communicated to individuals?
4. How specific and operational is the advice given to individuals undergoing health checks about significantly abnormal findings (urgent or routine), abnormal findings of uncertain significance and normal findings?
5. What mechanisms are in place to ensure that any advice given is patient-centred, evidence-based, regularly updated and consistent (between members of a health check organisation)?
6. What safety netting is in place to address unforeseen issues?

Table 3.9 Assessing effectiveness

| Does the FOBT/FIT contribute to the health-related outcome? | FOBT/FIT and bowel cancer |
|---|---|
| *Efficacy – Strength of association*<br>Is there good-quality research evidence demonstrating a strong association between the test and the outcomes from bowel cancer that is unlikely to be due to other factors? | As discussed in Chapter 7, there is sound evidence that testing brings about a reduction in death rates from bowel cancer. Moreover, the statistical association is strong and not attributable to other factors (confounders). |
| *Efficacy – Consistency of association*<br>Has the issue been looked at by a number of different and good-quality research studies and is there consistency between the results? | As discussed in Chapter 7, there is sound evidence from a number of different studies undertaken in a variety of settings in relation to the likely impact of testing on bowel cancer–related outcomes. |
| *Plausibility*<br>Is the association between the test and the outcome biologically plausible in relation to the stated purpose of the test? | The biological rationale behind FOBT/FIT in improving outcomes is that occult bleeding occurs from both early bowel cancers and pre-malignant polyps. Moreover, surgically removing these will prevent any further development or spread of malignancy/pre-malignancy. |
| *Effectiveness: Pathway*<br>Is there a clearly agreed – and accessible – pathway of care which, if followed, is likely to bring about improvements in outcomes in a cost-effective manner following the initial testing based? | This is about ensuring that there is a clearly agreed approach to dealing with negative results, positive results, equivocal results and lost results/samples.<br>Moreover, results need to be dealt with in a cost-effective manner in order to deliver the best value. There is a requirement to minimise the inappropriate or excessive use of subsequent testing with increased delays and costs.<br>In order to evaluate testing against this question it is useful to refer to the 'Programme Specific Operating Model for Quality Assurance of Bowel Cancer Screening Programmes' (29). |

(*Continued*)

Table 3.9 (*Continued*) Assessing effectiveness

| Does the FOBT/FIT contribute to the health-related outcome? | FOBT/FIT and bowel cancer |
|---|---|
| *Effectiveness: Temporal relationship audit*<br>Is the time interval between the testing and the initial diagnosis of bowel cancer consistent with a causal link between the two elements? | For FOBT/FIT, there will be a need to ensure that the next steps in the process (i.e. colonoscopy) were linked to the test and not already arranged due to another factor such as overt rectal bleeding. |
| *Effectiveness: Audit of positives*<br>Has a post–health check audit been undertaken to determine the subsequent diagnoses made following the initial positive screening result (false-positive and true-positive results)? | As FOBT/FIT are screening tests any positive result then needs to be evaluated by colonoscopy. A simple way to identify what the definitive diagnosis turns out to be (including any false positives) is by contacting the individual 3–6 months following their health check. If possible, it might also be useful to gain consent to obtain further information from their own doctor about their future progress. |
| *Effectiveness: Audit of negatives*<br>Is a system in place to identify those who subsequently turn out to have a problem that was not picked up at the screen (false negatives)? | Most private health check companies undertake customer satisfaction surveys after a health check. This provides an opportunity to identify important/significant conditions that might have been diagnosed in the 6- to 12-month period following a health check such as new bowel cancers. Another issue is to identify any delayed diagnoses (e.g. due to false re-assurance or inadequate safety netting). |

Following a health check most individuals will receive a written report. Ideally, this should arrive as soon as possible and contain clear, operational and tailored explanations of findings. In general, test results will fall into three categories:

1. *Normal finding*: In this situation, it is very important that the tailored text emphasises the requirement to continue to work to maintain a healthy lifestyle in relation to weight, diet, exercise, smoking and alcohol irrespective of the normal result. It is also critical to emphasise that with, for example, cancer markers such as FIT, PSA or cancer antigen 125 (CA-125) a normal finding should be treated with caution in the presence of certain unexplained

symptoms (see Chapters 7, 12 and 13). In addition, it might be suggested to have a further check in, perhaps, 1–2 years depending on the result.
2. *Possibly abnormal finding*: In this situation, it might be suggested that the test be repeated after a pre-defined interval or additional investigations be considered (e.g. ultrasound in the context of abnormal liver fibrosis score). Again advice should also be included on maintaining a healthy lifestyle.
3. *Definitely abnormal finding*: In this situation, the individual will generally be directed back to their usual doctor but with clear advice about possible next steps – for example, colonoscopy in the context of a positive FIT result (see Chapter 7).

In addition, the tailored text will need to vary according to individual circumstances – for example, the information provided linked to an abnormal HbA1c result will require adjustment according to whether or not the individual is already known to have diabetes.

However, to deliver value I would suggest that individuals require more than just a written report – no matter how well constructed. Two specific areas to consider are the personalised health plan and patient activation.

#### 3.3.3.3.1 Personalised health plan

One of the major criticisms of many health check packages (both from customers and their regular physicians) is that there is no opportunity for a detailed and unhurried discussion about any findings with a doctor. This includes the provision of clear and operational advice concerning the follow-up of any issues identified at the health check.

Face-to-face consultations immediately after the initial clinical data collection can also become rushed and insufficiently focused on an individual's needs if there are additional requirements to produce a final report for the person to take away with them at the conclusion of the health check.

The 'personalised health plan' (PHP) incorporates an extended conversation between an individual who has undergone clinical data collection in the context of a health check and a GP or family practitioner. The focus of the PHP is on an individual's particular healthcare concerns combined with a more structured review of their baseline health risks, continuing health problems and the findings from the health check. The overarching purpose of the PHP is to enhance value along the whole care pathway after a health check.

There are three specific aspects to the PHP:

1. Review
   a. Assessing the clinical significance of all the clinical data findings (normal, abnormal, uncertain)
   b. Evaluating any reported/elicited symptoms or signs
   c. Discussing any continuing health problems, investigations and treatments
   d. Determining family and social circumstances (including any significant family medical history)
   e. Assessing and addressing individual values, concerns and expectations

f. Reviewing relative and absolute 10-year cardiovascular and osteoporosis risks (see Chapters 4 and 6)
g. Stratifying diabetes, mental health and cancer risks (see Chapters 9 and 11)
h. If appropriate undertaking an informant interview (see Chapter 15)

Most importantly, the review needs to be scheduled *after* all the test results have been assembled and the individual has received a copy of their interim health report and had time to reflect on the findings. They might also need to discover some additional information themselves in relation to, for example, their family medical history.

The content and times of the assessments can also be tailored to individual requirements but, in general, a personalised health plan takes around 20 minutes and is best undertaken by phone or Skype.

2. Plan
    a. Advising on health risk reduction (especially in relation to cancer or cancer recurrence, cardiovascular disease, diabetes, mental health and osteoporosis – prevention, screening and surveillance)
    b. Advising on the management of continuing health problems (with an emphasis on reducing disability, morbidity and mortality and enhancing quality of life; from a company's perspective additional key outcomes might include facilitating more rapid recovery, return to work and relapse prevention)
    c. Signposting to relevant health and wellbeing resources
    d. Providing appropriate information and education
    e. Recommending additional investigations (diagnosis, screening, monitoring) (e.g. imaging, endoscopies, pathology, physiological testing as appropriate)
    f. Recommending specialist referrals (if appropriate)
    g. Recommending referrals to other services as appropriate (e.g. physiotherapy, counselling/cognitive behavioural therapy [CBT], podiatry, audiology, health coaching and nutrition)
3. *Concierge service (action)*: This is about enabling the plan to be put into action. It might include the following elements:

1. Arranging additional investigations (as detailed in the plan)
2. Arranging specialist referrals (as detailed in the plan)
3. Arranging referrals to other services as appropriate (e.g. physiotherapy, counselling/CBT, podiatry, audiology, health coaching)
4. Communicating to the individual's usual clinician (subject to agreement) using a standardised format
5. Establishing appropriate follow-up arrangments

*NB*: For some issues such as rectal bleeding or breast problems, direct booking for investigations or specialist referrals might even be made without the requirement for a face-to-face consultation.

Table 3.10 Criteria for UK doctors delivering personalised health plans

| Criteria |
|---|
| On the NHS performers list and participating in the NHS appraisal system (in accordance with the General Medical Council revalidation criteria) |
| Member or fellow of the Royal College of General Practitioners in good standing |
| At least 10 years NHS general practice experience and remain active in NHS general practice |
| Commitment to enhancing the quality and consistency of health checks with a particular emphasis on safety, accessibility (time and place), efficiency/acceptability, value and patient satisfaction/convenience |
| Commercially aware and supportive of the work of both the private medical insurance industry and the private healthcare providers |
| Excellent communications (written and verbal) and interpersonal skills |
| Experience and/or additional training/qualifications in clinical general practice, education, research or public health medicine; interests in health checks and early diagnosis |

In seeking to ensure high value, my own experience has been that the doctors delivering health checks are of variable experience, qualifications, confidence and quality. In relation to selecting doctors to undertake PHPs in the United Kingdom, I have therefore developed some explicit criteria (see Table 3.10).

### 3.3.3.3.2 Patient activation

An important aspect of helping individuals to act appropriately on the findings from a health check with a view to improving their outcomes is to seek to better understand their perspectives. This of course echoes, builds on and links to the shared decision making undertaken before the health check.

Patient activation (30) is an approach to understanding the knowledge, skills and confidence a person has in managing their own health and healthcare. Individuals who have low levels of activation are less likely to play an active role in staying healthy and following advice – with adverse effects on both outcomes and healthcare costs. But, those who are more activated are more likely to engage in healthy behaviours such as eating a well-balanced diet or taking regular exercise.

To measure patient activation a valid and reliable tool has been developed (patient activation measure [PAM]). In common with PROMs the PAM is a measure that the individual completes themselves. It consists of 13 statements about beliefs, confidence in the management of health-related tasks and self-assessed knowledge. People are asked to rate the extent to which they agree or disagree with each statement with the responses scored and totalled.

Examples of questions include the following:

- I am confident that I can maintain lifestyle changes like eating right and exercising even during times of stress.

- I am confident that I can help prevent or reduce problems associated with my health.
- I know how to prevent problems with my health.

Tailoring support, advice and actions according to initial PAM levels represents better value health with impacts of care costs and outcomes such as quality of life or cholesterol or blood pressure levels. Moreover, patient activation can be altered using techniques such as peer support, health coaching, educational initiatives, skills development and confidence building.

Following a health check it is worth considering tailoring any initial interventions to a person's level of activation, possibly using health coaching (Table 3.11).

#### 3.3.3.4 AUGMENTING IMPACTS FOR GROUPS (E.G. ORGANISATIONS)

If a group of individuals within an organisation undergoes health checks the data can be aggregated into a 'public health plan'. As will be discussed in Chapter 16, it is recommended to undertake careful baseline assessments of body size and composition, fitness and physical activity, smoking status, blood pressure and lipids, alcohol misuse and the extent of any anxiety or depression for all members of an organisation prior to designing a workplace wellness improvement programme.

Having developed and presented a variety of 'public health plans' to a number of organisations the following issues warrant highlighting:

- Caution needs to be exercised in seeking to draw too many inferences from small numbers. Consequently, my focus is often confined mainly to cardiovascular or diabetes risk factors (e.g. smoking, weight, blood pressure and lipids), mental wellbeing and, following some further detailed analysis of the biochemistry results, liver fibrosis (see Chapter 8). It is also often possible to examine the wellbeing of specific employee subgroups (e.g. by gender, age, work location and work type).
- In the plan, after examining the data, I then promote evidence-based interventions in order to facilitate appropriate changes in risk factors and to improve both individual and organisational outcomes.
- Personally presenting the public health plan to the key stakeholders within an organisation always facilitates some very productive discussions; often bringing in other sources of information and insight to enhance or modify my initial wellbeing suggestions. The ideal outcome from this dialogue is the development of a realistic and effective workplace wellness programme.
- Offering annual or biannual health checks to staff allows health trends to be monitored and programme effectiveness to be assessed.

#### 3.3.3.5 TRENDING

Although a single health check episode will generally involve no more than two or three separate dealings between an individual undergoing a health check and

Table 3.11 Patient activation levels

| PAM levels (based on aggregated questionnaire scores) | Characteristics of individuals | Tailored support and advice (health coaching) |
|---|---|---|
| Level 1 | Tend to be passive and feel overwhelmed by managing their own health. They may not understand their role in the care process. | Focus on building self-awareness and understanding behaviour patterns, and begin to build confidence through small steps. |
| Level 2 | May lack the knowledge and confidence to manage their own health. | Help individuals to continue taking small steps, such as adding a new fruit or vegetable to their diet each week or reducing their portion sizes at two meals a day. Assist them to build up their basic knowledge. |
| Level 3 | Appear to be taking action but may still lack the confidence and skill to support their behaviours. | Work with individuals to adopt new behaviours and to develop some level of condition-specific knowledge and skills. Support the initiation of new 'full' behaviours (those that are more than just small changes – e.g. 30 minutes of exercise three times a week) and work on the development of problem-solving skills. |
| Level 4 | Have adopted many of the behaviours needed to support their health but may not be able to maintain them in the face of life stressors. | Focus on preventing a relapse and handling new or challenging situations as they arise. Problem solving and planning for difficult situations to help individuals maintain their behaviours. |

those delivering the service, subsequent checks on an annual or biannual basis can provide valuable additional information.

Trending involves harnessing changes in measurements or findings between two consecutive health checks in order to improve the ability to monitor an individual's or an organisation's health. It can also help to motivate individuals to make healthy choices or lifestyle changes and to spot serious and important conditions earlier such as prostate or ovarian cancers.

Change occurs when something becomes different. In relation to periodic health checks, there are a number of types of change that might be considered:

- *Continuous change*: This occurs when any continuous numerical measure increases or decreases. Examples include age, weight and laboratory measures such as the estimated glomerular filtration rate (eGFR) or the full blood count.
- *Discrete change*: This is a type of change in which the measurements are restricted to specific numerical values such as the numbers of moles on a person's arm or the frequency of urinary symptoms.
- *Categorical change*: Here, the change is focused on one of a limited number of possible categories. For example, a smoker might be classified as a non-smoker, light smoker, heavy smoker or very heavy smoker. One specific type of categorical change of particular relevance for health checks is dichotomous or binary change where the data can only exist in two forms. Examples of dichotomous change include a new cancer diagnosis in a first-degree relative (i.e. a dichotomous change in the individual's family history) or a new finding of a left bundle branch block on a person's ECG. There might also be a change in an individual's general health status that can impact on their risk profile such as a new diagnosis of coeliac disease, ulcerative colitis or diabetes.
- *Episodic change*: Some conditions – for example, atrial fibrillation – can be paroxysmal with episodic changes in the ECG. The lung function in individuals with possible asthma can also exhibit significant variability over time.

It is important to appreciate that more than one type of change will often be taking place in the same individual. For example, in seeking to spot cancer earlier there is good evidence that trends in the haemoglobin level matter but, in parallel the person's baseline risk of bowel cancer might change due to, for example, dichotomous changes in their FIT test result or their bowel cancer family history. We are all getting older with consequent increases in our baseline risks for a variety of illnesses.

In seeking to incorporate the assessment of change into a better value health check a number of specific issues need to be considered:

- *Measurement characteristics*: In accordance with Section 3.2.5, it is important to ensure that the measure is valid and reliable but, also, over time, responsive to change with a predictable association with alterations in a condition. For example, if used on an annual basis HbA1c exhibits particularly good responsiveness to change in terms of both monitoring diabetes control (for those with diabetes) and assessing future risk for diabetes (for those who do not have diabetes).

- *Signal-to-noise ratio*: The signal is the true longitudinal trend in a measure whereas the 'noise' reflects the measurement variability due to biological and technical factors. In order for a measure to be able to differentiate clinically important change from background variability the signal-to-noise ratio should be as large as possible. Biological variability may sometimes be addressed by measuring individuals at specific times. Technical measurement variability can be reduced by ensuring that, for example, blood samples are taken, stored and handled in a way that preserves the stability of the specimen. From the health check perspective, two simple innovations that can make a considerable difference to reducing noise from blood test results are centrifuging samples on-site before transportation to the laboratory and consistently using one accredited laboratory for all analyses.
- *Prospective approach*: It is much more accurate to collect any additional data prospectively as retrospective estimates of change are fraught with errors. For example, in a study of Israeli soldiers suffering from post-traumatic stress disorder there was poor correlation between their subjective estimates of change and a variety of standardised symptom scales applied at specific intervals. In considering how best to spot ovarian cancer earlier, a prospective annual assessment of CA-125 is also much more effective than a retrospective assessment of symptom variations (see Chapter 13). However, re-measurement needs to take place after a pre-defined interval linked to the natural history of the condition, the speed at which important changes are likely to occur, the signal-to-noise ratio and the responsiveness of the measure.
- *Pre-define and plan* the clinical actions to be taken based on the trend results. Moreover, the advice needs to be consistent with that given for individually raised results.

## REFERENCES

1. Porter ME. What is value in health care? *N Engl J Med* 2010;363:2477–2481.
2. Summerton N. *Primary Care Diagnostics: The Patient-Centred Approach in the New Commissioning Environment*. Abingdon: Radcliffe Medical Press, 2011.
3. Zerillo JA, Schouwenburg MG, van Bommel ACM et al. An international collaborative standardizing a comprehensive patient-centered outcomes measurement set for colorectal cancer. *JAMA Oncol* 2017;3:686–694.
4. Brooks R. EuroQol: The current state of play. *Health Policy* 1996;37:53–72.
5. Reynolds EE, Hefferman J, Mehrotra A, Libman H. Should patients have periodic health examinations? Grand rounds discussion from Beth Israel Deaconess Medical Center. *Ann Intern Med* 2016;164:176–183.

6. Prochazka AV, Caverly T. General health checks in adults for reducing morbidity and mortality from disease. Summary review of primary findings and conclusions. *JAMA Intern Med* 2013;173:371–372.
7. Sharp L, Timmons A. *The Financial Impact of a Cancer Diagnosis*. Dublin: National Cancer Registry Ireland, 2010.
8. Mold JW, Hamm RM, Jafri B. The effect of labelling on perceived ability to recover from acute illnesses and injuries. *J Fam Pract* 2000;49:437–440.
9. Haynes RB, Sackett DL, Taylor DW et al. Increased absenteeism from work after detection and labelling of hypertensive patients. *N Engl J Med* 1978;299:741–744.
10. Halpern JA, Chughtai B, Ghomrawi H. Cost-effectiveness of common diagnostic approaches for evaluation of asymptomatic microscopic haematuria. *JAMA Intern Med* 2017;177:800–807.
11. Tufts Medical Center. *Center for the Evaluation of Value and Risk in Health Value Databases*. https://www.tuftsmedicalcenter.org/Research-Clinical-Trials/Institutes-Centers-Labs/Center-for-Evaluation-of-Value-and-Risk-in-Health/CEVR-Value-Databases
12. Ndase P, Celum C, Kidoguchi L et al. Frequency of false positive rapid HIV serologic tests in African men and women receiving PrEP for HIV prevention: Implications for programmatic roll-out of biomedical interventions. *PLoS ONE* 2015;10:e0123005. doi:10.1371/journal.pone.0123005
13. Bossuyt PMM, Reitsma JB, Linnet K, Moons KGM. Beyond diagnostic accuracy: The clinical utility of diagnostic tests. *Clin Chem* 2012;58:1636–1643.
14. Vassy JL, Bates DW, Murray MF. Appropriateness: A key to enabling the use of genomics in clinical practice? *Am J Med* 2016;129:551–553.
15. Hoffman RM, Elmore JG, Fairfield KM et al. Lack of shared decision making in cancer screening discussions. Results from a national survey. *Am J Prev Med* 2014;47:251–259.
16. Trikalinos TA, Wieland LS, Adam GP et al. *Decision Aids for Cancer Screening and Treatment*. Rockville, MD: Agency for Healthcare Research and Quality, 2014.
17. Lillie SE, Partin MR, Rice K et al. *The Effects of Shared Decision Making on Cancer Screening: A Systematic Review*. Minneapolis, MN: Evidence-Based Synthesis Program Center, 2014.
18. Frosch DL, Bhatnagar V, Tally S et al. Internet patient decision support: A randomized controlled trial comparing alternative approaches for men considering prostate cancer screening. *Arch Intern Med* 2008;168:363–369.
19. Mathieu E, Barratt AL, McGeechan K et al. Helping women make choices about mammography screening: An online randomized trial of a decision aid for 40-year-old women. *Patient Educ Couns* 2010;81:63–72.

20. Ruffin MT, Fetters MD, Jimbo M. Preference-based electronic decision aid to promote colorectal cancer screening: Results of a randomized controlled trial. *Prev Med* 2007;45:267–273.
21. Sheridan SL, Harris RP, Woolf SH et al. Shared decision making about screening and chemoprevention. A suggested approach from the U.S. Preventive Services Task Force. *Am J Prev Med* 2004;26:56–66.
22. Lee EO, Emanuel EJ. Shared decision making to improve care and reduce costs. *N Engl J Med* 2013;368:6–8.
23. Stacey D, Légaré F, Lewis K et al. Decision aids for people facing health treatment or screening decisions. *Cochrane Database of Systematic Reviews* 2017;(4). Art. No.: CD001431. doi: 10.1002/14651858.CD001431.pub5
24. Elwyn G, Frosch D, Thomson R et al. Shared decision making: A model for clinical practice. *J Gen Intern Med* 2012;27:1361–1367.
25. Bijlsma M, Rendering A, Chin-On N et al. Quality criteria for health checks: Development of a European Consensus agreement. *Prev Med* 2014;67:238–241.
26. Eckel RH. LDL cholesterol as a predictor of mortality, and beyond. To fast or not to fast, that is the question? *Circulation* 2014;130:528–529.
27. Sidhu D, Naugler C. Fasting time and lipid levels in a community-based population. *Arch Intern Med* 2012;172:1707–1710.
28. Gill JP, Shephard MDS. The conduct of quality control and quality assurance testing for PoCT outside the laboratory. *Clin Biochem Rev* 2010;31:85–88.
29. Public Health England. *Programme Specific Operating Model for Quality Assurance of Bowel Cancer Screening Programmes.* London: PHE, 2017.
30. Hibbard J, Gilburt H. *Supporting People to Manage Their Health: An Introduction to Patient Activation.* London: King's Fund, 2014.

# 4

# Cardiovascular health

## KEY RECOMMENDATIONS

- For those designing a better value heath check incorporating a focus on cardiovascular health it is suggested that the following conditions warrant particular consideration: atherosclerotic cardiovascular disease, atrial fibrillation and abdominal aortic aneurysms.
- A three-stage approach is recommended to facilitate the earlier recognition of individuals at elevated cardiovascular risk: baseline clinical assessment, baseline investigations followed, if appropriate, by risk scoring.
- A computer-based risk scoring tool needs to be selected appropriate to the population undergoing the health check.
- For those individuals estimated to be at an intermediate level of cardiovascular risk (i.e. a total risk estimate of between 10% and 20% at 10 years) it is recommended that consideration is given to undertaking one or more of the following additional investigations: C-reactive protein, HbA1c, urinary albumin excretion, lipoprotein-associated phospholipase A2, ankle-brachial blood pressure index measurement, computed tomography (CT) calcium scoring, carotid ultrasound for intima-media thickness, or exercise electrocardiogram (ECG) testing. Measurement of homocysteine might also be undertaken.
- Screening for atrial fibrillation is advocated.
- Abdominal aortic aneurysm screening is suggested for all men over the age of 65 years and, also, for individuals at elevated cardiovascular risk.

## 4.1 OVERVIEW

In terms of developing a better value health check incorporating a focus on cardiovascular health, it is suggested that the key priorities are atherosclerotic cardiovascular disease, atrial fibrillation and abdominal aortic aneurysms.

There are some other areas that have been considered for inclusion within this chapter but, at present, I felt that the evidence of benefit in terms of delivering value was insufficient. Key amongst these are hypertrophic cardiomyopathy screening in young adults and case-finding for heart failure amongst individuals at elevated cardiovascular risk using natriuretic peptide.

Although there does appear to be a relationship between serum homocysteine levels and cardiovascular disease, there are differing views as to whether reducing homocysteine levels by group B vitamins (more specifically $B_{12}$, $B_6$ and folate) has any effect on the level of risk. However, the studies assessing the impacts of such interventions on health outcomes have often been poorly designed. Based on some new analyses, it is now suggested that the lowering of elevated homocysteine levels does reduce cardiovascular risk (including stroke risk) in individuals *not* currently taking antiplatelet therapy and with *normal* renal function (i.e. estimated glomerular filtration rate [eGFR] $>60$ mL/min/1.73 $m^2$).

Finally, as smoking is a key element of cardiovascular health there are strong links between this chapter and Chapter 5 (Lung Health). Interventions to identify and address smoking are covered in Chapter 16.

## 4.2 ATHEROSCLEROTIC CARDIOVASCULAR DISEASE

### 4.2.1 Importance

Atherosclerotic cardiovascular disease (ACVD) includes the following:

- Coronary heart disease (CHD) (i.e. fatal or non-fatal myocardial infarction [MI], angina pectoris and/or heart failure)
- Cerebrovascular disease (i.e. fatal or non-fatal stroke and transient ischemic attack [TIA])
- Peripheral artery disease (i.e. intermittent claudication and critical limb ischemia)
- Aortic atherosclerosis and thoracic or abdominal aortic aneurysms

ACVD is the primary cause of premature death and disability worldwide, contributing largely to the escalating costs of healthcare. A substantial proportion of these deaths (46%) are in people under 70 years of age, in their most productive period of life.

In the United Kingdom, heart and circulatory diseases cause more than one in three of all deaths, and a fifth of hospital admissions at an estimated cost of £30 billion per annum. In the United States, 35% of the total deaths in 2010 were attributed to ACVD compared to 45% in Germany, 31% in Denmark, 48% in Greece, 32% in Japan, 26% in Mexico and 38% in China.

Globally, deaths from ACVD increased by 41% between 1990 and 2013. Only in Central Europe and Western Europe did the annual number of deaths from cardiovascular disease decline. South Asia experienced the largest jump in total deaths due to ACVD, with 1.8 million more deaths in 2013 than in 1990 – a rise of 97%. In line with global trends, the increase in deaths from cardiovascular disease in India is driven by population growth and aging.

### 4.2.2 Prevention

According to the INTERHEART study, nine potentially modifiable risk factors account for more than 90% of the risk for acute MI: smoking, abnormal lipids, a history of hypertension or diabetes, abdominal obesity, alcohol consumption, psychological stress, a low daily consumption of fruit and vegetables and a lack of regular physical exercise. The effect of these risk factors was consistent in men and women across different geographical regions and by ethnic group.

At an individual level the following adjustments can reduce the chances of developing ACVD:

- All people who smoke should be advised to stop and be offered support including pharmacotherapy and behavioural interventions.
- Exposure to passive (secondary) smoking must be minimised.
- Individuals should maintain an ideal body weight (body mass index [BMI] 20–25 kg/m$^2$) and avoid central obesity (waist circumference in white Caucasians <102 cm in men and <88 cm in women, and in Asians <90 cm in men and <80 cm in women).
- Diets low in saturated fats should be recommended to all. Ideally, the intake of saturated fats should be kept to under 10% of total fat intake (or less than 30 g per day).
- Increase the intake of fresh fruit and vegetables to at least five portions per day.
- Ensure a regular intake of fish and other sources of omega 3 fatty acids. All individuals should aim to eat at least two portions of fish per week, one of which should be a fatty fish.
- Reduce alcohol consumption and limit alcohol intake to no more than 21 units/week for men or 14 units/week for women.
- All individuals should aim to consume less than 6 g of salt per day. People with hypertension should be advised to reduce their salt intake as much as possible to lower blood pressure.
- Physical activity of at least moderate intensity (e.g. breathing faster than normal) is recommended for the whole population (unless contraindicated by an individual's condition). Aim for regular aerobic physical activity of at least 30 minutes per day, most days of the week (e.g. fast walking/swimming).
- Physical activity may include occupational and/or leisure-time activity and should incorporate accumulated bouts of moderate-intensity activities such as brisk walking.
- Those who are moderately active and are able to increase their activity should be encouraged to do so. Activity can be increased through a combination of changes to intensity, duration or frequency.
- Those who are already moderately active without contraindications can safely be encouraged to undertake vigorous-intensity exercise to achieve additional benefits.
- Individuals should be advised to minimise the amount of time spent being sedentary (sitting) over extended periods.
- All individuals, irrespective of health, fitness or activity level, should be encouraged to increase activity levels gradually.

For those at high risk (i.e. >20% cardiovascular disease [ACVD] risk at 10 years), there is a need for intensive risk factor intervention through a combination of lifestyle improvement and medical therapy – such as antithrombotic therapy, anti-hypertensive therapy and lipid-lowering therapy.

There is often substantial room for improvement in risk factor control especially in those at high risk. According to the Scottish Intercollegiate Guidelines Network, adopting a Mediterranean diet pattern supplemented with 30 g extra virgin olive oil or unsalted nuts per day is recommended for adults at high risk of ACVD or with established ACVD. Individuals at risk of cardiovascular disease, who are overweight or obese, should also be targeted with interventions designed to reduce weight by at least 3 kg, and to maintain this reduction.

The overarching principle is that the higher a person's overall ACVD risk the greater the benefit that will be derived from treating all modifiable risk factors. The desirable levels for cholesterol and blood pressure might need to be set lower than for individuals at lesser risk – for example, low-density lipoprotein (LDL) cholesterol targets of <2.5 mmol/L or <1.8 mmol/L for those at high or very high ACVD risk, respectively. For individuals at high ACVD risk due to, for example, diabetes or chronic renal disease a lower blood pressure target of <135/85 mm Hg should also be considered.

## 4.2.3 Earlier recognition

Although it is recommended that general lifestyle advice about the maintenance of cardiovascular health should be given to *all* individuals attending for a health check, it is also important to recognise those at elevated risk who might benefit from more intensive interventions. There is a particular requirement to spot people at high (i.e. a total ACVD risk estimate greater than 20% at 10 years) or intermediate (i.e. a total ACVD risk estimate of between 10% and 20% at 10 years) risk.

There are four elements to the earlier recognition of individuals at elevated cardiovascular risk: baseline clinical assessment, baseline investigations, risk scoring and, if appropriate, refining risk. However, it is always important to emphasise that assessing someone's ACVD risk does not actually change their ACVD risk. In short, there is no point in seeking to identify individuals at increased risk without the ability to intervene and to make changes to lower that risk.

### 4.2.3.1 BASELINE CLINICAL ASSESSMENT

*Symptoms* such as a history of exertional chest pain, dyspnoea, syncope, claudication or palpitations need to be carefully evaluated. A clear cardiovascular symptom history places an individual in the high-risk group.

Cardiovascular risk might also be intermediate or high in individuals with erectile dysfunction (see Chapter 12).

*Age* is associated with increasing ACVD risk. All individuals over the age of 75 years should be considered as being at intermediate or high risk.

*Smoking* has greater impacts on atherosclerosis progression (and ACVD risk) for individuals with hypertension or diabetes.

*Alcohol* consumption impacts on ACVD risk. Heavy drinking is associated with the highest risk of ACVD and light to moderate consumption carries a lower risk.

*Current treatments* for hypertension, hyperlipidaemia, HIV and psychosis are associated with increased ACVD risk. Treatment with corticosteroids and atypical antipsychotics also impacts on risk. In general individuals will be *at least* at an intermediate level of risk.

*Diseases and disorders* such as systemic lupus erythematosus, rheumatoid arthritis, premature menopause and obstructive sleep apnoea increase ACVD risk. In general such individuals will be *at least* at an intermediate level of risk. Conditions conferring a *high risk* of ACVD include the following:

- *Cardiovascular disease*: i.e. Angina, MI, stroke, TIA, aortic aneurysm or peripheral arterial disease
- *Stage 3 or higher chronic kidney disease or micro- or macro-albuminuria*
- *Diabetes over the age of 40 years*
- *Diabetes under the age of 40, and*
  - At least 20 years duration of disease, or
  - Target organ damage (e.g. proteinuria, micro- or macro-albuminuria, proliferative retinopathy or autonomic neuropathy), or
  - Significantly elevated cardiovascular risk factors

*Depression, anxiety and social isolation or lack of quality social support* are additional risk factors for the development and prognosis of ACVD and should also be taken into account when assessing individual risk.

*A family history* of clinically proven ACVD (angina, MI, TIA or ischaemic stroke) in a first-degree relative before the age of 60 years doubles the risk of a coronary event.

*Familial hypercholesterolaemia (FH)* is associated with a high ACVD risk. According to the National Institute for Health and Care Excellence (NICE), an individual with a total cholesterol of 7.5 mmol/L or greater should be considered as a possible candidate for a diagnosis of FH if they also have

- A family history of MI: Aged younger than 50 years in a second-degree relative or aged younger than 60 years in a first-degree relative or,
- A family history of raised total cholesterol: greater than 7.5 mmol/L in adult first- or second-degree relative or greater than 6.7 mmol/L in child, brother or sister aged younger than 16 years

*Blood pressure* of greater than 160/100 is associated with at least an intermediate level of ACVD risk. Elevated blood pressure together with clinical evidence of end organ damage such as hypertensive/diabetic retinopathy; or generalised vascular disease (such as bruits, diminished peripheral pulses or abdominal aortic aneurysm) will place an individual within the high ACVD risk group. Unfortunately the clinical examination can be highly unreliable (e.g. kappa = 0.07 for peripheral pulse, normal or diminished). Furthermore, some findings might be helpful if present (e.g. positive likelihood ratio = 7.3 for a limb bruit related to vascular disease) but much less helpful in excluding a diagnosis if absent (e.g. negative likelihood ratio for limb bruit related to vascular disease = 0.7).

There is also a growing body of evidence that there is an association between long-term variability in clinic-based blood pressure readings and cardiovascular risk.

#### 4.2.3.1.1 Weight and waist circumference

Individuals with a BMI >30 kg/m$^2$ have a 40-fold increased risk of developing diabetes and a two- to threefold increased risk of CHD and stroke compared to individuals with a normal BMI (<25 kg/m$^2$). However, central obesity, as measured by waist circumference, is a better predictor of cardiovascular risk than BMI. Central obesity is present if the waist circumference is >102 cm in men (>90 cm in Asian men) and >88 cm in women (>80 cm in Asian women).

### 4.2.3.2 BASELINE INVESTIGATIONS

As discussed in Chapter 3, fasting is often unnecessary in undertaking blood testing in relation to assessing cardiovascular risk.

#### 4.2.3.2.1 Lipids

The optimal recommended total cholesterol level is ≤5 mmol/L, LDL cholesterol ≤3 mmol/L and high-density lipoprotein (HDL)-cholesterol ≥1 mmol/L. The risk of ACVD is also increased by a factor of 1.3 in those individuals with hypertriglyceridaemia (>1.7 mmol/L). HDL cholesterol is inversely related to the risk of ACVD and for this reason the ratio of total cholesterol to HDL cholesterol is used for ACVD risk assessment.

#### 4.2.3.2.2 Glucose

Impaired glucose tolerance (see Chapter 9) is associated with an increased risk of death from ACVD. Amongst individuals *without* established diabetes there is evidence that small increases in glycated haemoglobin (HbA1c) levels are associated with significantly increased risks for CHD and stroke. A 1% rise in haemoglobin A1c levels has been linked with a 20%–30% increase in cardiovascular events for individuals with HbA1c levels of 5% (31 mmol/mol) to 6.5% (48 mmol/mol).

#### 4.2.3.2.3 Renal function

An eGFR of <60 mL/min/1.73 m$^2$ is indicative of stage 3 renal disease and such individuals are at increased risk of cardiovascular events. However, the eGFR may be falsely low in people with large muscle bulk and should be interpreted with caution in non-white ethnic groups, pregnancy, oedematous states, muscle-wasting diseases, amputees and the malnourished. There is also evidence of a dose-response relationship between albuminuria and the risk of CHD.

#### 4.2.3.2.4 Electrocardiogram

In terms of assessing cardiovascular risk the resting electrocardiogram (ECG) has roles in identifying ischaemia, arrhythmias and ventricular hypertrophy. Specific ECG findings that have been linked to cardiovascular risk in population-based cohorts and asymptomatic individuals with hypertension include QRS prolongation, ST-segment depression, T-inversion and pathological Q waves. It is also important to appreciate that subtle ECG abnormalities detectable only by computer analysis may be associated with increased risk.

#### 4.2.3.3 RISK SCORING

If an individual has already been clearly categorised as intermediate or higher risk following the baseline clinical assessment or investigations, risk scoring may not be appropriate. But in other situations risk scoring can be extremely helpful – for example, an individual with several mildly raised risk factors may be at a higher total risk of ACVD than someone with just one elevated risk factor.

A number of risk scoring tools have been developed to seek to integrate both modifiable (e.g. smoking, blood pressure, cholesterol) and non-modifiable (e.g. age, gender) risk factors. These tools generate a single quantitative estimate of risk that can be used to target preventive interventions.

All of the risk scoring tools consider age, gender, total cholesterol, HDL cholesterol, systolic blood pressure and smoking. However, there are variations in some other elements (Table 4.1).

In determining which scoring system should be applied it is useful to consider the additional elements included in Table 4.1 but also to take note of the following:

- *Framingham* is based on data from a group of U.S. volunteers in Framingham, Massachusetts, and tends to underestimate or overestimate risk for certain populations such as those from Europe and Asia in addition to individuals older than 85 years.
- *SCORE* has been developed from a very large European data set from 11 countries and can be customised to any European country. The risk in middle-aged subjects is provided in greater detail.
- *QRISK2* and *QRISK3* are based on the records of individuals attending UK general practices and include a number of features not incorporated in most of the other scoring systems. However, it is not based on a random population sample.

In selecting a scoring system, it is also important to be aware that a variety of other risk assessment tools have been derived or adjusted from these risk scores. For example, JBS2, the Sheffield Table, and the New Zealand Risk Charts have been developed from the Framingham data and JBS3 from the QRISK data. The ETHRISK calculator is a modified version of the Framingham risk assessment tool that has been designed for UK ethnic groups.

Although the earliest age at which risk scores should be applied has not been rigorously established, there is a growing consensus that periodic risk scoring might be considered from the age of 20 until the age of 80. Within QRISK3 the age range is now 25–84 years.

Heart age is a simple way of expressing how prone individuals are to atherosclerotic heart disease due to modifiable risk factors such as smoking, poor diet, high blood pressure, raised cholesterol and lack of exercise. It can be derived from a number of the risk scoring systems and the reasons for any differences between the heart age and an individual's chronological age can be explored

Table 4.1 Cardiovascular risk scores

| Cardiovascular risk score and version year | Additional risk factors considered |
|---|---|
| Framingham (2008) | • Blood pressure treatment<br>• Diabetes mellitus |
| Reynolds (2007/2008) | • Serum high-sensitivity C-reactive protein (hs-CRP)<br>• Parental history of MI before age 60 years<br>• HbA1c (women only) |
| SCORE (2003) | • Region of Europe (high-risk or low-risk region) |
| QRISK2 (2008) | • Ethnic origin<br>• Deprivation<br>• BMI<br>• Family history of CHD in a first-degree relative aged less than 60 years<br>• Blood pressure treatment<br>• Rheumatoid arthritis<br>• AF<br>• Chronic kidney disease |
| QRISK3 (2017) | In addition to QRISK2<br>• Migraine<br>• Treatment with corticosteroids<br>• Systemic lupus erythematosus<br>• Treatment with atypical antipsychotics<br>• Severe mental illness<br>• Erectile dysfunction<br>• Systolic blood pressure variability |
| China-PAR (2016) | • Lipid-lowering treatment<br>• Blood pressure treatment<br>• Diabetes mellitus<br>• Waist circumference<br>• Geographical region (northern or southern China)<br>• Urbanisation (males)<br>• Family history of atherosclerotic CVD |

in the context of a health check. I find it quite straightforward to emphasise to individuals that, by addressing the various modifiable risk factors, it is possible to 'dial back' their heart age.

#### 4.2.3.4 REFINING RISK

In some circumstances further, non-invasive investigations may be of value in enhancing the precision of the risk estimate and guiding subsequent patient management. Thus, for those assessed as being at an intermediate level of risk (e.g. based on the scoring system [i.e. a total ACVD risk estimate 10%–20% at 10 years], those with a strong family history of ACVD or those having at least one major ACVD risk factor [e.g. identified on the history, examination or from the simple investigations detailed above]) a subsequent non-invasive test might raise the post-test probability of ACVD events to more than 20% at 10 years (i.e. high risk). Conversely a negative non-invasive test may sufficiently lower estimated risk and provide evidence against the need for intensive risk factor measures (especially medications). In the United States, this intermediate-risk group constitutes 40% of the adult population (compared to 25% within the high-risk group).

Possible approaches to refine risk are listed in Table 4.2.

## 4.3 ATRIAL FIBRILLATION

### 4.3.1 Importance

Atrial fibrillation (AF) is the most common arrhythmia of clinical significance and is estimated to affect 33.5 million people worldwide – or 0.5% of the world's population. Prevalence also increases significantly with age from 0.1% among adults younger than 55 years to 9% in persons aged 80 years or older.

Unrecognised and untreated atrial fibrillation can lead to strokes – especially severe or recurrent strokes – in addition to dementia and heart failure. It is estimated that 20% of such individuals die prematurely and around 60% are left with some form of disability. There are also significant impacts on quality of life.

Several regional studies suggest rising prevalence and incidence of AF globally due to aging populations in addition to the impacts of co-morbidities, cardiovascular risk factors and lifestyle changes. In the United States, it is estimated that the number of adults with AF will more than double by the year 2050. Although deaths linked to AF are rising around the world, more women with AF are now dying in developing countries.

The economic burden of AF is also considerable. In the United Kingdom, it has been calculated that the annual costs to the health service amount to £2.8 billion with a further £2.4 billion being spent on home care each year. In addition, there are significant financial impacts on employers and insurers due to, for example, reduced productivity and disability. The annual cost to the wider economy has been estimated at £1.8 billion per annum.

### 4.3.2 Prevention

All of the approaches adopted to seek to prevent ACVD covered in the previous section also apply to the prevention of AF.

Moreover, individuals with conditions that are linked to AF such as diabetes, hypertension, heart disease and hyperthyroidism also need to ensure that the management of the underlying condition is optimised.

Table 4.2 Approaches to refine cardiovascular risk

| Approach | Key points |
| --- | --- |
| C-reactive protein (CRP) measurement | • Inflammation is considered to be central to the pathogenesis of atherosclerosis.<br>• High-sensitivity CRP (hs-CRP) has been associated with an increased risk for CVD.<br>• There is also some evidence that CRP measurement can refine the assessment of an individual's cardiovascular risk and has been incorporated within the Reynolds algorithm.<br>• The American College of Cardiology Foundation (ACCF)/American Heart Association (AHA) guideline suggests that the measurement of CRP can be useful in the selection of individuals for statin therapy. |
| Glycated haemoglobin (HbA1c) testing | • See Section 4.2.3.2.2. |
| Urinary albumin excretion testing | • The ACCF/AHA guideline recommends that urinalysis to detect albumin might be particularly helpful in asymptomatic individuals assessed as being at intermediate risk (see 4.2.3.2.3). |
| Lipoprotein-associated phospholipase A2 (Lp-PLA2) measurement | • Lp-PLA2 is an enzyme linked to the progression of early, relatively stable atherosclerotic plaques to unstable plaques. Unstable plaques are more likely to rupture leading to thrombus formation.<br>• There is some evidence that individuals with elevated levels of Lp-PLA2 are at heightened risk for MI and strokes irrespective of other risk factors. |
| Ankle-brachial pressure index (ABPI) measurement | • ABPI-detectable peripheral arterial disease correlates with clinical disease in the coronary and cerebral vascular beds.<br>• Test reliability and validity are excellent.<br>• Around 20% of the population over 60 years have peripheral arterial disease (PAD), although only a quarter of these are symptomatic.<br>• Even if there are no symptoms, the presence of a reduced blood pressure at the ankle signifies a three- to fourfold increase in the risk of cardiac and cerebrovascular morbidity and mortality. |

(*Continued*)

Table 4.2 (*Continued*) Approaches to refine cardiovascular risk

| Approach | Key points |
| --- | --- |
| Carotid intima-media thickness measurement on ultrasound | • Measures of carotid intima media thickness are independent predictors of transient cerebral ischaemia, stroke and coronary events.<br>• The ACCF/AHA guideline concluded that it may be helpful in asymptomatic adults at intermediate risk.<br>• Published recommendations on required equipment, technical approach plus operator training and experience must be followed to achieve high-quality results. |
| Computed tomography (CT) calcium scoring | • The presence of calcification within the coronary arterial wall is a marker for atherosclerosis.<br>• The approach combines CT with a scoring system.<br>• Calcium scores correlate with the extent of anatomical atherosclerosis and with the risk of subsequent CHD.<br>• Due to the radiation exposure and general low prevalence of calcium in men younger than 40 years and women younger than 50 years of age, individual selection is an important consideration. |
| Exercise ECG testing | • The ACCF/AHA guideline suggests that an exercise ECG may be considered in intermediate-risk asymptomatic adults.<br>• Several findings on exercise testing are associated with subsequent mortality and cardiovascular events such as ST-segment changes, heart rate recovery and exercise capacity.<br>• Although the serious effects of exercise testing such as MI are rare (1 per 2500 tests), false-positive results are common amongst adults at low cardiovascular risk (especially at younger ages), leading to unnecessary further testing plus anxiety. This can also have serious adverse consequences in relation to work and insurance. |

*Note:* A judgement about the advisability and appropriateness of the two imaging technologies (and other alternatives such as CT angiography) is best made in discussion with a consultant radiologist and a consultant cardiologist.

## 4.3.3 Earlier recognition

The traditional way in which AF was recognised involved checking the pulse in an individual complaining of palpitations. Moreover, there is some evidence that individuals experiencing short-lasting bouts of palpitations or palpitations affected by sleeping are less likely to have AF. Other symptoms that might be linked to AF include breathlessness, syncope or dizziness and chest discomfort.

However, by relying on symptoms alone it seems that AF remains undetected in between 30% and 50% of individuals. In a recent international survey, there was an average delay of 2.6 years between the onset of symptoms and the diagnosis of AF. Moreover, around one-quarter of individuals with AF are only diagnosed following a stroke.

Based on a systematic review, the Cochrane Heart Group concluded that both systematic and opportunistic screening for AF increased the rate of detection of new cases compared with routine practice. The recognition and treatment of AF reduces the stroke risk by at least 60% and, in relation to costs it is also worth bearing in mind that AF-related strokes cost, on average, 20% more than other strokes. Screening for AF has therefore been advocated as a way of reducing the burden of stroke by detecting individuals who would benefit from prophylactic anticoagulation before the onset of any symptoms.

At present, there are three main approaches to screening for AF: pulse palpation, recording a screening (six-lead) ECG or using an oscillometric blood pressure monitor that, while recording blood pressure, also automatically detects pulse irregularity. Newer smartphone applications are currently being evaluated.

According to Taggar and colleagues, screening ECGs and oscillometric blood pressure monitors are the most accurate tools for detecting pulse irregularities caused by AF with sensitivities and specificities greater than 90%. Pulse palpation is more likely to lead to false-positive findings in individuals with transient pulse irregularities due to, for example, ventricular extra-systoles.

One further issue to consider is that a proportion of individuals with AF may have an intermittent rhythm disturbance. Such people with paroxysmal AF present a particular screening challenge and, according to Svennberg and colleagues, ambulatory ECG recordings might have a key role in screening for all forms of AF.

Once AF has been detected by screening, a formal diagnostic ECG is then required. In addition, the CHA$^2$DS$^2$VASc stroke risk score needs to be applied in order to assess an individual's chances of having a stroke. The following features included within this tool help to stratify people with AF according to their stroke risk: heart failure, hypertension, age, diabetes, gender, and a history of vascular disease/stroke/TIA.

Finally, in the context of a health check it is also important to be aware of other conditions that might be associated with AF such as diabetes, thyroid disease, chronic obstructive pulmonary disease, obesity and excessive alcohol intake.

## 4.4 ABDOMINAL AORTIC ANEURYSMS

### 4.4.1 Importance

An abdominal aortic aneurysm (AAA) is a focal dilation 50% greater than the average diameter of the aorta. The normal diameter of the abdominal aorta is approximately 2 cm so an AAA is defined by an aortic diameter exceeding 3 cm. The abdominal aorta is the most common site of arterial aneurysms affecting, predominantly, the segment of aorta below the renal arteries. Large AAAs are at increased risk for rupture, with high mortality.

In Western countries, such as the United Kingdom, AAAs are present in 5%–7.5% of Caucasian males but are four times less common in Caucasian females and are rare in individuals of African and Asian heritage (0.45% of Asian men). The prevalence also varies considerably by region – for example, in Japan and South Korea the figures are 0.3% and 0.55%, respectively.

In designing a better value heath check it is important to be aware that, although the global prevalence of AAAs seems to be decreasing, some regions such as South Asia, South Africa and Latin America are seeing increases. This matters as the research evidence suggests that screening programmes for AAA in 65-year-old males reduce mortality and are cost-effective where disease prevalence is 1% or higher.

### 4.4.2 Prevention

All of the approaches adopted to seek to prevent ACVD covered in the first section also apply to AAA prevention. Conversely, it is recommended that individuals found to have an AAA should be considered at high cardiovascular risk with careful attention being paid to blood pressure, smoking and cholesterol levels.

### 4.4.3 Earlier recognition

Risk factors associated with the development of AAAs include older age; male gender; Caucasian race; positive smoking history; one or more first-degree relatives with an AAA; and having a history of other vascular aneurysms, coronary artery disease, cerebrovascular disease, atherosclerosis, hypercholesterolemia, obesity or hypertension.

Abdominal examination can detect abnormal widening of the aortic pulsation. However, although palpation *specifically directed* at measuring aortic width has moderate sensitivity for detecting an AAA (positive likelihood ratio = 15.6 for AAA >4 cm), it cannot be relied on to exclude an AAA. Therefore, a routine abdominal assessment as part of a health check should not be viewed as a screening test for AAAs.

Based on a comprehensive review of the research evidence, the U.S. Preventive Services Task Force recommends one-time screening for AAA with ultrasonography in men aged 65–75 years who have ever smoked and opportunistic screening for AAA in men aged 65–75 years who have never smoked.

Abdominal ultrasonography, performed in a setting with adequate quality assurance, is the preferred screening test for AAAs. No significant physical harms have been associated with ultrasound screening, and it is accurate (sensitivity 94%–100%, specificity 98%–100%), and reliable (reproducible) in detecting AAAs.

An invitation to attend AAA screening using abdominal ultrasonography can reduce AAA mortality by 43% in men age 65–75 years. Although AAAs may be asymptomatic for years, as many as one in three eventually rupture if left untreated, and the prognosis for ruptured AAAs is grim. Since most patients with ruptured AAAs die out of hospital or before surgery, and since the operative mortality rate for emergency AAA repair is high, only 10%–25% of individuals with ruptured AAAs survive until hospital discharge.

In general, the risk of rupture is principally determined by the AAA diameter, but rupture rates are also increased in individuals who smoke, people with hypertension and those with a strong family history (Table 4.3).

It is also important to appreciate that elective AAA repair is associated with significant risks for operative death (4.2%) and complications (32.4%) including MI, respiratory failure and renal failure. However, such risks may be acceptable to men with AAAs greater than 5.5 cm that are most prone to rupture. Operative mortality also varies by the patient's age and co-morbidities in addition to hospital/surgeon case load. Clearly, individuals can only benefit from surgery if they have a reasonable life expectancy, and this should be taken into account when discussing screening.

As with any screening test it is extremely important to consider the pathway following the initial ultrasound. For example, the national programme in the United Kingdom includes the following recommendations:

- Those patients identified with an aortic diameter greater than 3 cm should undergo regular surveillance:
  a. 3–4.4 cm, a follow-up will be arranged in 1 year
  b. 4.5–5.4 cm, a follow-up will be arranged in 3 months
- All individuals with AAAs >5.5 cm should be referred for a vascular surgical opinion.
- An urgent referral should be made to a vascular surgeon if the AAA has a diameter of over 7 cm, if there has been rapid expansion of the AAA or if there are potentially sinister symptoms such as back or abdominal pain or tenderness.

Table 4.3 AAA diameter and rupture rate

| Aneurysm diameter (cm) | Annual rupture rate (%) |
|---|---|
| 4.0–5.4 | 1 |
| 5.5–6.0 | 9.4 |
| 6.0–6.9 | 10.2 |
| 7.0–7.9 | 32.5 |
| >8.0 | 50 |

There is continuing debate about screening within low-prevalence populations, amongst younger men and in women. In such circumstances targeted screening based on risk profiling (case-finding) might be a better value option. For example, women older than 65 years with multiple risk factors (smoking history, cerebrovascular disease or family history) should be considered for screening according to Canadian guidance. Screening has also been suggested as an option for men younger than 65 years who are at higher risk (e.g. those who smoke, have other cardiovascular diseases or have a positive family history) by the European Society for Vascular Surgery.

## FURTHER READING

### Overview

Ganguly P, Alam SF. Role of homocysteine in the development of cardiovascular disease. *BMC Nutr J* 2015;14:1–10.

Hankey GJ, Eikelboom JW, Yi Q et al. Antiplatelet therapy and the effects of B vitamins in patients with previous stroke or transient ischaemic attack: A post-hoc subanalysis of VITATOPS, a randomised, placebo-controlled trial. *Lancet Neurol* 2012;11:512–520.

Mishra N. Hyperhomocysteinemia: A risk of CVD. *Int J Res Biol Sci* 2016;6:13–19.

Spence JD, Yi Q, Hankey GJ. B vitamins in stroke prevention: Time to reconsider. *Lancet Neurol* 2017;16:750–760.

### Atherosclerotic cardiovascular disease

Berger JS, Jordan CO, Lloyd-Jones D, Blumenthal RS. Screening for cardiovascular disease in asymptomatic patients. *J Am Coll Cardiol* 2010;55:1169–1177.

Chou R, Arora B, Dana T et al. Screening asymptomatic adults with resting or exercise electrocardiography: A review of the evidence for the U.S. Preventive Services Task Force. *Ann Intern Med* 2011;155:375–385.

Conroy RM, Pyörälä K, Fitzgerald AP et al. Estimation of ten-year risk of fatal cardiovascular disease in Europe: The SCORE project. *Eur Heart J* 2003;24:987–1003.

Cooney MT, Dudina AL, Graham IM. Value and limitations of existing scores for the assessment of cardiovascular risk. A review for clinicians. *J Am Coll Cardiol* 2009;54:1209–1227.

D'Agostino RB Sr, Vasan RS, Pencina MJ et al. General cardiovascular risk profile for use in primary care: the Framingham Heart Study. *Circulation* 2008;117:743–753.

Greenland P, Alpert JS, Beller GA et al. 2010. ACCF/AHA Guideline for assessment of cardiovascular risk in asymptomatic adults: A report of the American College of Cardiology Foundation/American Heart Association Task Force on Practice Guidelines. *J Am Coll Cardiol* 2010;56:e50–e103.

Hippisley-Cox J, Coupland C, Brindle P. Development and validation of QRISK3 risk prediction algorithms to estimate future risk of cardiovascular disease: Prospective cohort study. *BMJ* 2017;357:j2099 doi:10.1136/bmj.j2099

Hippisley-Cox J, Coupland C, Vinogradova Y et al. Predicting cardiovascular risk in England and Wales: Prospective derivation and validation of QRISK2. *BMJ* 2008;336:1475–1482.

Khaw KT, Wareham N, Bingham S et al. Association of hemoglobin A1c with cardiovascular disease and mortality in adults: The European Prospective Investigation into Cancer in Norfolk. *Ann Intern Med* 2004;141:413–420.

Marmot M, Elliott P. *Coronary Heart Disease Epidemiology*. Oxford: OUP, 2005.

National Institute for Health and Clinical Excellence (NICE). *Cardiovascular Disease: Risk Assessment and Reduction, Including Lipid Modification*. London: NICE, 2016 [Update].

National Institute for Health and Clinical Excellence (NICE). *Familial Hypercholesterolaemia: Identification and Management*. London: NICE, 2016 [Update].

Perk J, De Backer G, Gohlke H et al. European guidelines on cardiovascular disease prevention in clinical practice. *Eur Heart J* 2012;33:1635–1701.

Ridker PM, Buring JE, Rifai N, Cook NR. Development and validation of improved algorithms for the assessment of global cardiovascular risk in women: The Reynolds Risk Score. *JAMA* 2007;297:611–619.

Ridker PM, Paynter NP, Rifai N et al. C-reactive protein and parental history improve global cardiovascular risk prediction: The Reynolds Risk Score for men. *Circulation* 2008;118:2243–2251.

Roth GA, Forouzanfar MH, Moran AE et al. Demographic and epidemiologic drivers of global cardiovascular mortality. *N Engl J Med* 2015;372:1333–1341.

Scottish Intercollegiate Guidelines Network (SIGN). *Risk Estimation and the Prevention of Cardiovascular Disease*. Edinburgh: SIGN, 2017.

Stevens SL, Wood S, Koshiaris C et al. Blood pressure variability and cardiovascular risk. *BMJ* 2016;354:i4098.

The Lp-PLA2 Studies Collaboration. Lipoprotein-associated phospholipase A2 and risk of coronary heart disease, stroke and mortality: Collaborative analysis of 32 prospective studies. *Lancet* 2010;375:1536–1544.

U.S. Preventive Services Task Force. Statin use for the primary prevention of cardiovascular disease in adults: Recommendation statement. *Am Fam Phys* 2017;95:108A–108G.

World Health Organization. Cardiovascular Diseases. *Fact Sheet*. http://www.who.int/mediacentre/factsheets/fs317/en/

Yang X, Li J, Hu D et al. Predicting the 10-year risks of atherosclerotic cardiovascular disease in Chinese population: The China-PAR project (prediction for ASCVD Risk in China). *Circulation* 2016;134:1430–1437.

Yusuf S, Hawken S, Ôunpuu S et al. Effect of potentially modifiable risk factors associated with myocardial infarction in 52 countries (the INTERHEART study): Case-control study. *Lancet* 2004;364:937–952.

## Atrial fibrillation

Chugh SS, Havmoeller R, Narayanan K et al. Worldwide epidemiology of atrial fibrillation: A global burden of disease 2010 study. *Circulation* 2014;129:837–847.

Lown M, Garrard J, Irving G et al. Should we screen for atrial fibrillation? *Brit J Gen Pract* 2017;67:296–297.

Moran PS, Teljeur C, Ryan M, Smith SM. Systematic screening for the detection of atrial fibrillation. *Cochrane Database of Systematic Reviews* 2016;(6). Art No: CD009586. DOI: 10.1002/14651858.CD009586.pub3.

National Institute for Health and Clinical Excellence (NICE). *WatchBP Home A for Opportunistically Detecting Atrial Fibrillation during Diagnosis and Monitoring of Hypertension.* London: NICE, 2013.

National Institute for Health and Clinical Excellence (NICE). *Atrial Fibrillation: Management.* London: NICE, 2014.

Svennberg E, Engdahl J, Al-Khalili F et al. Mass screening for untreated atrial fibrillation: The STROKESTOP study. *Circulation* 2015;131:2176–2184.

Taggar JS, Coleman T, Lewis S et al. Accuracy of methods for detecting an irregular pulse and suspected atrial fibrillation: A systematic review and meta-analysis. *Eur J Prev Cardiol* 2016;23:1330–1338.

Thavendiranathan P, Bagai A, Khoo C et al. Does this patient with palpitations have a cardiac arrhythmia? *JAMA* 2009;302:2135–2143.

## Abdominal aortic aneurysms

Lederle FA Simel DL. The rational clinical examination. Does this patient have an abdominal aortic aneurysm? *JAMA* 1999;281:77–82.

Mastracci TM, Cina CS, Canadian Society for Vascular Surgery. Screening for abdominal aortic aneurysm in Canada: Review and position statement of the Canadian Society for Vascular Surgery. *J Vasc Surg* 2007;45:1268–1276.

Moll FL, Powell JT, Fraedrich G et al. European society for vascular surgery. Management of abdominal aortic aneurysms clinical practice guidelines of the European Society for Vascular Surgery. *Eur J Vasc Endovasc Surg* 2011;41(Suppl 1):S1–58.

Public Health England. *NHS Abdominal Aortic Aneurysm (AAA) Screening Programme. Essential Elements in Providing an AAA Screening and Surveillance Programme.* London: Public Health England, 2017.

Sampson UK, Norman PE, Fowkes FG et al. Estimation of global and regional incidence and prevalence of abdominal aortic aneurysms 1990–2010. *Glob Heart* 2014;9:159–170.

U.S. Preventative Services Task Force. Screening for abdominal aortic aneurysm: U.S. Preventive Services Task Force recommendation statement. *Ann Intern Med* 2014;161:281–290.

# 5

# Lung health

## KEY RECOMMENDATIONS

- For those designing a better value health check incorporating a focus on lung health it is suggested that the following conditions warrant particular consideration: chronic obstructive pulmonary disease (COPD), $\alpha$-1 antitrypsin (AAT) deficiency, tuberculosis (TB) and lung cancer.
- Encourage and facilitate smoking cessation using evidence-based interventions with a view to preventing lung cancer and COPD.
- Undertake case-finding for COPD by considering an individual's baseline risk and using a symptom questionnaire or microspirometry.
- Offer screening for AAT deficiency for individuals with COPD (and other family members) in areas of increased prevalence and case-finding amongst individuals at increased risk.
- Provide influenza and pneumococcal immunisation to individuals with COPD.
- Offer Bacille Calmette-Guérin (BCG) immunization against TB in specific risk groups.
- Consider case-finding for active TB together with targeted screening for latent TB infection.
- Annual screening for lung cancer with low-dose computed tomography (CT) is suggested for adults who are smokers or former smokers.

## 5.1 OVERVIEW

In terms of developing a better value health check incorporating a focus on lung health it is suggested that the key priorities are chronic obstructive pulmonary disease (COPD), $\alpha$-1 antitrypsin (AAT) deficiency, tuberculosis (TB) and lung cancer. However, it is important to be aware that many countries already have high-quality TB prevention and screening programmes in place and, therefore, those developing health checks need to carefully consider whether they can enhance value in relation to any current services.

There are some other areas that have been considered for inclusion within this chapter but, at present, I felt that the evidence of benefit in terms of delivering value was insufficient. Key amongst these are asthma prevention and screening in adults and case-finding for sarcoidosis.

Finally, as smoking is a key element of lung health there are strong links between this chapter and cardiovascular health (see Chapter 4). Interventions to identify and address smoking are covered in Chapter 16.

## 5.2 CHRONIC OBSTRUCTIVE PULMONARY DISEASE

### 5.2.1 Importance

COPD is a lung disease characterized by obstruction of lung airflow that interferes with normal breathing and is not fully reversible.

In the United States, around 14% of adults aged 40–79 years have COPD, and it is a significant cause of premature mortality. Worldwide, more than 3 million people died of COPD in 2012, and it is projected to be the third leading cause of death by 2020.

Within the United Kingdom, there is evidence that COPD is under-recognised and, while 3 million people might be affected by COPD, a further 2 million individuals remain undiagnosed. It has also been estimated that 60% of individuals living in the United States with COPD have not been diagnosed.

In 2010, the cost of COPD in the United States was approximately $50 billion, which included $20 billion in indirect costs and $30 billion in direct healthcare expenditure.

Once COPD is recognised, pharmacological interventions and smoking cessation initiatives can alleviate COPD symptoms, reduce the frequency and severity of exacerbations and improve health status and exercise tolerance.

AAT deficiency is one of the most common hereditary disorders, especially in populations of European descent. The abnormally reduced serum AAT levels found in individuals with the condition are associated with an increased risk for the development of early onset COPD and liver disease. AAT is produced in the liver, and one of its functions is to protect the lungs from neutrophil elastase, an enzyme that can disrupt connective tissue. More than 120 genetic variants (Pi types) of AAT exist and in individuals with the PiZZ genotype, AAT levels are less than 15% of normal.

In North America, the prevalence of AAT deficiency is about 1 per 3000–5000 people. Up to 5% of people with COPD are thought to have AAT deficiency and yet only 4%–5% of these have been identified. Even when the deficiency is diagnosed there has typically been a delay of 5–10 years.

### 5.2.2 Prevention

Smoking cessation is key to preventing lung health problems. As discussed in Chapter 16, there are a number of approaches that can be harnessed to seek to increase long-term smoking abstinence rates.

Individuals with AAT deficiency are particularly at risk from the adverse effects of smoking on lung health. Those with stable COPD who continue to smoke should be strongly encouraged and supported to quit. Offering immunisations against influenza and pneumonia is also important for individuals with established COPD in order to decrease the incidence of lower respiratory tract infections.

## 5.2.3 Earlier recognition

### 5.2.3.1 RISK ASSESSMENT

In seeking to identify individuals at elevated risk for the development of COPD the following features warrant consideration:

- A history of exposure to tobacco smoke from cigarettes, pipes, cigars and water-pipes (including passive smoking).
- A history of exposure to indoor air pollution from biomass fuel used for cooking and heating in poorly ventilated dwellings. This is a particular risk for women in developing countries.
- Occupational exposures including organic and inorganic dusts, chemical agents and fumes.
- AAT deficiency.

A diagnosis of COPD should always be considered in any patient over 40 years old who has persistent and progressive breathlessness (especially on exercise), chronic cough, recurrent wheeze or sputum production or a history of risk factors for the disease, especially cigarette smoking. There might also be a history of repeated lower respiratory tract infections.

### 5.2.3.2 CASE-FINDING

To improve the recognition of COPD in a cost-effective and efficient manner a case-finding approach is suggested. In this, individuals are selected for more formal diagnostic spirometry testing after first harnessing symptoms (using a questionnaire), microspirometry or peak flow measurement in order to rule out those individuals less likely to have COPD.

#### 5.2.3.2.1 Symptom questionnaires

In the context of a health check case-finding questionnaires are particularly helpful in identifying those individuals in whom formal diagnostic spirometry testing might be especially appropriate (Table 5.1).

Applying a cutoff of 4 or greater the COPD Population Screener has a sensitivity of 67% and specificity of 73% in a general population within Japan. Using a cutoff of greater than 16.5, the COPD Diagnostic Questionnaire has a sensitivity of about 90% and specificity of about 40% for identifying people with COPD in a primary care population.

In terms of logistics, the questions on the COPD Population Screener can be answered by individuals prior to attending a health check, whereas the COPD Diagnostic Questionnaire needs to be completed in conjunction with a primary care clinician.

Table 5.1 COPD case-finding questionnaires

| Authors | Questions |
|---|---|
| Martinez et al. (2008) COPD Population Screener | 1. During the past 4 weeks, how much of the time do you feel short of breath?<br>2. Do you ever cough up any 'stuff' such as mucus or phlegm?<br>3. Please select the answer that best describes you in the past 12 months. I do less than I used to because of my breathing problems (strongly agree/agree/unsure/disagree/strongly disagree).<br>4. Have you smoked at least 100 cigarettes in your entire life?<br>5. How old are you? |
| Price et al. (2006a,b) COPD Diagnostic Questionnaire | 1. Age group (year)<br>2. Body mass index (tertiles)<br>3. Smoking intensity (pack-years)<br>4. Does the weather affect your cough?<br>5. Do you ever cough up phlegm (sputum) from your chest when you do not have a cold?<br>6. Do you usually cough up phlegm (sputum) from your chest first thing in the morning?<br>7. How frequently do you wheeze?<br>8. Do you have or have you had any allergies? |

### 5.2.3.2.2 Microspirometry

Microspirometry with a hand-held spirometer can easily be used at a health check to exclude those individuals at very low likelihood of having COPD while selecting others for more formal diagnostic spirometry. Moreover, it has also been proposed that, for such stratification, it is acceptable to perform a less specific but more sensitive test (see Chapter 3).

According to Price, suitable spirometry parameters for such case-finding are forced expiratory volume in 1 second (FEV1), FEV1/forced vital capacity (FVC) ratio and the FEV1/forced expiratory volume in 6 seconds (FEV6) ratio. The following cutoff points are also proposed for identifying individuals in whom the possibility of COPD cannot be excluded and who therefore require more formal diagnostic spirometry:

- FEV1 ≤80% predicted value *or*
- FEV1/FVC ≤80% *or*
- FEV1/FEV6 ≤80%

The rationale for including a ratio of FEV1/FVC of ≤80% rather than 70% is that underestimation of FVC can result in a normal ratio. Moreover, many technically bad results from spirometry are in the direction of a low FVC through early stopping.

FEV6 measures the volume of air that can be forcibly expired in 6 seconds. It approximates the FVC and in normal people the two values would be identical. It is also suggested that using FEV6 instead of FVC may be helpful in patients with more severe airflow obstruction who might take up to 15 seconds to fully exhale. According to guidance developed by the Global Initiative for Chronic Obstructive Lung Disease (GOLD), the FEV1/FEV6 ratio is well validated and an acceptable alternative to FEV1/FVC.

Rytila and colleagues undertook a cross-sectional study of case-finding microspirometry in Finland. Amongst a population of 611 smokers or ex-smokers an FEV1 of <80% was found in 44.6% of cases. Furthermore, in a subgroup of 50 individuals who also underwent concomitant full diagnostic spirometry, a good correlation was found between the FEV1 measurements using the two approaches. They concluded that case-finding microspirometry is quick to perform, does not take longer than checking blood pressure and the measurements can easily be performed by a clinical nurse specialist in the community.

A major issue about case-finding microspirometry in the context of a health check is to ensure that patients with abnormal results do actually *progress* along the pathway to formal diagnostic spirometry and are not managed simply on the basis of the results from the case-finding. The message needs to be got across that formal diagnostic spirometry (with reversibility testing) should *always* be used to confirm the diagnosis of COPD.

The following microspirometers have been suggested for case-finding: One Flow FVC Screen, One Flow Tester Screen, PulmoLife, PiKo-6 and Vitalograph COPD-6.

#### 5.2.3.2.3 Peak expiratory flow measurement

Traditionally, peak flow measurements have not been recommended for ruling out COPD. However, data from the PLATINO and BOLD studies demonstrate that a normal peak expiratory flow (PEF) measurement might be used to exclude more severe COPD in smoking adults.

### 5.2.3.3 ALPHA-1 ANTITRYPSIN DEFICIENCY SCREENING

Universal screening for AAT deficiency is recommended for all patients with COPD (under the age of 65) in areas with a high prevalence of AAT deficiency. Family members should also be screened. In other areas AAT case-finding should be undertaken in those at increased risk based on the following features:

- Early onset COPD (aged 45 years or less)
- COPD in the absence of a recognised risk factor such as smoking
- Otherwise unexplained liver disease
- A family history of COPD, liver disease or AAT deficiency
- Asthma that is poorly responsive to standard treatments
- Northern European (Scandinavian and British) or Iberian (Spanish and Portuguese) descent

#### 5.2.3.4 IDENTIFYING CO-MORBIDITIES

COPD often co-exists with other diseases that may have a significant impact on outcomes such as

- Lung cancer
- Cardiovascular disease
- Osteoporosis
- Depression/anxiety

As part of a better value health check these co-morbidities should be actively sought as they can influence mortality and hospitalisations independently of the underlying COPD.

## 5.3 TUBERCULOSIS

### 5.3.1 Importance

TB remains a worldwide problem. One-third of the world's population is thought to be affected and new infections arise in about 1% of the population each year. In 2014, there were 9.6 million cases of TB which resulted in 1.5 million deaths with more than 95% of these occurring in developing countries. About 80% of people in many Asian and African countries test positive while 5%–10% of individuals in the United States test positive by tuberculin skin testing.

Almost all cases of TB in the United Kingdom are acquired from an individual with infectious respiratory TB. The initial infection may be eliminated, remain latent – where the individual has no symptoms but the TB bacteria remain in the body – or progress to active TB over the following weeks or months.

In relation to health checks, it is very important to distinguish between active TB and latent TB. Active TB is highly contagious and symptomatic but, in contrast, latent TB cases are asymptomatic and cannot spread to others. However, about 10% of individuals with latent infections (5% in the first 2 years after infection and 0.1% per year thereafter) will progress to active disease that, if left untreated, kills about half of those infected. Such re-activation is particularly likely if an individual's immune system has become weakened, for example by disease (e.g. HIV), certain medical treatments (e.g. cancer chemotherapy, corticosteroids) or due to old age.

The delay in diagnosing TB and initiating appropriate treatment is often long, especially in those with poor access to healthcare. Moreover, many individuals with active TB do not experience typical TB symptoms in the early stages of the disease.

### 5.3.2 Prevention

TB prevention continues to hinge on raising and sustaining awareness about TB and TB risks amongst the public and healthcare professionals. This needs to be combined with appropriately targeted Bacille Calmette-Guérin (BCG) immunization.

## 5.3.3 Earlier recognition

### 5.3.3.1 RISK ASSESSMENT

In seeking to identify individuals at elevated risk for the development of TB the features listed in Table 5.2 warrant consideration.

### 5.3.3.2 ACTIVE TB CASE-FINDING

Active TB is characterized by symptoms and signs such as the following:

- A persistent cough that lasts more than 3 weeks typically productive of phlegm, which may be bloody
- Weight loss
- Night sweats
- Fever
- Tiredness and fatigue
- Loss of appetite
- Lymph node swellings in the neck

Table 5.2 Tuberculosis risk factors

| | |
|---|---|
| Geography | Areas with a high TB prevalence<br>Areas with poor access to healthcare<br>Immigrants from settings with a high prevalence of TB |
| Possible TB history | People previously treated for TB<br>People with an untreated fibrotic lesion identified by chest radiography |
| Medical history and patient characteristics | People living with HIV and people attending HIV testing<br>People with diabetes mellitus<br>People with chronic respiratory diseases and smokers<br>Undernourished people<br>People with a history of gastrectomy or jejunoileal bypass<br>People with an alcohol-use disorder and intravenous drug users<br>People with chronic renal failure<br>People having treatments that compromise their immune system<br>Older people |
| Environment | People in mental health clinics or institutions<br>Prisoners and prison staff<br>People residing in shelters<br>Members of other congregate institutions (such as the military)<br>People in refugee camps<br>Healthcare workers<br>Miners or others who are exposed to silica |

Although the symptoms of active TB can be variable depending on the site of infection, the most common form remains pulmonary TB which accounts for 60% of cases in the United Kingdom.

According to the World Health Organization (WHO), case-finding is often the most cost-effective strategy to detect active TB. More specifically the following groups should be considered for case-finding for active TB:

- Household contacts and other close contacts of people with TB
- People living with HIV
- Current and former workers in silica-exposed workplaces
- People in prisons and other penitentiary institutions, and prison staff
- People with untreated fibrotic lesions on chest X-ray
- People in settings where TB prevalence in the general population is greater than 100/100,000 population who are seeking healthcare
- Individuals who are in care or belong to selected risk groups (see Table 5.2)
- Healthcare workers
- Geographically defined subpopulations with extremely high levels of undetected TB (1% prevalence or higher) and other sub-populations with very poor access to healthcare, such as homeless individuals or people living in remote areas with poor access to healthcare

Symptom assessment, chest X-ray and sputum smear are the primary tools for any case detection programme. Further information on the sensitivities and specificities of these approaches is detailed in Table 5.3.

Varying the threshold of cough duration (e.g. 2 weeks, 3 weeks) affects the sensitivity and specificity of case-finding. Three weeks of cough has better specificity, but 2 weeks has somewhat higher sensitivity.

Sputum smear microscopy is the least expensive and most rapid case-finding tool. Culture will increase yield in areas with high rates of smear-negative disease (i.e. HIV populations), but at increased cost. Chest X-rays should also always be

Table 5.3 Tuberculosis case-finding tools

| Case-finding tool | Sensitivity (%) | Specificity (%) |
|---|---|---|
| Chest X-ray with any abnormality compatible with TB (active or inactive) | 98 | 75 |
| Chest X-ray abnormalities suggestive of active TB | 87 | 89 |
| History of a prolonged cough (lasting >2–3 weeks) | 35 | 95 |
| History of any cough | 57 | 80 |
| History of any TB symptom (settings with low prevalence of HIV) | 70 | 61 |
| History of any TB symptom (settings with high prevalence of HIV) | 84 | 74 |
| Sputum-smear microscopy | 61 | 98 |

used to augment symptom-based case-finding in settings with a high prevalence of TB and HIV.

#### 5.3.3.3 LATENT TB SCREENING

Latent TB occurs where a person is infected with the TB mycobacterium but does not have active TB. However, 5%–10% of individuals with latent TB will progress to active TB.

There are four main categories of people who should be screened for latent TB infection:

- Individuals at risk of exposure to persons with active TB by virtue of geography, environment, residence or occupation (see Table 5.2).
- Individuals at risk of exposure to persons with active TB by virtue of close contact or travel from (or residence within) TB-endemic areas of the world (or TB high-burden countries). According to the WHO, the 30 TB high-burden countries (2016) are Angola, Bangladesh, Brazil, Cambodia, China, Congo, Central African Republic, DPR Korea, DR Congo, Ethiopia, India, Indonesia, Kenya, Lesotho, Liberia, Mozambique, Myanmar, Namibia, Nigeria, Pakistan, Papua New Guinea, the Philippines, the Russian Federation, Sierra Leone, South Africa, Thailand, the United Republic of Tanzania, Vietnam, Zambia and Zimbabwe.
- Individuals with evidence of previous TB infection including radiographic evidence of prior healed TB.
- Individuals with conditions or other factors associated with progression from latent TB to active TB such as individuals who are HIV positive; misuse alcohol, are injecting drug users, have had a solid organ transplantation, have a haematological malignancy, are having chemotherapy, have had a jejunoileal bypass, have diabetes, have chronic kidney disease or receive haemodialysis, have had a gastrectomy, are having treatment with anti-tumour necrosis factor-alpha or other biologic agents, or have silicosis.

There is no direct test to determine the presence of latent TB. The two screening tests – the tuberculin skin test and the interferon-gamma release assay – rely on measurements of an individual's immune response.

##### 5.3.3.3.1 Tuberculin skin test

This assesses an individual's response to a solution of *Mycobacterium tuberculosis*–complex antigens, known as purified protein derivative. However, it has limitations, including precise intradermal administration, the need for a follow-up visit to interpret the results, specific criteria for interpretation of the results and the possibility of false-positive results with BCG immunisation or other environmental mycobacteria.

##### 5.3.3.3.2 Interferon-gamma release assays

Interferon-gamma release assays (IGRAs) measure a person's immune reactivity to *Mycobacterium tuberculosis*. White blood cells from most people who have been infected with TB will release interferon-gamma when mixed with antigens derived from *Mycobacterium tuberculosis*. These assays are performed in the laboratory, requiring one blood draw and only one patient visit to obtain results. However, blood samples must be processed within 8–30 hours after collection while white blood cells are still viable and errors in collecting or transporting blood specimens or in running and interpreting the assay can decrease the accuracy of IGRAs.

The results from IGRAs are not confounded by BCG vaccination and are also less likely to be affected by exposure to non-TB mycobacteria.

According to a systematic review undertaken for the U.S. Preventive Services Task Force, tuberculin skin testing at a positivity threshold of 10 mm has a sensitivity of 79% and a specificity of 97% for the diagnosis of latent TB infection. The IGRA T-SPOT TB test has a sensitivity of 90% and specificity of 95%.

Individuals with a positive screening result need further evaluation to determine if positivity is due to latent TB infection or active TB disease. A clinical evaluation and chest radiograph should be performed on all people with a positive screening test to check for active TB disease. If the individual does not have clinical signs or symptoms, and the chest radiograph does not have findings suggestive of active TB; the patient should be diagnosed with latent TB infection and offered a treatment course to diminish the risk of progressing to active TB.

## 5.4 LUNG CANCER

### 5.4.1 Importance

Lung cancer has been the most common cancer and the most frequent cause of cancer deaths across the world for several decades. There were around 1.8 million new cases in 2012, 58% of which occurred in the less-developed regions.

In men the highest incidence rates are found in Central and Eastern Europe and Eastern Asia. In women, the incidence rates are generally lower and the geographical pattern is different, reflecting different historical exposure to tobacco smoking. For them, the highest rates are in Northern America and Northern Europe.

About 12% of lung cancers diagnosed in the United Kingdom and the United States are small cell lung cancer (SCLC). Most of the rest are non-small cell lung cancer (NSCLC). Both types of lung cancer are potentially curable but, due to late diagnosis, only about 5% of SCLC patients and 10%–20% of NSCLC patients survive beyond 5 years in the United Kingdom.

The most important cause of lung cancer is tobacco smoking (including passive/secondhand smoking). However, the proportion of lung cancer deaths attributable to smoking varies across populations, ranging from more than 80% in the United States and France to 61% in Asia and 40% in sub-Saharan Africa. Most of the lung cancer deaths due to passive smoking and indoor air pollution occur in low- and middle-income countries, particularly China.

## 5.4.2 Prevention

In common with COPD, lung cancer prevention depends on smoking avoidance, smoking cessation and eliminating secondhand smoke. There is also a need for employers and construction companies to work to reduce or eliminate occupational exposure to lung carcinogens and radon.

## 5.4.3 Earlier recognition

### 5.4.3.1 RISK ASSESSMENT

In seeking to identify individuals at elevated risk for the development of lung cancer the following features warrant consideration:

- In the United Kingdom, 44% of people diagnosed with lung cancer are aged 75 and older.
- Tobacco smoking can be linked to 86% of people who are diagnosed with lung cancer in the United Kingdom (including passive smoking). Both the amount smoked and the length of time as a smoker matter.
- Radiation exposure from any of the following: radiotherapy to the breast or chest, radon exposure in the home or workplace, medical imaging tests, such as computed tomography (CT) scans.
- Occupational exposure to asbestos, arsenic, chromium, beryllium, nickel and cadmium.
- A history of other lung diseases such as TB or COPD.
- A family history of lung cancer. A first-degree relative with lung cancer increases the risk by 50%.
- Lowered immunity due to HIV infection or immunosuppressant drugs.
- Indoor air pollution because of unventilated combustion of coal in the household for heating and cooking and outdoor air pollution.

### 5.4.3.2 SYMPTOMS

The following symptoms might indicate lung cancer:

- An unexplained cough lasting at least 3 weeks
- Coughing up blood
- Unexplained shortness of breath
- Aches or pains when breathing
- A hoarse voice
- Unexplained weight loss
- Extreme tiredness
- A chest infection that does not go away after treatment

Unfortunately, relying on symptoms to spot lung cancer earlier has proved disappointing. Part of this problem might relate to a poor awareness amongst the general public about lung cancer symptoms and risk factors. However, this is compounded by a continuing tendency to use an inadequate test – the chest X-ray – as the next step in the investigation of possible lung cancer–related symptoms.

According to Stapley and colleagues, nearly a quarter of chest X-rays requested from primary care in lung cancer patients are negative.

Based on the findings from the Philadelphia Pulmonary Neoplasm Research Project, in which 6027 men aged 45 or older underwent a chest X-ray every 6 months for 10 years and were questioned about symptoms and smoking habits, it is clear that the chest X-ray should simply be viewed as a risk marker for lung cancer. If the lung fields on a chest X-ray are non-specifically unclear the risk of lung cancer is 2.64% (compared to 1.78% if the lung fields are clear).

In spotting lung cancer earlier, it might also be useful to look beyond symptoms to an individual's health behaviour – for example, there is evidence that spontaneous smoking cessation may be a presenting feature of lung cancer. Also, it is important to be alert to those who arrange an appointment – perhaps for a health check – after not having seen a clinician for a while and mention a possible cancer symptom as such individuals are more likely to have a cancer than those who attend their own doctor regularly.

#### 5.4.3.3 SCREENING

Routine screening for lung cancer with chest X-rays and/or sputum cytology is not effective in reducing long-term mortality. Moreover, three randomised controlled trials conducted in the 1970s (Mayo Clinic, Johns Hopkins and Memorial-Sloane Kettering hospitals) demonstrated high false-negative rates, high follow-up testing requirements and low yields.

More recently, the National Lung Screening Trial compared annual screening with low-dose CT scanning against that by routine chest X-rays in heavy smokers (30 pack-years).

As can be seen from Table 5.4, in this trial many more cancers were detected at an early stage (1 or 2) by CT scanning. Importantly, this translated into a 20% lung cancer mortality difference between the two arms of the trial.

As a result of this study, the U.S. Preventive Services Task Force now recommends annual screening for lung cancer with low-dose CT in adults aged 55–80 years who have a 30 pack-year smoking history and currently smoke or have quit within the past 15 years. They also recommend that screening should be discontinued once a person has not smoked for 15 years or develops a health

Table 5.4 Lung cancer staging in the National Lung Screening Trial

| Lung cancer stage | Computed tomography (% of cancers detected by stage) | Chest X-ray (% of cancers detected by stage) |
|---|---|---|
| 1 | 50 | 31.1 |
| 2 | 7.1 | 7.9 |
| 3 | 21.2 | 24.8 |
| 4 | 21.7 | 36.2 |

problem that substantially limits life expectancy or the ability or willingness to have curative surgery.

The harms associated with low-dose CT screening include false-negative and false-positive results, incidental findings, overdiagnosis, radiation exposure and psychological distress. In the National Lung Screening Trial, the most significant adverse effect related to the high number of false-positive results. In over three rounds of screening with CT, 24.2% of the test results were positive with 96.4% of these being false positives. Most positive test results were followed by additional imaging but approximately 2.5% of positive test results required invasive diagnostic procedures such as bronchoscopy, needle biopsy or thoracoscopy. Moreover, of the 17,053 positive results evaluated there were approximately 61 complications and 6 deaths following a diagnostic procedure.

Incidental findings can also lead to a cascade of testing and treatment. Therefore, appropriately informed shared decision making is particularly important for individuals contemplating lung cancer screening.

Newer approaches to screening continue to be evaluated such as the *Early* CDT-Lung test that measures an individual's antibody response to seven proteins produced by lung cancer cells.

## FURTHER READING

### Chronic obstructive pulmonary disease


Guarascio AJ, Ray SM, Finch CK, Self TH. The clinical and economic burden of chronic obstructive pulmonary disease in the USA. *Clinicoecon Outcomes Res* 2013;5:235–245.

Martinez FJ, O'Connor GT. Screening, case-finding, and outcomes for adults with unrecognized COPD. *JAMA* 2016;315:1343–1344.

Martinez FJ, Raczek AE, Seifer FD et al. Development and initial validation of a self-scored COPD population screener questionnaire (COPD-PS). *COPD* 2008;5:85–95.

NHS Purchasing and Supply Agency. *Buyers' Guide. Spirometers*. London: CEP, 2009.

Perez-Padalla R, Vollmer WM, Vázquez-Garcia JC et al. Can a normal peak flow exclude severe chronic obstructive pulmonary disease? *Int J Tuber Lung Dis* 2009;13:387–393.

Pocket Guide to COPD Diagnosis, Management and Prevention. A Guide for Health Professionals: 2017. Global Initiative for Chronic Obstructive Lung Disease. http://goldcopd.org/wp-content/uploads/2016/12/wms-GOLD-2017-Pocket-Guide.pdf

Price DB, Tinkelman DG, Halbert RJ et al. Symptom-based questionnaire for identifying COPD in smokers. *Respiration* 2006a;73:285–295.

Price DB, Tinkelman DG, Nordyke RJ et al. Scoring system and clinical application of COPD diagnostic questionnaires. *Chest* 2006b;129:1531–1539.

Rytila P, Helin T, Kinnula V. The use of microspirometry in detecting lowered FEV1 values in current or former cigarette smokers. *Prim Care Respir J* 2008;17:232–237.

U.S. Preventive Services Task Force. Screening for chronic obstructive pulmonary disease: U.S. Preventive Services Task Force recommendation statement. *JAMA* 2016;315:1372–1377.

## Alpha-1 antitrypsin deficiency

American Thoracic Society/European Respiratory Society. American Thoracic Society/European Respiratory Society statement: Standards for the diagnosis and management of individuals with alpha-1 antitrypsin deficiency. *Am J Respir Crit Care Med* 2003;168:818–900.

Brode SK, Ling SC, Chapman KR. Alpha-1 antitrypsin deficiency: A commonly overlooked cause of lung disease. *CMAJ* 2012;184:1365–1371.

Stoller JK, Aboussouan LS. A review of alpha-1 antitrypsin deficiency. *Am J Respir Crit Care Med* 2012;185:246–259.

## Tuberculosis

Kahwati LC, Feltner C, Halpern M et al. Primary care screening and treatment for latent tuberculosis infection in adults. Evidence report and systematic review for the U.S. Preventive Services Task Force. *JAMA* 2016;316:970–983.

National Institute for Health and Care Excellence (NICE). *Tuberculosis*. London: NICE, 2016.

World Health Organization (WHO). *Systematic Screening for Active Tuberculosis: Principles and Recommendations*. Geneva: WHO, 2013.

## Lung cancer

Boucot KR, Seidman H, Weiss W. The Philadelphia Pulmonary Neoplasm Research Project. *Envir Res* 1977;13:451–469.

Campling BG, Collins BN, Algazy KM et al. Spontaneous smoking cessation before lung cancer diagnosis. *J Thorac Oncol* 2011;6:517–524.

Hamilton W, Peters TJ, Round A, Sharp D. What are the clinical features of lung cancer before the diagnosis is made? A population-based case-control study. *Thorax* 2005;60:1059–1065.

Islami F, Torre LA, Jemal A. Global trends of lung cancer mortality and smoking prevalence. *Transl Lung Cancer Res* 2015;4:327–338.

Jett JR, Peek LJ, Fredericks L et al. Audit of autoantibody test, *Early*CDT-Lung, in 1600 patients: An evaluation of its performance in routine clinical practice. *Lung Cancer* 2014;83:51–55.

Simon AE, Juszczyk D, Smyth N et al. Knowledge of lung cancer symptoms and risk factors in the UK: Development of a measure and results from a population-based survey. *Thorax* 2012;67:426–432.

Stapley S, Sharp D, Hamilton W. Negative chest x-rays in primary care patients with lung cancer. *Br J Gen Pract* 2006;56:570–573.

The National Lung Screening Trial Research Team. Reduced lung-cancer mortality with low-dose computed tomographic screening. *N Eng J Med* 2011;365:395–409.

U.S. Preventative Services Task Force. Screening for lung cancer: U.S. Preventive Services Task Force recommendation statement. *Ann Intern Med* 2014;160:330–338.

Wolpaw DR. Early detection in lung cancer. *Med Clin North Am* 1996;80:63–82.

# 6

# Musculoskeletal health

## KEY RECOMMENDATIONS

- For those designing a better value health check incorporating a focus on musculoskeletal health it is suggested that the following conditions warrant particular consideration: low back pain, osteoporosis, vitamin D, rheumatoid arthritis and gout.
- Recommend exercise alone or in combination with education to prevent low back pain.
- For individuals with low back pain seek to rule out any red flags.
- Apply the Örebro Musculoskeletal Pain Screening Questionnaire or the STarT Back Screening Tool to identify individuals at risk of persistent disability from low back pain.
- Undertake screening for osteoporosis-related fracture risk using the Fracture Risk Assessment Tool (FRAX) in combination with dual-energy X-ray absorptiometry (DXA).
- Consider ensuring adequate calcium and vitamin D intake, antiresorptive therapy, weight-bearing exercise, tobacco avoidance, reducing alcohol intake, and the avoidance of trip or fall hazards for osteoporosis-fracture prevention.
- Recommend that individuals in northern latitudes consider vitamin D supplementation during the autumn and winter months in addition to offering vitamin D case-finding in certain circumstances.
- Adopt a case-finding approach to rheumatoid arthritis using anti-cyclic citrullinated peptide (anti-CCP) antibody in individuals with musculoskeletal symptoms.
- Consider targeted measurement of uric acid based on risks.

## 6.1 OVERVIEW

In terms of developing a better value health check incorporating a focus on musculoskeletal health it is suggested that the key priorities are low back pain, osteoporosis, vitamin D, rheumatoid arthritis and gout.

There are some other areas that have been considered for inclusion within this chapter but, at present, I felt that the evidence of benefit in terms of delivering value was insufficient. Key amongst these is case-finding for carpal tunnel syndrome using a validated questionnaire and electrophysiology.

Musculoskeletal health also has very important links to older people's health (see Chapter 15) in relation to falls and frailty.

## 6.2 LOW BACK PAIN

### 6.2.1 Importance

Low back pain is one of the most burdensome symptoms worldwide. It has a lifetime prevalence of approximately 40% and is most common among females and persons aged 40–80 years. Approximately one-half of individuals experience a recurrence of low back pain within 1 year after recovering from a previous episode.

There is some evidence that low back pain might have a lower prevalence in less economically prosperous countries such as Nepal, Cuba and Pakistan. This has been attributed to higher levels of exercise, shorter height and differences in pain thresholds.

Low back pain has adverse effects on physical and psychological wellbeing. It also affects work performance and social responsibilities, such as family life, and is increasingly a major factor in escalating healthcare costs. As the population ages over the coming decades, the number of individuals with low back pain is likely to increase substantially.

It is becoming clear that, although deranged anatomy and physiology contribute to back pain, psychological factors including anxiety and depression may amplify or prolong the pain. Moreover, social factors such as the demands of work, the work environment or legal action related to back pain affect the nature of the pain and responses to therapy.

### 6.2.2 Prevention

A systematic review and meta-analysis of 21 good-quality studies concluded that exercise alone or in combination with education is effective for preventing low back pain. The available research evidence suggests that individual interventions such as education, back belts, shoe insoles and ergonomics do not help.

Employers also need to recognise that low back pain is more common in occupational roles that involve repetitive tasks (e.g. manual packing of goods; heavy manual labour; poor or awkward postures such as stooping, bending over or crouching; maintaining the same position for long periods of time, e.g. working with computers or driving long distances; operating vibrating tools); and working in low-temperature environments, e.g. outdoors during winter.

There are a variety of things that employers and their occupational health departments can do to seek to prevent back problems such as making modifications to the work environment and work style as far as is practical. This might include varying tasks to give employees a range of postures, moving loads on wheels, providing better handles on loads and adjusting the heights of worktops.

## 6.2.3 Earlier recognition

In the context of a health check the challenges are to

- Identify individuals with back problems that might be due to serious underlying conditions such as cancers, infections, fractures or inflammatory conditions (e.g. ankylosing spondylitis) – *red flags*. Importantly, back problems due to such issues may often not be spotted immediately and the clinical picture might also develop over time. Therefore, a health check presents a great opportunity to review the diagnosis and prognosis of an individual's back problems.
- Identify individuals likely to have poor outcomes from any recent onset back pain (i.e. starting within the preceding 3 months) with a risk of progression to long-term distress, disability and pain – *yellow flags*. Such yellow flags relate to issues such as attitudes, beliefs, emotions, behaviours, family and workplace.

### 6.2.3.1 RED FLAGS

My own consolidated list of red flags is as follows:

- A personal history of cancer (however long ago).
- Unexplained weight loss or fever. This points to an infection especially if there is any evidence of a recent bacterial infection (e.g. urinary infection).
- Significant trauma (e.g. a recent fall from a height or motor vehicle accident at any age; or a recent minor fall in an older patient or a person with osteoporosis).
- Possible immune deficiency – for example, being HIV positive, recreational needle drug use, taking steroids or on immunosuppressant medicines.
- Rapidly worsening pain or constant back pain that does not ease after lying down.
- Back pain starting for the first time in an individual over the age of 50 years.

Moreover, there might be some neurological effects due to, for example, the local effects of the cancer, fracture, inflammation or infection on the cauda equina:

- Sudden onset of urinary retention or incontinence
- Loss of bowel control
- Numbness around the genitals, buttocks or back passage
- Pain or weakness affecting either leg

However, as serious underlying problems are relatively uncommon accounting for around 1% of back problems, it is also helpful to seek to differentiate between some of these features in terms of their discriminatory power. There is always a risk that the unthinking application of such lists to individuals will result in low-value care with the overinvestigation of individuals with back problems. Lumbar spine imaging has certainly been significantly overused in the past with a low yield of clinically useful findings and a high number of misleading findings together with radiation exposure and costs.

Downie and colleagues undertook a systematic review of the red flags to screen for malignancy and fractures in patients with low back pain and discovered that some features are significantly better than others in terms of the magnitude of their likelihood ratios.

Likelihood ratios for cancer red flags are as follows:

- History of cancer: LR+ 15.3
- Age > 50: LR+ 2.7
- Unexplained weight loss: LR+ 2.6
- Not improved after a month: LR+ 3

Likelihood ratios for spinal fracture red flags are as follows:

- Age > 70: LR+ 11.2
- Prolonged use of corticosteroids: LR+ 48.5
- Significant trauma: LR+ 10

Back pain that is insidious in onset, in a patient younger than 40 years, persisting for at least 3 months, associated with morning stiffness (lasting for more than 1 hour) and improving with exercise is characteristic of ankylosing spondylitis with an overall sensitivity of 95% (specificity 85%).

Frequently, during the course of a health check, the spine is examined. However it is salutary to note that the positive likelihood ratios (in the hands of a generalist) for muscle spasm and spine tenderness are 0.5 and 0.4, respectively. Even in a specialist setting the likelihood ratio for spine tenderness only achieves 0.8. Moreover, it seems that most examination procedures demonstrate very poor reliability – local tenderness has a reported kappa of 0.35 (slight agreement) and muscle spasm a kappa of 0.43 (moderate agreement).

Blood tests that might be arranged for the assessment of back pain in the context of a health check include prostate-specific antigen (PSA) testing in men, bone biochemistry (calcium, phosphate, alkaline phosphatase) and plasma viscosity/erythrocyte sedimentation rate (ESR)/C-reactive protein (CRP). Human leukocyte antigen B27 testing can also assist when the clinical picture is suggestive of ankylosing spondylitis.

Although back pain is not an indication for bone densitometry, osteoporosis should always be considered if vertebral fractures are present (see Section 6.3). In such circumstances, myeloma may also need to be ruled out using serum protein electrophoresis.

#### 6.2.3.2 YELLOW FLAGS

A proportion of individuals become severely disabled by their back pain – often requiring significant periods away from work. Some might benefit from a course of treatment by a physiotherapist, osteopath or chiropractor. For others, it is now clear that psychological factors such as anxiety, depression and a tendency to adopt a pessimistic view about the future can also have a major impact on a person's ability to recover from back problems.

In relation to the persistence of back pain, the key issues to address are as follows:

- Beliefs that the pain is harmful or severely disabling
- Fear-avoidance behaviours (i.e. stopping doing certain activities because of worries about pain)
- Low mood and social withdrawal
- Expectations that passive treatment rather than active participation will help

The Örebro Musculoskeletal Pain Screening Questionnaire is designed to identify people at risk of developing chronic low back pain associated with psychosocial factors. There are 21 scored questions (plus three unscored items) concerning attitudes and beliefs, behaviour in response to pain, affect, perception of work and activities of daily living. The items screen for six key issues: self-perceived function, pain experience, fear-avoidance beliefs, distress, return-to-work expectancy, and pain coping. It is a highly reliable tool (kappa 0.83) and external validity has been established in a variety of populations and settings.

A cutoff score of 105 and below predicts, with 95% accuracy, those who will recover from their back problem and, with 81% accuracy, those who will have no further sick leave during the subsequent 6 months. A cutoff score of 130 and above correctly identifies 86% of those who failed to return to work. Recently a shorter form of the tool has been developed with 10 items which is almost as accurate as the long version but takes less time to complete and score.

The STarT Back Screening Tool incorporates nine items enquiring about radiating leg pain, pain elsewhere, disability, fear, anxiety, pessimistic expectations, low mood and how much the individual is bothered by their pain. It focuses on many of the same prognostic factors as the Örebro questionnaires but is better at forecasting persistent disability whereas Örebro is preferable for predicting time off work.

In the context of a health check the purpose of both questionnaires is to categorise individuals with acute low back pain into different management groups. Those at low risk of persistent disability might simply need an explanation about the biopsychosocial nature of back pain, analgesia and advice on exercise and activity. Whereas people scoring higher may benefit from cognitive behavioural-type therapies and other psychological approaches.

Importantly, the questionnaires are only a guide and even if the score is low psychological therapies might still be indicated if any individual has, for example, co-existing anxiety or depression (see Chapter 11).

## 6.3 OSTEOPOROSIS

### 6.3.1 Importance

Osteoporosis is best defined as a skeletal disorder characterised by compromised bone strength predisposing a person to an increased risk of fracture (fragility fractures).

It affects an estimated 75 million people in Europe, the United States and Japan. Globally, it accounts for 9 million fractures each year. The lifetime risk for developing any osteoporotic fracture is 40%–50% for women and 13%–22% for men. This risk increases exponentially with age.

By 2050 the worldwide incidence of hip fracture is projected to grow by 310% in men and by 240% in women compared to current levels. Moreover, the greatest increase in the number of osteoporotic fragility fractures (mainly hip fractures) is expected to occur in the Middle East, Asia and Latin America due to increasing life expectancy. It is estimated that, in these regions, the total number of hip fractures will rise more than fivefold between 1990 and 2050.

Men sustain 20%–30% of all osteoporotic fractures and this proportion is also expected to increase. Indeed, it is suggested that, by 2025, the number of hip fractures occurring worldwide in men will be similar to that observed in 1990 in women. Unfortunately, osteoporosis in older men continues to be underestimated and insufficiently diagnosed and treated.

Osteoporotic fractures are a major public health problem worldwide because of the associated morbidity, mortality and costs. The financial burden of osteoporosis-related fractures includes direct costs (hospital acute care, in-hospital rehabilitation, outpatient services, long-term nursing care) and indirect costs (morbidity, loss of working days). In the United States, the direct cost of osteoporosis was $19 billion in 2005 and this is expected to increase by 50% by 2025. Trends are similar in Europe, where the cost of osteoporotic fractures was €36 billion in 2000 and this is predicted to rise to €77 billion by 2050.

## 6.3.2 Prevention

Osteoporosis-related fragility fractures are preventable. Prevention strategies include adequate combined calcium and vitamin D intake (calcium alone has not been shown to reduce fractures), weight-bearing exercise, tobacco avoidance, and moderating alcohol intake. However, based on a systematic review of the evidence the U.S. Preventive Services Task Force advised against the routine treatment of pre- and post-menopausal women or men (without osteoporosis or vitamin D deficiency) using vitamin D and calcium supplements.

It is important to recognise that fracture prevention also needs to consider factors that might increase the risk of falls such as

- Environmental hazards (e.g. steps)
- General health (e.g. poor vision, postural hypotension, joint disease, stroke, Parkinson's disease)
- Medications, especially sedating drugs or anti-hypertensives

Cost-effectiveness analyses support early detection and treatment of high-risk patients with anti-resorptive medications, and optimisation of bone health throughout life to help prevent osteoporosis.

## 6.3.3 Earlier recognition

### 6.3.3.1 RISK ASSESSMENT

An enormous number of risk factors have been identified for osteoporosis as presented in Table 6.1.

It is necessary to be aware of these risk factors and also that some of these act, at least in part, independently of bone mineral density (BMD); for example,

*BMD-independent risk factors*: Age, previous fragility fracture, maternal history of hip fracture, oral glucocorticoid therapy, current smoking, excessive alcohol intake, rheumatoid arthritis, low body mass index

*BMD-dependent risk factors*: Malabsorption, endocrine disease, chronic renal disease, chronic liver disease, chronic obstructive pulmonary disease, immobility, medications (e.g. aromatase inhibitors)

The Fracture Risk Assessment Tool (FRAX) algorithm uses selected risk factors with or without BMD to estimate the 10-year fracture probability and is available online (https://www.sheffield.ac.uk/FRAX/).

Factors included in the FRAX algorithm are

- Age
- Gender
- Height
- Weight
- Personal history of fragility fracture
- Parental history of hip fracture
- Smoking status
- Alcohol intake
- Current glucocorticoid treatment
- Known rheumatoid arthritis
- Bone mineral density (optional)
- Secondary causes of osteoporosis (including diabetes [insulin dependent], osteogenesis imperfecta in adults, untreated long-standing hyperthyroidism, premature menopause in women or hypogonadism in men, chronic malnutrition or malabsorption, chronic liver disease, drugs such as aromatase inhibitors and androgen deprivation therapy)

Specific FRAX models have been developed applicable to populations from Europe, North America, Asia and Australia. One disadvantage of FRAX is an inability to include all known clinical risk factors that are important in considering treatment options, so it needs to be viewed as part of the overall assessment.

### 6.3.3.2 SCREENING

The most commonly used bone mineral density tests to screen for osteoporosis are dual-energy X-ray absorptiometry (DXA) of the hip and lumbar spine and

Table 6.1 Risk factors for osteoporosis

| Risk factor | Example |
|---|---|
| Demographics | All women 65 years of age or older and men aged 75 years or older (especially if of Caucasian or Asian race) |
| Lifestyle | Excessive alcohol intake (more than 14 units per week)<br>Prolonged loss of mobility (e.g. unable to move around outside the home without a wheelchair for longer than a year)<br>Body weight lower than 57.5 kg or a BMI of 19 or less<br>Diet deficient in calcium or vitamin D without adequate supplementation<br>Current smoker |
| Fracture and fall history | Personal history of hip fracture<br>Prior fracture with minor trauma (i.e. fall from standing height or less)<br>Frequent falls |
| Genetic factors | History of non-traumatic fracture after age 45 years in a first-degree relative<br>Family history (maternal, paternal or sororal) of osteoporosis, 'brittle bones' or kyphosis<br>Haemochromatosis |
| Hypogonadal state | Anorexia nervosa and bulimia<br>Menopause before age 40 (particularly in those not taking hormone replacement therapy) |
| Endocrine and metabolic disorders | Cushing syndrome<br>Adrenal insufficiency<br>Diabetes mellitus<br>Hyperparathyroidism<br>Thyrotoxicosis<br>Chronic renal disease |
| Gastrointestinal disorders | Coeliac disease<br>Inflammatory bowel disease<br>Chronic liver disease<br>Chronic pancreatitis |
| Respiratory disorders | Cystic fibrosis<br>COPD |
| Haematological disorders | Sickle cell disease<br>Thalassaemia<br>Multiple myeloma |
| Rheumatic and autoimmune diseases | Ankylosing spondylitis<br>Rheumatoid arthritis |

(*Continued*)

Table 6.1 (*Continued*) Risk factors for osteoporosis

| Risk factor | Example |
|---|---|
| Medications | Aromatase inhibitors<br>Glucocorticoids (e.g. prednisolone at a dose of 5 mg or more per day for at least 3 months) |
| X-ray findings | Radiographic osteopenia or vertebral deformity consistent with fracture |

quantitative ultrasonography of the calcaneus. Quantitative ultrasonography is less expensive and more portable than DXA and does not expose people to ionising radiation. Quantitative ultrasonography of the calcaneus also predicts fractures of the femoral neck, hip and spine as effectively as DXA. However, current diagnostic and treatment criteria for osteoporosis rely on DXA measurements only, and criteria based on quantitative ultrasonography or a combination of quantitative ultrasonography and DXA have not been defined.

Osteoporosis in women is classified as a BMD 2.5 or more standard deviations below the average value for pre-menopausal women – that is a T-score $\leq -2.5$. However, it is important to appreciate that many fragility fractures occur in women with bone density values above the defined level (and, conversely, some individuals with very low negative T-scores will never sustain an osteoporotic fracture). Fractures can therefore be better predicted by also considering clinical risk factors and the likelihood of an individual falling. Combining BMD and clinical risk factors (using FRAX) increases sensitivity and maintains specificity.

The most important clinical factors independent of BMD are as follows:

*Age >65 years*: For example, a lumbar T-score of −2 in an 80-year-old woman represents nearly 10 times the risk of fracture as the same T-score in a 50-year-old newly menopausal woman.

*Presence or history of a previous fragility fracture*: A fragility fracture is defined as a fracture occurring after a fall from standing height or less. This includes fractures resulting from activities such as coughing, sneezing or abrupt movements (e.g. opening a window). A particularly tricky group to identify are individuals with vertebral fractures as many are asymptomatic but some helpful pointers are

- A reported high loss over several years (6 cm is considered significant)
- Vertebral fractures documented on radiographs

*A strong family history of fracture*: A generic family history of osteoporosis is a relatively weak risk factor, but a specific maternal history of hip fracture doubles the fracture risk.

Although the U.S. Preventive Services Task Force found insufficient evidence to recommend screening for osteoporosis in men; other organisations such as the National Osteoporosis Foundation and the American College of Physicians advocate screening all men aged 70 years or older.

Following a DXA suggesting osteoporosis, further investigations might need to be considered to search for underlying (secondary) causes. Secondary osteoporosis is particularly likely if multiple vertebral fractures are present; causes are found in about 30% of women and 55% of men with vertebral crush fractures.

To search for any underlying reasons for osteoporosis a careful patient assessment is required in addition to undertaking a full blood count and erythrocyte sedimentation rate, bone biochemistry (serum calcium, phosphate and alkaline phosphatase concentrations), liver and kidney function tests, serum thyroid-stimulating hormone, vitamin D and coeliac serology. In patients with vertebral fractures myeloma should also be excluded using serum protein electrophoresis.

DXA is a non-invasive test with a short test time so the radiation exposure is low. Consequently, the harms of screening for osteoporosis relate more to the management of the osteoporosis than to the screening itself. In addition to adequate calcium and vitamin D intake, weight-bearing exercise, moderating alcohol consumption and stopping smoking, a variety of drug treatments are available to reduce fractures including bisphosphonates and raloxifene. Occasionally, such therapies can lead to ulcers, atrial fibrillation, osteonecrosis of the jaw and an increased risk for thromboembolic events.

## 6.4 VITAMIN D

### 6.4.1 Importance

Vitamin D has been known to have a role in calcium homeostasis and bone health for nearly 100 years. It is obtained primarily from skin exposure to ultraviolet B (UVB) radiation in sunlight and from dietary sources such as oily fish, mushrooms and fortified foods (milk, juices, margarines, yoghurts, cereals and soy).

Adequate vitamin D intake is important for the regulation of calcium and phosphorus absorption, and maintenance of healthy bones and teeth. It might confer a protective effect against multiple conditions such as cancer, cardiovascular disease, type 1 diabetes and multiple sclerosis. However, meta-analyses of randomised controlled trials of vitamin D on non-musculoskeletal health outcomes suggest ongoing uncertainty about the broader health impacts of vitamin D supplementation.

Worldwide, naturally occurring dietary sources of vitamin D are limited, and food fortification is optional, inconsistent, inadequate or non-existent. Therefore, for most people, vitamin D is primarily obtained by cutaneous production from sun exposure. However, many variables influence the amount of UVB from sunlight that reaches the skin and its effectiveness. These include time of day, season, latitude, altitude, clothing, sunscreen use, pigmentation and age.

For example, significant levels of vitamin D deficiency (<30 nmol/L) have been identified amongst 35% of individuals in Scotland (due to latitude) and 26% of women in Bangladesh (due to clothing). In winter 16% of individuals in the

United Kingdom are deficient compared to 3% in the summer. Older people are particularly at risk with reports of 44% of women over the age of 80 severely lacking vitamin D.

### 6.4.2 Prevention

The U.S. Preventive Services Task Force recommends against vitamin D and calcium supplementation for fracture prevention in otherwise healthy post-menopausal women.

Based on a more recent review of the evidence, Public Health England advises that in spring and summer, the majority of the population get enough vitamin D through sunlight on the skin and from dietary sources. But during autumn and winter, it is difficult for people to meet the 10 micrograms recommendation by dietary means alone. Therefore, it is now suggested that all individuals in the United Kingdom should consider taking a daily supplement containing 10 micrograms of vitamin D during these two seasons.

### 6.4.3 Earlier recognition

Universal screening for vitamin D is not recommended. However, in the context of a health check it is suggested that case-finding should be considered in the following risk groups:

- Individuals aged 65 years or older
- People who have low or no sun exposure to the skin (e.g. those who cover their skin for cultural reasons, are housebound or are confined indoors for long periods)
- Individuals who have a darker skin, for example, people of African, Afro-Caribbean and South Asian origin
- Women considering becoming pregnant
- Those with a poor diet or conditions causing malabsorption (e.g. coeliac disease, inflammatory bowel disease)
- Individuals with liver or kidney disease
- People taking treatments for epilepsy
- Those found to have an elevated alkaline phosphatase level or a low serum calcium on core testing
- Individuals with decreased bone mineral density (osteopenia or osteoporosis) or a history of a non-traumatic (fragility) fracture (see Section 6.3)

It has also been suggested that it is worth considering testing individuals with musculoskeletal symptoms, such as bone pain, myalgias and generalised weakness, because these symptoms are often associated with low vitamin D and might be misdiagnosed as fibromyalgia, chronic fatigue or age-related weakness.

Testing for vitamin D might also be helpful in individuals already taking supplements in order to check that they are not being over-treated. Vitamin D toxicity leads to hypercalcaemia which can cause poor appetite, nausea and vomiting. Weakness, fatigue, frequent urination, constipation and kidney stones might also occur.

Both ingested and cutaneously produced vitamin D is rapidly metabolised to 25-hydroxy vitamin D (25[OH]D), but only a fraction of 25(OH)D is converted to its active metabolite 1,25-dihdroxy vitamin D. Thus, measurement of the total serum 25(OH)D level is the best test to assess body stores of vitamin D.

## 6.5 RHEUMATOID ARTHRITIS

### 6.5.1 Importance

Rheumatoid arthritis is a common autoimmune systemic inflammatory disease affecting approximately 1% of the worldwide population. The incidence appears to be highest in Pima and Chippewa Indians (6%), and lowest in people from China and Japan (0.2%–0.3%).

The interaction of genetic and environmental factors results in a cascade of immune reactions, which ultimately ends in the development of joint and structural bone damage. These, in turn, lead to pain and disability with up to one-third of individuals becoming work-disabled within 2 years of disease onset, and 50% after 10 years. The physical, emotional and social impact of rheumatoid arthritis contributes to poor health-related quality of life.

Unfortunately the disease burden of rheumatoid arthritis is not restricted to joints. It is also associated with a number of systemic complications related to the underlying disease process such as osteoporosis (see Section 6.3), lung fibrosis, atherosclerotic cardiovascular disease (see Chapter 4) and to eye problems such as episcleritis. The majority of the deaths amongst individuals with rheumatoid arthritis are linked to cardiovascular disease and cardiovascular mortality appears to be at least 1.5-fold higher than in the general population.

### 6.5.2 Prevention

There is no known way to prevent rheumatoid arthritis, although progression of the disease usually can be stopped or slowed by early, aggressive treatment. This emphasises the importance of earlier recognition.

### 6.5.3 Earlier recognition

Traditionally, the diagnosis of rheumatoid arthritis is made clinically based on the history and physical examination findings such as the number of joints involved, the types of joints affected, the existence of morning stiffness and duration of symptoms. However, such an approach has been criticised due to its inability to identify patients with early disease, who could gain the most benefit from available therapies.

The vast majority of patients with rheumatoid arthritis will first present to their GP when they develop symptoms. Unfortunately, in general, GPs and those undertaking health checks will have less expertise in assessing early arthralgia.

Within the United Kingdom, it is estimated that patients with rheumatoid arthritis visit their GP on average four times before being referred to a specialist for definitive diagnosis.

Rheumatoid factor (an antibody) is often measured as an aid to the diagnosis of rheumatoid arthritis. But only about half of people with rheumatoid arthritis have a positive rheumatoid factor present in their blood when the disease starts. Moreover, around 1 in 20 people without rheumatoid arthritis will also test positive.

A better approach – and applicable to individuals attending for health checks – is to undertake case-finding for early rheumatoid arthritis using anti-cyclic citrullinated peptide (anti-CCP) in any individual presenting with a new musculoskeletal complaint (especially those with a family history of rheumatoid arthritis). People who test anti-CCP positive are at high risk of imminent rheumatoid arthritis, with 45% progressing to clinical arthritis, the majority within 1 year.

Following a positive anti-CCP test, additional clinical, serological and imaging tests can then be harnessed to quantify the risk of progression to arthritis more accurately. However, for individuals with negative anti-CCP results further assessment might still be required for continuing unexplained joint symptoms or signs.

An individual attending for a health check with known rheumatoid arthritis should also always undergo blood pressure and lipid testing. Despite the excess risk of vascular disease in patients with rheumatoid arthritis being of a similar magnitude to that seen in diabetes; people with rheumatoid arthritis often do not receive focused screening for atherosclerotic cardiovascular disease. Moreover, the traditional cardiovascular risk assessment tools, such as Framingham, substantially underestimate the risk of cardiovascular disease in patients with rheumatoid arthritis. QRISK2 and QRISK3 are the only validated cardiovascular risk assessment tools to include rheumatoid arthritis as an independent risk factor for atherosclerotic cardiovascular disease (see Chapter 4).

## 6.6 GOUT

### 6.6.1 Importance

Gout is the most common form of inflammatory arthritis. In its initial stages, it is recognised by acute, intermittent episodes of joint swelling and pain that may progress to chronic and persistent symptoms with a reduced quality of life. Gout is the result of excess uric acid crystallising in the joints (in the form of monosodium urate) or as renal stones.

The self-reported prevalence in the United States was recently estimated as 3.9% of adults. It is less common in Malaysia, the Philippines, Saudi Arabia, Japan, South Korea and most African countries. Hyperuricaemia is a necessary – but not sufficient – risk factor for the development of gout, occurring in 21% of the U.S. population.

Over the last few decades the prevalence of gout has risen in many countries (e.g. New Zealand, China, United States, United Kingdom, Singapore), possibly mediated by increases in conditions that are associated with hyperuricaemia, including hypertension, obesity, metabolic syndrome, type 2 diabetes and chronic kidney disease. Other factors linked to the rising prevalence of gout include certain dietary trends together with the widespread prescription of thiazide and loop diuretics for cardiovascular diseases. Meat, seafood and alcohol also all elevate levels of uric acid.

There is a continuing debate as to whether a raised uric acid level is an independent and causal risk factor for cardiovascular disease mortality (as for rheumatoid arthritis). Even if this is the case it remains unclear whether altering the level of uric acid in the blood would impact this risk.

### 6.6.2 Prevention

Although some might argue for lowering the level of uric acid in the blood by avoiding high-purine foods such as offal, game and seafood; losing weight; reducing alcohol consumption; and reviewing the use of medications known to affect urate levels such as diuretics there is, as yet, no evidence that such interventions will prevent progression to symptomatic gout or improve outcomes.

### 6.6.3 Earlier recognition

Although hyperuricaemia is a requirement for the development of symptomatic gout, it is not sufficient, and the majority of individuals with hyperuricaemia will never develop clinical evidence of gout. But it is clear that gout becomes more likely at higher levels of uric acid in the blood.

Over a 3-year period, approximately 18% of people with severe hyperuricaemia ($\geq$0.55 mmol/L) will develop gout. Initiating treatment on the basis of uric acid levels alone would, therefore, result in up to 82 out of 100 people who might never develop gout receiving therapy.

Generating a clinical risk score to guide targeted case-finding for hyperuricaemia would be extremely useful. However, in the meantime, the following groups should be considered for uric acid testing in the context of a health check:

- People undergoing chemotherapy or radiation therapy when uric acid levels might increase due to tumour lysis
- Those with a family history of gout
- Individuals classified as having possible metabolic syndrome
- Individuals taking diuretics

## FURTHER READING

### Overview

D'Arcy CA, McGee S. Does this patient have carpal tunnel syndrome? *JAMA* 2000;283:3110–3117.

## Back pain

Brown G. The Örebro musculoskeletal pain questionnaire. *Occup Med* 2008;58:447–448.

Calin A, Porta J, Fries JF, Schurman DJ. Clinical history as a screening test for ankylosing spondylitis. *JAMA* 1977;237:2613–2614.

Deyo RA. Biopsychosocial care for chronic back pain. *BMJ* 2015;350:8.

Deyo RA, Jarvick JG, Chou R. Low back pain in primary care. *BMJ* 2014;349:30–33.

Downie A, Williams CM, Henschke N et al. Red flags to screen for malignancy and fracture in patients with low back pain: Systematic review. *BMJ* 2013;347:f7095.

Hill JC, Dunn KM, Main CJ, Hay EM. Subgrouping low back pain: A comparison of the STarT Back Tool with the Örebro Musculoskeletal Pain Screening Questionnaire. *Eur J Pain* 2010;14:83–89.

Hockings RL, McAuley JH, Maher CG. A systematic review of the predictive ability of the Örebro musculoskeletal pain questionnaire. *Spine* 2008;33:E494–E500.

Hoy D, Bain C, Williams G et al. A systematic review of the global prevalence of low back pain. *Arthritis Rheum* 2012;64:2028–2037.

Health and Safety Executive for Northern Ireland (HSENI). Back pain – Advice for employers. https://www.hseni.gov.uk/articles/back-pain-advice-employers

Karran EL, McAuley JH, Traege AC et al. Can screening instruments accurately determine poor outcome risk in adults with recent onset low back pain? A systematic review and meta-analysis. *BMC Med* 2017;15:13. doi:10.1186/s12916-016-0774-4

Linton SJ, Nicholas M, MacDonald S. Development of a short form of the Örebro Musculoskeletal Pain Screening Questionnaire. *Spine* 2011;36:1891–1895.

Manchikanti L, Singh V, Falco FJ, Benyamin RM, Hirsch JA. Epidemiology of low back pain in adults. *Neuromodulation* 2014;17(Suppl 2):3–10.

May S, Littlewood C, Bishop A. Reliability of procedures used in the physical examination of non-specific low back pain: A systematic review. *Aust J Physiother* 2006;52:91–102.

Steffens D, Maher CG, Pereira LSM et al. Prevention of low back pain: A systematic review and meta-analysis. *JAMA Intern Med* 2016;176:199–208.

## Osteoporosis

Green AD, Colón-Emeric CS, Bastian L et al. Does this woman have osteoporosis? *JAMA* 2004;292:2890–2900.

Jeremiah MP, Unwin BK, Greenawald MH, Casiano VE. Diagnosis and management of osteoporosis. *Am Fam Physician* 2015;92:261–268.

Kling JM, Clarke BL, Sandhu NP. Osteoporosis prevention, screening, and treatment: A review. *J Womens Health* 2014;23:563–572.

National Institute for Health and Clinical Excellence. *Osteoporosis: Assessing the Risk of Fragility Fracture*. London: NICE, 2012.
Premaor MO, Compston JE. Testing for secondary causes of osteoporosis. *BMJ* 2010;341:c6959.
Szulc P, Bouxsein ML. *Vertebral Fracture Initiative Part I. Overview of Osteoporosis: Epidemiology and Clinical Management*. Lyon: International Osteoporosis Foundation, 2010.
U.S. Preventive Services Task Force. Screening for osteoporosis: U.S. Preventive Services Task Force recommendation statement. *Ann Intern Med* 2011;154:356–364.
U.S. Preventive Services Task Force. Vitamin D and calcium supplementation to prevent fractures in adults: U.S. Preventive Services Task Force recommendation statement. *Ann Intern Med* 2013;158:691–696.

## Vitamin D

Bolland MJ, Avenell A, Grey A. Should adults take vitamin D supplements to prevent disease? *BMJ* 2016;355:i6201.
Kennel KA, Drake MT, Hurley DL. Vitamin D deficiency in adults: When to test and how to treat. *Mayo Clin Proc* 2010;85:752–758.
National Osteoporosis Society. *Vitamin D and Bone Health: A Practical Clinical Guideline for Patient Management*. Bath: National Osteoporosis Society, 2013.
Palacios C, Gonzalez L. Is vitamin D deficiency a major global public health problem? *J Steroid Biochem Mol Biol* 2014;144:138–145.
Public Health England. PHE publishes new advice on vitamin D. 2016. www.gov.uk/government/news/phe-publishes-new-advice-on-vitamin-d.
U.S. Preventive Services Task Force. Vitamin D and calcium supplementation to prevent fractures in adults: U.S. Preventive Services Task Force recommendation statement. *Ann Intern Med* 2013;158:691–696.
U.S. Preventive Services Task Force. Screening for vitamin D deficiency in adults: U.S. Preventive Services Task Force recommendation statement. *Ann Intern Med* 2015;162:133–140.

## Rheumatoid arthritis

Gibofsky A. Overview of epidemiology, pathophysiology, and diagnosis of rheumatoid arthritis. *Am J Manag Care* 2012;18:S295–S302.
Mankia K, Emery P. Imminent rheumatoid arthritis can be identified in primary care. *Ann Rheum Dis* 2017;76:e14.
Mankia K, Nam J, Emery P. Identifying arthralgia suspicious for progression to rheumatoid arthritis. *Ann Rheum Dis* 2017;76:e14.
Monk HL, Muller S, Mallen CD, Hider SL. Cardiovascular screening in rheumatoid arthritis: A cross-sectional primary care database study. *BMC Fam Pract* 2013;14:150.

Villeneuve E, Nam JL, Bell MJ et al. A systematic literature review of strategies promoting early referral and reducing delays in the diagnosis and management of inflammatory arthritis. *Ann Rheum Dis* 2013;72:13–22.

## Gout

Kuo CF, Grainge MJ, Zhang W, Doherty M. Global epidemiology of gout: Prevalence, incidence and risk factors. *Nat Rev Rheumatol* 2015;11:649–662.

Roddy E, Doherty M. Epidemiology of gout. *Arthritis Res Ther* 2010;12:223–234.

Stamp L, Dalbeth N. Screening for hyperuricaemia and gout: A perspective and research agenda. *Nat Rev Rheumatol* 2014;10:752–756.

# 7

# Gastrointestinal health

## KEY RECOMMENDATIONS

- For those designing a better value health check incorporating a focus on gastrointestinal health it is suggested that the following conditions warrant particular consideration: colorectal cancer, gastric cancer and coeliac disease.
- Suggest aspirin use for the prevention of colorectal cancer, if appropriate, in adults aged 50–69 years.
- Encourage screening for colorectal cancer using faecal occult blood testing, flexible sigmoidoscopy or colonoscopy.
- Do not undertake routine digital rectal examination as a screening test for rectal cancer.
- Consider routine stool testing for *Helicobacter pylori* antigen.
- Screen populations for gastric cancer if they are at higher risk, particularly those resident in (or recently emigrated from) Eastern Asia, Russia or South America or who have a family history of gastric cancer.
- Undertake case-finding for coeliac disease in individuals with symptoms, and in asymptomatic individuals at increased risk.
- Seek expert advice before offering any testing for food allergies or intolerances.

## 7.1 OVERVIEW

In terms of developing a better value health check incorporating a focus on gastrointestinal (GI) health it is suggested that the key priorities are colorectal cancer, gastric cancer and coeliac disease.

There are some other areas that have been considered for inclusion within this chapter but, at present, I felt that the evidence of benefit in terms of delivering value was insufficient. Key amongst these are pancreatitis case-finding (using amylase), pancreatic cancer screening (using cancer antigen 19-9 alone or in combination with other markers) and oesophageal cancer screening.

Barrett's oesophagus is a pre-malignant condition that might be identified endoscopically in individuals with chronic or recalcitrant gastro-oesophageal reflux disease. However, although surveillance is recommended once the condition has been picked up, there is not universal support for the suggestion that case-finding should be undertaken in men over the age of 60 with symptoms of reflux for at least 10 years as an approach to improve oesophageal cancer outcomes.

Routine food allergy or food intolerance investigations have also not been included within this chapter as this is a particular tricky area requiring expert advice and testing. Before incorporating such components into a health check detailed consideration always needs to be given to the available research evidence for any test (including validity, reliability and utility), the quality assurance processes (with a view to reducing false-positive results) and the aftercare recommendations. Moreover, there is a requirement to take care in testing individuals with irritable-bowel-type symptoms and to always consider other conditions such as coeliac disease (see Section 7.4), ovarian cancer (Chapter 13), colorectal cancer (see Section 7.2), thyroid dysfunction (Chapter 9) and HIV (Chapter 14) in addition to calprotectin testing to rule out inflammatory bowel diseases.

As discussed in Chapter 2, digital rectal examination has been recommended and practised in the context of many health checks in the hope that it will lead to the earlier discovery and the more effective treatment of rectal cancer and adenomatous polyps. However, this seems to be a low-value intervention as the test characteristics of the rectal examination are very poor. Moreover, aside from the time required to undertake the procedure, it is also suggested that there might be an opportunity cost by deterring individuals from attending general health checks due to concerns about the discomfort and the embarrassment of having a digital rectal examination.

## 7.2 COLORECTAL CANCER

### 7.2.1 Importance

Colorectal cancer is the third most common cancer worldwide and a major cause of premature deaths. Almost 55% of the cases occur in the more developed regions such as Australia, New Zealand, Canada, the United States and Western Europe. The lowest rates are found in Western Africa.

However, over recent years, the incidence rates have begun to rise in many low- and middle-income countries but have stabilised elsewhere. It has been estimated that the global burden of colorectal cancer will increase by 60% to more than 2.2 million new cases and 1.1 million deaths by 2030.

There is now good evidence that earlier colorectal cancer recognition reduces premature deaths. Moreover, there is also a significant impact on total healthcare expenditure as it is clear that picking up an early stage colon cancer is cheaper both in relation to the initial treatment and the costs linked to recurrence (Table 7.1).

These health costs will also be mirrored by the costs for individuals and organisations.

Table 7.1 Colon cancer treatment costs by disease stage

| Colon cancer stage | Treatment costs per person (UK) | Treatment costs per person if any recurrence (UK) |
|---|---|---|
| 1 | £3373 | £376 |
| 2 | £7809 | £2003 |
| 3 | £9220 | £4757 |
| 4 | £12,519 | N/A |

## 7.2.2 Prevention

For the vast majority of individuals, the key risk factor for colorectal cancer is aging. Most cases of colorectal cancer occur among adults older than 50 years with the median age at diagnosis being 68 years.

However, the following modifiable risk factors also increase the chances of developing colorectal cancer: obesity, lack of exercise, smoking and excessive alcohol intake. Therefore, serious consideration should be given to stopping smoking, reducing alcohol consumption, maintaining a healthy weight and exercising for 30 minutes most days of the week.

There is also a growing body of evidence that long-term treatment with aspirin (75 mg per day) can reduce the risk of developing colorectal cancer by around 40%. The U.S. Preventive Services Task Force suggests considering aspirin use for the prevention of colorectal cancer in adults aged 50–69 years who are not at any increased risk for bleeding, have a life expectancy of at least 10 years, and are willing to take an aspirin every day for at least 10 years.

## 7.2.3 Earlier recognition

### 7.2.3.1 RISK ASSESSMENT

In seeking to identify individuals at elevated risk for the development of colorectal cancer the following features warrant particular consideration:

- *Symptoms*: In the context of a health check attention should be paid to reports of any rectal bleeding, changes in bowel habits, abdominal pain or unexplained weight loss. Although such symptoms are not uncommon and can have a variety of causes, it is important to appreciate that having combinations of these symptoms greatly increases the risk of an underlying colorectal cancer.
- *Past medical history*: Patients with long-standing ulcerative colitis or Crohn's disease are at higher risk of developing colorectal cancer than the general population. A history of colorectal cancer or adenomas also increases the risk as does having type 2 diabetes, primary sclerosing cholangitis or acromegaly.
- *Family history*: Colorectal cancer has a large (and complex) familial component; it has been estimated that a quarter of new colorectal cancers

may arise in individuals with an inherited genetic predisposition. Two specific genetic syndromes are often specifically highlighted—familial adenomatous polyposis (FAP) and Lynch syndrome/hereditary non-polyposis colorectal cancer (HNPCC)—but many cases do not fall within these two syndromes.

In the context of a health check it is suggested that particular attention is paid to identifying those at increased risk:

1. One first-degree relative affected, diagnosed with colorectal cancer or adenomatous polyps before the age of 60 years.
2. At least two first-degree relatives of any age affected with colorectal cancer.
3. Families with at least two individuals with colorectal cancer, plus endometrial, ovarian, stomach, urinary tract, biliary tract or small bowel cancers (i.e. evidence of a dominant family cancer trait).

- *Investigations*: It is recommended that the possibility of colorectal cancer should be considered in all patients with iron-deficiency anaemia. There is also recent evidence that haemoglobin concentrations begin to decline at least 2 years before the diagnosis of colorectal cancer.

#### 7.2.3.2 SCREENING

It is now generally accepted that screening for colorectal cancer in average-risk, asymptomatic adults aged 50–75 years is of substantial benefit. Three main screening modalities are currently recommended: faecal occult blood testing, flexible sigmoidoscopy or colonoscopy.

- *Faecal occult blood testing*: Multiple randomised clinical trials including those undertaken in Minnesota (United States), Nottingham (United Kingdom), Funen (Denmark) and Gothenberg (Sweden) have shown that screening for faecal occult blood reduces colorectal cancer deaths. Most used biennial screening except for Minnesota where the testing interval was 12 months. Interestingly, this study also produced the greatest reduction in mortality (33%).

  The first generation of tests using guaiac-based assays (FOBT) for occult blood have now largely been replaced by faecal immunochemical testing (FIT), which identifies intact human haemoglobin in the stool. FIT has improved sensitivity and does not detect haemoglobin from non-human dietary sources or partially digested haemoglobin from the upper respiratory or GI tracts.

  Multitargeted stool DNA testing (FIT-DNA) is an emerging screening strategy that combines a FIT with the measurement of altered DNA biomarkers in cells shed into the stool. Such testing has increased single-test sensitivity for detecting colorectal cancer compared with FIT alone. However, the specificity of FIT-DNA is lower than that of FIT alone, with an increased number of false-positive results and a higher likelihood of follow-up colonoscopy.

- *Flexible sigmoidoscopy*: Several randomised controlled trials including NORCCAP (Norway), Telemark (Norway), SCORE (Italy), the UK trial and PLCO (United States) have demonstrated that flexible sigmoidoscopy alone reduces deaths from colorectal cancer by around 25%. Flexible sigmoidoscopy combined with FIT has also been studied in a single trial and seems to reduce the colorectal cancer–specific mortality rate more than flexible sigmoidoscopy alone. However, flexible sigmoidoscopy can result in serious complication rates of around 0.03% due to perforations and bleeding.
- *Colonoscopy*: Although optical colonoscopy has been suggested as a further screening tool the evidence base is – as yet – not as robust as for the other two modalities. Moreover, harms may be caused by bowel preparation prior to the procedure (e.g. dehydration and electrolyte imbalances), the sedation used during the colonoscopy (e.g. cardiovascular events) or the procedure itself (e.g. infection, colonic perforations, or bleeding).

  Computed tomography colonography is an alternative mechanism to visualise the whole bowel but, aside from the radiation exposure, this technique can often result in unnecessary diagnostic testing or treatment of incidental findings. Extra-colonic findings are common, occurring in about 40%–70% of screening examinations. Between 5% and 37% of these findings result in diagnostic follow-up, and about 3% require definitive treatment.

About one-third of eligible adults in the United States have never been screened for colorectal cancer and offering choice in colorectal cancer screening strategies might increase screening uptake. For example, colonoscopy requires a relatively greater time commitment over a short period (bowel preparation, procedure and recovery) but allows for much longer periods between screenings. Faecal occult blood testing that involves individuals sampling their own faeces may be difficult or unacceptable for some.

It is also always important to appreciate that, following initial screening with anything other than optical colonoscopy, a subsequent colonoscopy (plus biopsy) will generally be required to establish a definitive diagnosis. This needs to be borne in mind as harms can occur from such follow-up colonoscopies for positive (true or false) findings on preliminary testing.

In 2015, the American College of Physicians categorised colorectal cancer screening using one of the following four strategies as a high-value intervention in average-risk adults aged 50–75 years:

- Annual high-sensitivity FOBT or FIT
- Flexible sigmoidoscopy every 5 years
- High-sensitivity FOBT or FIT every 3 years plus flexible sigmoidoscopy every 5 years
- Colonoscopy every 10 years

It is also recommended that an individualised assessment of risk is undertaken for all adults in order to target screening more appropriately. Key issues to consider are a personal history of colorectal cancer, colonic adenomas, ulcerative colitis, Crohn's disease, primary sclerosing cholangitis, acromegaly or a significant family history. In this group, the American College of Physicians makes the following evidence-based recommendations:

- Screening in high-risk adults should commence at the age of 40 years (or 10 years younger than the age at which the youngest affected relative was diagnosed with colorectal cancer).
- Optical colonoscopy is the preferred screening test for those at high risk but patient preferences also need to be considered.

## 7.3 GASTRIC CANCER

### 7.3.1 Importance

Gastric cancer is an important condition in terms of mortality and incidence but with significant geographical variability.

Worldwide there are almost one million new cases of gastric cancer each year making it the fifth most common cancer globally. The highest incidence rates are seen in Eastern Asia (50% of cases), Russia and South America, with lower rates in North America and Western Europe.

Rates are about twice as high in men as in women. The incidence also increases with age with most cases occurring over the age of 50.

The highest estimated mortality rates are found in Eastern Asia, Central and Eastern Europe (including Russia) and in South America with the lowest in Northern America. According to the UK Oesophago-Gastric Cancer Audit, the 5-year survival for gastric cancer is 18%, with the poor outcomes being largely attributable to late diagnosis. Only 1 in 20 cases are spotted at an early – and potentially curable – stage.

Gastric cancer also represents a significant economic burden both to the individual and the healthcare system. Using U.S. administrative claims data it has been calculated that patients with gastric cancer incurred more than 10 times the healthcare costs than those without cancer ($96,571 versus $8338), particularly individuals with advanced disease ($131,663).

### 7.3.2 Prevention

The major preventative approaches for gastric cancer focus on dietary and lifestyle modifications and reduction in the prevalence of *Helicobacter pylori* (*H. pylori*). Prevention through dietary intervention is about increasing fruit and vegetable intake and decreasing the consumption of salt or salt-preserved foods. Lifestyle modifications such as increasing physical activity and smoking cessation may also help reduce the risk of developing the disease.

There is consistent evidence that *H. pylori* infection of the stomach is strongly associated with both the initiation and the promotion of gastric cancer and gastric lymphoma. A meta-analysis of seven randomised studies suggests that treatment of *H. pylori* may reduce gastric cancer risk by around 1.7%.

*H. pylori* causes chronic gastritis, which can slowly progress via intestinal metaplasia and dysplasia to gastric cancer. This process takes decades and provides an excellent window of opportunity for the detection and treatment of *H. pylori*.

Four main approaches have been developed to check for *H. pylori*: blood testing, stool testing, urea breath testing and various endoscopy-related tests. In the context of a health check both blood antibody testing and faecal antigen testing have been used. However, based on decision analysis, it seems that the testing for the presence of *H. pylori* antigen in a stool sample offers the best value in terms of outcomes and costs. Moreover, a positive blood serology result for *H. pylori* antibodies is unable to differentiate between a current infection and a previous infection.

## 7.3.3 Earlier recognition

### 7.3.3.1 RISK ASSESSMENT

In seeking to identify individuals at elevated risk for the development of gastric cancer the following issues warrant particular consideration:

- Residents of geographical areas with increased incidence are at elevated risk. First-generation immigrants to other countries from these areas (i.e. from Eastern Asia, Russia and South America) are also at increased risk.
- A history of *H. pylori* infection (see Section 7.3.2).
- Having a first-degree relative with gastric cancer. This increases the risk by between 2- and 10-fold. Certain hereditary cancer syndromes such as Lynch syndrome also confer an enhanced risk.
- Stomach problems such as atrophic gastritis, metaplasia and some types of stomach adenomas (polyps) raise the risk as does a history of partial gastrectomy.
- Pernicious anaemia due to a lack of intrinsic factor produced by the stomach has also been associated with an increased risk for gastric cancer.

Symptoms of gastric cancer include poor appetite; unexplained weight loss; abdominal pain or discomfort; a sense of fullness in the upper abdomen after eating a small meal; heartburn or indigestion; nausea; vomiting, with or without blood; and anaemia (e.g. leading to tiredness and breathlessness). There is also some evidence that haemoglobin concentrations begin to decline at least 3 years before the diagnosis of gastric cancer.

### 7.3.3.2 SCREENING

Screening for gastric cancer has the potential to impact on mortality and morbidity. Stage IA cancer, where there is no spread beyond the stomach, has a 5-year survival of 71%, whereas Stage IB cancer, where there has also been spread to one or two lymph nodes near the stomach (N1) but not to any distant tissues or organs, is associated with a 5-year survival of 57%. Moreover, in Japan (where there is a well-established screening programme), the proportion of early stage gastric cancers is more than 50% of all cancers diagnosed (compared to only 15% in Europe).

In South Korea, where a screening programme commenced in 1999, over 67% of the screen-detected cancers were being picked up at an early stage by 2009.

Several techniques, including barium-meal photofluorography, gastric endoscopy and serum pepsinogen have been proposed as screening tools for the early detection of gastric cancer:

- *Barium-meal photofluorography* (*upper GI series*) screening has been ongoing since the 1960s in Japan and participation rates have been in the range of 10%–20%. Case-control studies show decreases in gastric cancer mortality in people who have undergone screening. Exposure to the low doses of radiation (about 0.6 mSv in photofluorography) carries a theoretical but poorly quantified risk of cancer development.
- *Endoscopy* appears to be more sensitive than photofluorography for the detection of gastric cancer. Time-trend analysis and case-control studies of gastric endoscopy suggest a twofold decrease in gastric cancer mortality in screened versus unscreened individuals. In Japan and South Korea, endoscopy has now become the primary method for gastric cancer screening given its superior test characteristics, availability and affordability. Rare complications of screening may include adverse effects of premedication and bleeding or perforation from the endoscopy.
- *Serum pepsinogen testing* is a non-invasive screening test that measures the levels of pepsinogen I and II from the gastric mucosa. Although some concerns have been raised about the test characteristics, it might have some value if combined with *H. pylori* serology testing. However, it is always important to appreciate that, following screening with anything other than endoscopy, a subsequent endoscopy (plus biopsy) will generally be required to establish a definitive diagnosis.

Although the evidence for gastric cancer screening is not as strong as for bowel cancer there is some justification for screening populations at higher risk, particularly those resident in (or recently emigrated from) Eastern Asia, Russia or South America or who have a family history of gastric cancer.

## 7.4 COELIAC DISEASE

### 7.4.1 Importance

Coeliac disease is a multisystem autoimmune disorder in genetically predisposed individuals that is triggered by dietary gluten. Ingestion of gluten by persons with coeliac disease causes immune-mediated inflammatory damage to the small intestine, which can result in GI and non-GI problems. Coeliac affects all age groups but the average age at diagnosis is now between 40 and 60.

The prevalence in Western countries is around 1% of the general population, but it is also increasing in other parts of the world such as Asia due to the adoption of a more Westernised diet. However, it remains rare in Japan due to continuing low wheat consumption and reduced genetic susceptibility.

There is evidence that coeliac disease is associated with excess mortality, intestinal adenocarcinoma and lymphoma. Some studies have highlighted improved quality of life with gluten-free dietary treatment in individuals found to have coeliac disease.

Coeliac disease–associated costs represent a significant burden, particularly for diseased males and those with a delayed diagnosis. Some individuals may have had symptoms for up to 10 years before being recognised. Diagnosis and treatment of coeliac disease reduce the costs of care suggesting an economic advantage to earlier detection and treatment.

## 7.4.2 Prevention

Coeliac disease cannot be prevented. However, a gluten-free diet reverses disease manifestations - including symptoms - in most patients by facilitating mucosal repair.

The time it takes for the small bowel to heal varies from person to person but, on average, the excess risk of complications (including death) appears to resolve after 3–5 years on a strictly gluten-free diet.

## 7.4.3 Earlier recognition

The U.S. Preventive Services Task Force has recently concluded that the current evidence is insufficient to assess the balance of benefits and harms of routine screening for coeliac disease in individuals without any symptoms.

However, case-finding should be considered in individuals with symptoms and in asymptomatic individuals at increased risk as it has been estimated that up to 75% of adults with coeliac disease remain unrecognised.

### 7.4.3.1 SYMPTOMS FOR CASE-FINDING

Although it is important to appreciate that the clinical presentation, the severity of symptoms and the natural history of coeliac disease varies and includes asymptomatic (or silent) coeliac disease, the following features should lead to consideration of testing (in adults at any age):

- Persistent unexplained abdominal or GI symptoms
- Prolonged fatigue
- Unexpected weight loss
- Severe or persistent mouth ulcers
- Unexplained neurological symptoms (particularly peripheral neuropathy or ataxia)

### 7.4.3.2 RISK ASSESSMENT FOR CASE-FINDING

An increased risk for coeliac disease is conferred by the following features:

- A family history (in a first- or second-degree relative)

- Persons with other autoimmune diseases (e.g. type 1 diabetes mellitus or autoimmune thyroid disease)
- Irritable bowel syndrome; almost a quarter of people with coeliac disease have previously been told they had irritable bowel syndrome or were being treated for it before they were diagnosed with coeliac disease
- Individuals with Down's syndrome or Turner's syndrome and those with immunoglobulin A (IgA) deficiency
- Unexplained anaemia and/or iron, vitamin $B_{12}$ or folate deficiency
- Unexplained subfertility or recurrent miscarriage
- Persistently raised liver enzymes of unknown cause
- Dental enamel defects
- Osteoporosis

Based on guidance from the National Institute for Health and Care Excellence (NICE) a suggested investigative sequence for coeliac is as follows:

- Test for total IgA and IgA tissue transglutaminase (tTG) as the first choice
- Use IgA endomysial antibodies (EMA) if IgA tTG is weakly positive
- Consider using IgG EMA, IgG deamidated gliadin peptide (DGP) or IgG tTG if IgA is deficient

Individuals with positive serological test results will then need to be referred to a GI specialist for consideration of an endoscopic intestinal biopsy to establish a definitive diagnosis. However, it is also important to appreciate that none of these tests are accurate if a gluten-containing diet is not being consumed.

Coeliac disease is also associated with specific human leukocyte antigen (HLA) types DQ2.5 and DQ8 in most populations. But HLA testing should only be used to rule out coeliac as these genotypes are not uncommon (i.e. people who lack one of the specific genotypes are very unlikely to have coeliac but the converse does not apply).

## FURTHER READING

### Overview

Herrinton LJ, Selby JV, Friedman GD et al. Case-control study of digital-rectal screening in relation to mortality from cancer of the distal rectum. *Am J Epidemiol* 1995;142:961–964.

Jankowski J. BOB CAT: A large-scale review and Delphi consensus for management of Barrett's esophagus with no dysplasia, indefinite for, or low-grade dysplasia. *Am J Gastroenterol* 2015;110:662–682.

Lavine E. Blood testing for sensitivity, allergy or intolerance to food. *CMAJ* 2012;184:666–668.

Muris JW, Starmans R, Wolfs GG et al. The diagnostic value of rectal examination. *Fam Pract* 1993;10:34–37.

## Colorectal cancer

Arnold M, Sierra MS, Laversanne M et al. Global patterns and trends in colorectal cancer incidence and mortality. *Gut* 2017;66:683–691.
Edgren G, Bagnardi V, Belloco R et al. Pattern of declining haemoglobin concentration before cancer diagnosis. *Int J Cancer* 2010;127:1429–1436.
Incisive Health. *Saving Lives, Averting Costs. An Analysis of the Financial Implications of Achieving Earlier Diagnosis of Colorectal, Lung and Ovarian Cancer.* London: Cancer Research UK, 2014.
Qaseem A, Denberg TD, Hopkins RH et al. Screening for colorectal cancer: A guidance statement from the American College of Physicians. *Ann Intern Med* 2012;156:378–386.
U.S. Preventive Services Task Force. Aspirin use for the primary prevention of cardiovascular disease and colorectal cancer: U.S. Preventive Services Task Force recommendation statement. *Ann Intern Med* 2016;164:836–845.
U.S. Preventive Services Task Force. Screening for colorectal cancer: U.S. Preventive Services Task Force recommendation statement. *JAMA* 2016;315:2564–2575.
Wilt TJ, Harris RP, Qaseem A. High value care task force of the American College of Physicians. Screening for cancer: Advice for high-value care from the American College of Physicians. *Ann Intern Med* 2015;162:718–725.

## Gastric cancer

Elwyn G, Taubert M, Davies S et al. Which test is best for *Helicobacter pylori*? A cost-effectiveness model using decision analysis. *Brit J Gen Pract* 2007;57:401–403.
Hirst C, Ryan J, Tunceli O et al. *Cost Profile of Patients with Gastric Cancer Using U.S. Administrative Claims Data.* Wilmington, DE: AstraZeneca, 2014.
Kim GH, Liang PS, Bang SJ, Hwang JH. Screening and surveillance for gastric cancer in the United States: Is it needed? *Gastrointest Endosc* 2016;84:18–28.
Kmietowicz Z. Oesophageal and gastric cancer need to be detected earlier to improve outcomes, audit finds. *BMJ* 2014;349:g7340.
Park JY, von Karsa L, Herrero R. Prevention strategies for gastric cancer: A global perspective. *Clin Endosc* 2014;47:478–489.

## Coeliac disease

Bai JC, Ciacci C, Corazza GR et al. *Celiac Disease.* Milwaukee, WI: World Gastrenterology Organisation, 2016. http://www.worldgastroenterology.org/guidelines/global-guidelines/celiac-disease
Long KH, Rubio-Tapia A, Wagie AE et al. The economics of coeliac disease: A population-based study. *Aliment Pharmacol Ther* 2010;32:261–269.

Ludvigsson JF, Bai JC, Biagi F et al. Diagnosis and management of adult coeliac disease: Guidelines from the British Society of Gastroenterology. *Gut* 2014;63:1210–1228.

Mooney PD, Hadjivassiliou M, Sanders DS. Coeliac disease. *BMJ* 2014;348:g1561.

National Institute for Health and Care Excellence (NICE). *Coeliac Disease: Recognition, Assessment and Management.* London: NICE, 2015.

U.S. Preventive Services Task Force. Screening for celiac disease. U.S. Preventive Services Task Force recommendation statement. *JAMA* 2017;317:1252–1257.

# 8

# Liver health

## KEY RECOMMENDATIONS

- For those designing a better value health check incorporating a focus on liver health it is suggested that the following conditions warrant particular consideration: hepatitis B, hepatitis C, hereditary haemochromatosis, liver fibrosis and hepatocellular carcinoma.
- It is important to be aware of Gilbert's syndrome as a cause of isolated raised bilirubin levels.
- Undertake hepatitis B immunisation and case-finding in specific risk groups.
- Consider hepatitis C prevention and case-finding in specific risk groups.
- Encourage testing for hereditary haemochromatosis in individuals with abnormal iron studies, liver disease or those with a family history.
- Have a high index of suspicion about alcohol misuse with a low threshold for enquiring about consumption.
- Support and facilitate weight loss and alcohol reduction using evidence-based interventions with a view to preventing liver fibrosis.
- Undertake case-finding for liver fibrosis using serum biomarkers or transient elastography.
- Consider case-finding for hepatocellular carcinoma in specific risk groups using $\alpha$-fetoprotein and hepatic ultrasound.

## 8.1 OVERVIEW

In terms of developing a better value health check incorporating a focus on liver health it is suggested that the key priorities are hepatitis B, hepatitis C, hereditary haemochromatosis, liver fibrosis and hepatocellular carcinoma.

Those undertaking health checks also need to be aware of Gilbert's syndrome, a genetic variant of bilirubin metabolism affecting around 5% of the population in the United States and the United Kingdom. It is associated with an elevated level of bilirubin but generally requires no treatment and has no serious consequences. Mild jaundice may appear under conditions of exertion, stress, fasting and infections, but the condition is otherwise usually asymptomatic.

Liver health links to lung health (see Chapter 5) in relation to α-1 antitrypsin deficiency. Preventing secondary liver cancer due to metastatic spread from, for example, breast cancer, colorectal cancer, stomach cancer, lung cancer or melanoma is also dependent on the earlier recognition of these conditions.

Excess alcohol intake and being overweight are significant factors leading to liver fibrosis. However, obesity is much easier to spot than alcohol misuse – for example, in a study amongst a group of Australian GPs, only 28% of heavy drinkers were identified. Considering excessive alcohol use is also of importance in patients with known liver diseases. For example, it can exacerbate hepatitis C infection and the underlying liver injury, thereby accelerating disease progression. It also has adverse effects on the response rates to anti-viral treatments.

In the context of a health check, there is a need to have a high index of suspicion about alcohol with a low threshold for enquiring about consumption. Alcohol misuse can be associated with a broad range of issues: diseases, symptoms, psychological disorders, accidents and injuries, together with social problems such as divorce.

For employers, alcohol misuse leads to absenteeism, tardiness, reduced productivity, high rates of turnover, injuries and violence. Employees who abuse alcohol are 3.5 times more likely to be involved in a workplace accident than co-workers, and approximately 40% of industrial fatalities and injuries can be linked to alcohol misuse. Drinking outside of work has been shown to decrease performance at work, with losses of approximately 33% on a variety of tasks.

It is generally agreed that drinking becomes hazardous at above 21 units weekly for men and 14 units weekly for women. However, quantifying the number of units can sometimes be tricky (see Table 8.1).

In determining whether an individual is actually abusing alcohol, additional information is required. To assist with this several questionnaires (e.g. CAGE, Alcohol Use Disorders Identification Test [AUDIT]) are available as well as some

Table 8.1 Alcohol units for alcoholic drinks

| Alcoholic drink | Measure | Units |
|---|---|---|
| Beers, lagers, ciders | 1 pint | 2 |
| | 1 can | 1.5 |
| Low-alcohol beers, lagers, ciders | 1 pint | 0.6 |
| | 1 can | 0.5 |
| Strong beers, lagers, ciders | 1 pint | 3 |
| | 1 can | 2 |
| Table wines | 1 glass | 1 |
| | 1 bottle (75 cl) | 8 |
| Sherry | 1 standard small measure | 1 |
| | 1 bottle | 13 |
| Spirits | 1 standard measure | 1.5 |
| | 1 bottle | 30 |
| 'Alcopops' | 1 bottle | 1.5 |

laboratory tests (e.g. mean cell volume [MCV] and gamma-glutamyl transferase [GGT]). The information collected by the CAGE questionnaire and AUDIT tools are detailed in the following sections.

### CAGE QUESTIONNAIRE

Alcohol dependence is stated to be likely if the patient gives two or more positive answers to the following questions:

- Have you ever felt you should **C**ut down your drinking?
- Have people **A**nnoyed you by criticising your drinking?
- Have you ever felt bad or **G**uilty about your drinking?
- Have you ever had a drink first thing in the morning to steady your nerves or get rid of a hangover (**E**ye-opener)?

### AUDIT QUESTIONNAIRE

Alcohol dependence is assessed by grading the following questions out of a total of 40. A cumulative score of greater than eight suggests hazardous drinking:

- How often do you have a drink containing alcohol?
- How many units of alcohol do you drink on a typical day when you are drinking?
- How often have you had six or more units if female, or eight or more if male, on a single occasion in the last year?
- How often during the last year have you found that you were not able to stop drinking once you had started?
- How often during the last year have you failed to do what was normally expected from you because of drinking?
- How often during the last year have you needed an alcoholic drink in the morning to get yourself going after a heavy drinking session?
- How often during the last year have you had a feeling of guilt or remorse after drinking?
- How often during the last year have you been unable to remember what happened the night before because you had been drinking?
- Have you or someone else been injured as a result of your drinking?
- Has a relative or friend or a doctor or another health worker been concerned about your drinking or suggested you cut down?

In research conducted within a European population similar to that likely to attend for a health check, discriminant characteristics were reported for the two questionnaires and the blood tests. The results indicate the general superiority of the questionnaires over the traditional blood tests (Table 8.2).

Table 8.2 Testing for alcohol abuse or dependence

| 'Test' | Sensitivity (%) | Specificity (%) | Positive predictive value (%) | Positive likelihood ratio |
|---|---|---|---|---|
| CAGE (men) | 48 | 92 | 49 | 6.2 |
| CAGE (women) | 37 | 97 | 35 | 11.6 |
| AUDIT (men) | 61 | 90 | 50 | 6.3 |
| AUDIT (women) | 50 | 99 | 64 | 37.5 |
| MCV (men) | 39 | 75 | 20 | 1.6 |
| MCV (women) | 41 | 79 | 8.6 | 2.0 |
| GGT (men) | 7 | 96 | 19 | 1.4 |
| GGT (women) | 7 | 92 | 4 | 0.8 |

However, some alternative biomarkers such as carbohydrate-deficient transferrin (CDT) might be worth considering. Within specialist settings, this test seems to have significantly better properties in identifying excessive drinkers than either GGT or MCV.

Once alcohol misuse has been identified, brief psychological intervention can be very effective in helping an individual to alter their drinking behaviour. They can take the form of personalised feedback following a health check, incorporating practical steps as to how to modify drinking habits and avoid the adverse consequences of alcohol misuse. For more problematic drinkers, formal counselling techniques might be required including cognitive behavioural therapy (CBT), motivational enhancement therapy and motivational interviewing.

## 8.2 HEPATITIS B

### 8.2.1 Importance

Around 2 billion of the world's population have been infected with hepatitis B. Of these, approximately 360 million become chronically infected (75% in Asia) and are at increased risk of developing cirrhosis and hepatocellular carcinoma. In the United States and the United Kingdom, it has been calculated that around 0.3% of the population is chronically infected, although rates may vary between individual communities.

Hepatitis B also represents a significant economic burden to individuals, families and society. For example, in a study undertaken in Iran and published in 2012, the total annual cost per patient for chronic hepatitis B, cirrhosis, and hepatocellular carcinoma was $3094, $17,483, and $32,958, respectively.

### 8.2.2 Prevention

Hepatitis B is highly preventable by immunisation. The choice of schedule depends on the local epidemiological situation and can be broadly divided into those that include a birth-dose and those that do not. In adults living in countries with a lower prevalence of hepatitis B such as the United Kingdom certain high-risk groups also warrant consideration for immunisation such as

- Injecting drug users (in addition to their sexual partners)
- Individuals who change sexual partners frequently
- Close family contacts of an individual with chronic hepatitis infection
- Families adopting children from countries with a high or intermediate prevalence of hepatitis B
- Foster carers
- Individuals receiving regular blood or blood products and their carers
- Patients with chronic renal failure
- Patients with chronic liver disease
- Inmates of custodial institutions
- Individuals and staff in residential accommodation for those with learning difficulties
- People travelling to or resident in areas of high or intermediate prevalence
- Individuals at occupational risk such as healthcare workers and laboratory staff

Specific hepatitis B immunoglobulin provides passive immunity and can give immediate but temporary protection after accidental inoculation or contamination with hepatitis B–infected blood.

### 8.2.3 Earlier recognition

One of the particular challenges of hepatitis B is that the primary infection can present in a variety of ways with some individuals having no symptoms or just a flu-like illness. The spectrum of disease and the subsequent natural history of hepatitis B infection are also diverse.

Many individuals clear the initial infection and develop lifelong immunity. Moreover, for some people with chronic hepatitis B the condition is inactive and does not lead to liver problems. However, in others it may cause progressive liver fibrosis (see Section 8.5), leading to cirrhosis with end-stage liver disease and a markedly increased risk of hepatocellular carcinoma.

In relation to hepatitis B, case-finding has two purposes:

1. To identify individuals who are not immune but are at risk and should be offered hepatitis B immunisation (see Section 8.2.2)
2. To identify individuals with chronic hepatitis B infection who might benefit from antiviral treatment

The general test used is hepatitis B surface antigen (HBsAg) and a positive result indicates acute or chronic infection.

Testing for hepatitis B surface antibody (anti-HBs) and hepatitis B core antigen (anti-HBc) is also sometimes done as part of a case-finding panel to help distinguish between infection and immunity.

Table 8.3 Tests for hepatitis B virus

| Test | Explanation | Purpose |
|---|---|---|
| Hepatitis B surface antigen (HBsAg) | Protein present on the surface of the virus, present in both acute and chronic infections | Used to screen for and detect infection – it is the earliest indicator of acute infection and may be present before symptoms appear. Also present in individuals with chronic infection. |
| Hepatitis B surface antibody (anti-HBs) | Antibody produced in response to HBsAg: levels rise during recovery phase of infection | Indicates previous exposure to the HBV but virus no longer present and cannot be passed on. It also protects against future infection. Antibodies can also be acquired from immunisation. |
| Hepatitis B core antibody (Anti-HBc) | Both IgM and IgG antibodies to hepatitis B core antigen | Can be used to help detect acute and chronic HBV infections; it is produced in response to the core antigen and usually persists for life. This antibody does not provide any protection against hepatitis B virus (unlike anti-HBs). |

Acute hepatitis B virus infection (acquired within 6 months after infection) is characterised by the appearance of HBsAg and followed by the development of anti-HBc. The disappearance of HBsAg and the presence of anti-HBs and anti-HBc indicate the resolution of hepatitis B virus infection and natural immunity. The persistence of HBsAg suggests a chronic infection. Anti-HBc, which persists for life, is present only after hepatitis B infection and does not develop in persons whose immunity to hepatitis B virus is due to vaccination. Persons who have received hepatitis B immunisation only have anti-HBs (Table 8.3).

The U.S. Preventive Services Task Force (USPSTF) suggests case-finding for hepatitis B as presented in Table 8.4.

## 8.3 HEPATITIS C

### 8.3.1 Importance

Hepatitis C affects around 143 million people (2%) worldwide, most of whom are chronically infected. Numbers have increased substantially in the last century due to a combination of intravenous drug abuse in addition to reused and poorly sterilised medical equipment.

Rates are high (>3.5% population infected) in central Asia, North Africa and the Middle East; they are intermediate (1.5%–3.5%) in South East Asia, Latin America, Australasia and Europe; and they are low (<1.5%) in North America.

Table 8.4 USPSTF hepatitis B case-finding recommendations

| Risk group | Recommended test(s) |
|---|---|
| Persons born in countries and regions with a high prevalence of hepatitis B virus infection (>2%) | HBsAg |
| Persons not vaccinated as infants whose parents were born in regions with a very high prevalence of hepatitis B virus (>8%) such as sub-Saharan Africa and South Eastern and Central Asia | HBsAg |
| Injecting drug users | HBsAg, anti-HBc, anti-HBs |
| Men who have sex with men | HBsAg, anti-HBc, anti-HBs |
| Household, needle-sharing, or sex contacts of persons with hepatitis B virus infection | HBsAg, anti-HBc, anti-HBs |
| HIV-positive persons | HBsAg, anti-HBc, anti-HBs |

The hepatitis C virus causes both acute and chronic infection. Acute hepatitis C infection is usually asymptomatic, and is only rarely associated with life-threatening disease. About 15%–45% of infected persons spontaneously clear the virus within 6 months of infection without any treatment. The remaining 55%–85% of people will develop a chronic infection.

Hepatitis C–infected individuals serve as a reservoir for transmission to others and are at risk for developing chronic liver disease, cirrhosis and hepatocellular carcinoma. It has been estimated that hepatitis C virus accounts for 27% of cirrhosis and 25% of hepatocellular carcinoma cases across the globe. As for hepatitis B, hepatitis C also imposes a very high-economic burden.

Once recognised, antiviral treatment prevents long-term complications of hepatitis C virus infection.

## 8.3.2 Prevention

Hepatitis C virus is most commonly transmitted by injecting drug use through the sharing of injection equipment; the reuse or inadequate sterilisation of medical equipment, especially syringes and needles in healthcare settings; and the transfusion of unscreened blood and blood products.

The virus can be transmitted sexually and may also be passed from an infected mother to her baby; however, these modes of transmission are much less common.

Currently, there is no vaccine for hepatitis C, therefore prevention of hepatitis C virus infection depends upon reducing the risk of exposure to the virus in healthcare settings and in higher-risk populations. The following list provides some examples of primary prevention interventions recommended by the World Health Organization:

- Hand hygiene: including surgical hand preparation, hand washing and use of gloves
- Safe and appropriate use of healthcare injections

- Safe handling and disposal of sharps and waste
- Provision of comprehensive harm-reduction services to people who inject drugs including sterile injecting equipment
- Testing of donated blood for hepatitis B and C (as well as HIV and syphilis)
- Training of healthcare personnel
- Promotion of correct and consistent use of condoms

### 8.3.3 Earlier recognition

Hepatitis C case-finding is particularly cost-effective for those individuals at high risk of infection:

- Those with a history of past or current injection drug use.
- People who use intranasal drugs.
- Recipients of infected blood products or invasive procedures in healthcare facilities with inadequate infection control practices. For example, in the United States it is recommended that adults be screened once if born between 1945 and 1965; if they received a blood transfusion before 1992; and if they are on long-term haemodialysis.
- Children born to mothers infected with hepatitis C virus.
- People with sexual partners who are infected with hepatitis C.
- People with HIV infection.
- Prisoners or previously incarcerated persons.
- People who have had tattoos or piercings.

Hepatitis C virus infection is diagnosed in two steps:

1. Screening for anti-hepatitis C virus antibodies (anti-HCV) with a serological test identifies people who have been infected with the virus.
2. If the test is positive for anti-HCV, a nucleic acid test for hepatitis C virus ribonucleic acid is then required to confirm chronic infection because about 15%–45% of people infected with hepatitis C virus spontaneously clear the infection by a strong immune response without the need for treatment. Although no longer infected, they will still test positive for anti-HCV.

## 8.4 HEREDITARY HAEMOCHROMATOSIS

### 8.4.1 Importance

Hereditary haemochromatosis is a relatively common genetic disorder with an estimated prevalence of 1 in 200 among individuals of European ancestry (the prevalence is lower in other ethnic groups). The gene responsible for hereditary haemochromatosis (known as *HFE* gene) is located on chromosome 6 and the known mutations of the *HFE* gene are C282Y and H63D.

Hereditary haemochromatosis is characterised by an accelerated rate of intestinal iron absorption and progressive iron deposition in various tissues including the liver, the pancreas, the joints, the skin and the heart. This typically begins to be expressed in the third to fifth decades of life.

### 8.4.2 Prevention

Hereditary haemochromatosis cannot be prevented. However, not everyone who inherits a haemochromatosis gene mutation develops the disease. The clinical penetrance of the mutation is probably much lower than the genetic prevalence.

### 8.4.3 Earlier recognition

Liver fibrosis, cirrhosis and hepatocellular carcinoma are the most serious complications of iron overload. Early diagnosis and treatment are important as the treatment is simple, involving regular therapeutic phlebotomy.

Unfortunately, haemochromatosis is underdiagnosed because it is often considered a rare disorder. It might only be recognised at a late stage in individuals presenting with cirrhosis, diabetes and skin pigmentation (so-called bronze diabetes).

A summary of the changes in iron test results seen in various diseases or disorders of iron status are shown in Table 8.5.

Transferrin is a glyco-protein that binds iron and acts as a carrier for iron in the bloodstream. Usually, about one-third of the transferrin measured is being used to transport iron, and this is called transferrin saturation. In iron deficiency, serum iron is low and fewer transferrin binding sites are used. This results in a low transferrin saturation, but an increased total iron-binding capacity. In conditions of iron overload, such as haemochromatosis, the serum iron and the transferrin saturation will be high and the total iron-binding capacity low or normal.

In 2011, based on a comprehensive review of the research evidence, the American Association for the Study of Liver Diseases made the following recommendations:

- All individuals with abnormal iron studies should be evaluated as patients with haemochromatosis, even in the absence of symptoms.
- All people with evidence of liver disease should be evaluated for haemochromatosis.
- For testing, a combination of transferrin saturation and ferritin should be obtained rather than relying on a single test. If either is abnormal then HFE mutation analysis should be performed.
- Screening should be undertaken (iron studies and HFE mutation analysis) of first-degree relatives of patients with HFE-related hereditary haemochromatosis (HFE-HC).

Table 8.5 Iron test results in various diseases/disorders of iron status

| Disease | Serum iron | Total iron-binding capacity (TIBC; transferrin) | Unsaturated iron-binding capacity | Transferrin saturation % | Ferritin |
|---|---|---|---|---|---|
| Iron deficiency | Low | High | High | Low | Low |
| Haemochromatosis | High | Low | Low | High | High |
| Chronic illness | Low | Low | Low/normal | Low | Normal/high |
| Iron poisoning | High | Normal | Low | High | Normal |

Siblings of individuals with HFE-HC have a 25% chance of being susceptible. However, general population genetic screening for HFE-HC is not recommended, as disease penetrance is low and only a few C282Y homozygotes will progress to iron overload.

## 8.5 LIVER FIBROSIS

### 8.5.1 Importance

Liver fibrosis is the scarring process that represents the liver's response to injury. It involves the excessive accumulation of extracellular matrix proteins, including collagen, within the liver disrupting liver structure and function. Advanced liver fibrosis results in cirrhosis, liver failure, hepatocellular carcinoma and portal hypertension.

All chronic liver diseases can lead to fibrosis. Worldwide, the following conditions are particularly important in the development and progression of liver fibrosis:

- Chronic viral hepatitis B
- Chronic viral hepatitis C
- Alcohol, which can lead to alcoholic liver disease
- Obesity, which can result in non-alcoholic fatty liver disease (NAFLD) that may progress to a more severe condition known as non-alcoholic steatohepatitis (NASH)

Around 6%–7% of the adult population have liver fibrosis, mostly associated with NAFLD. With the growing epidemic of obesity in many countries it is projected that the prevalence and impact of NAFLD will continue to increase, making NASH potentially the most common cause of advanced liver disease in future decades.

Other rarer risks for fibrosis include the following:

- Autoimmune hepatitis (more likely in individuals with other autoimmune disorders such as thyroid problems or pernicious anaemia)
- Alpha-1 antitrypsin deficiency (see Chapter 5)
- Wilson's disease (copper storage disorder)
- Hereditary haemochromatosis (see Section 8.4)
- Certain medications such as methotrexate
- Diseases affecting blood flow in the liver

### 8.5.2 Prevention

Preventing liver fibrosis hinges on forestalling, identifying and, if possible, addressing the underlying causes. Moreover, it seems that interventions to prevent the progression of liver fibrosis onto cirrhosis are more effective in the earlier stages of chronic liver diseases.

Suggested interventions include the following:

- Reducing alcohol consumption
- Losing weight
- Preventing or treating infections such as hepatitis B or C with antiviral therapies
- Therapeutic phlebotomy for haemochromatosis
- Medications such as steroids for autoimmune hepatitis

It can take years for fibrosis due to excessive alcohol consumption or being overweight to develop. So there is a great opportunity to make lifestyle changes to prevent the problem from getting worse. There is also good evidence from studies of patients undergoing bariatric surgery of the positive effects of weight loss on NASH and liver fibrosis.

## 8.5.3 Earlier recognition

Liver fibrosis itself does not cause symptoms. Symptoms may result from the disorder causing the fibrosis or, once fibrosis progresses to cirrhosis, from the complications of portal hypertension. These symptoms include variceal bleeding, ascites and encephalopathy. Cirrhosis can also result in hepatic insufficiency and potentially fatal liver failure.

To date, many health checks have simply incorporated the measurement of liver biochemistry with the reporting back of the results to an individual's usual doctor – this is insufficient. Faced with an abnormal result, there are further requirements to consider the possible causes for the finding followed by more precise assessment (by blood testing or imaging) of the extent of any fibrosis (Table 8.6).

It is also important to appreciate that liver function tests can be normal despite significant underlying liver fibrosis or even cirrhosis. Therefore, hepatic fibrosis should be suspected if individuals have known chronic liver disease (e.g. chronic viral hepatitis C and hepatitis B, alcoholic liver disease, α-1 antitrypsin deficiency or hereditary haemochromatosis) irrespective of the results of liver function tests.

Case-finding for liver fibrosis is also suggested for people with normal liver biochemistry who are overweight, have type 2 diabetes mellitus or consume excessive amounts of alcohol.

The gold standard to check for liver fibrosis remains biopsy but, in order to rapidly assess the likelihood of liver fibrosis in the context of a health check, various non-invasive methods have been developed: a 'biological' approach based on the quantification of biomarkers in serum samples or a 'physical' approach that measures liver stiffness.

Some example biomarker approaches are detailed in Table 8.7. The practical advantages of analysing serum biomarkers to assess fibrosis include their good inter-laboratory reproducibility, and their potential widespread availability and applicability. However, none are liver specific and the results may be influenced by changes in clearance and excretion of individual parameters. Increased levels

Table 8.6 Some causes of abnormal liver biochemistry results

| Possible cause of abnormal liver biochemistry results | Possible clinical clues | Further tests to consider |
|---|---|---|
| Alcohol related | Excessive alcohol consumption (e.g. AUDIT or CAGE questionnaires) | GGT<br>MCV<br>CDT |
| Hereditary haemochromatosis | Family history | Serum iron and ferritin levels, total iron-binding capacity |
| Hepatitis B | Immigration from endemic countries, non-monogamous sexual activity, injection drug use | Hepatitis B surface antigen testing |
| Hepatitis C | Injection drug use, HIV infection, blood transfusion before 1992 | Hepatitis C virus antibody testing |
| Medications | Prescribed, over the counter and herbal | Clinical history |
| Non-alcoholic fatty liver disease | Body mass index and body composition | Waist circumference |
| Alpha-1 antitrypsin deficiency | Early onset chronic obstructive pulmonary disease, family history | Serum alpha-1 antitrypsin level |
| Autoimmune hepatitis | Other autoimmune diseases such as thyroid disorders or pernicious anaemia | Antinuclear antibody and smooth muscle antibody testing |
| Wilson's disease | Younger than 40 years | Serum ceruloplasmin level |

of hyaluronate occur in the post-prandial state and, therefore, the marker should always be measured in fasting patients if possible.

Caution is needed in patients with HIV-hepatitis C virus co-infection because of the risk of false-positive results related to HIV-induced thrombocytopenia, antiretroviral treatment-induced hyperbilirubinemia or increased serum GGT levels.

In terms of costs, APRI and FIB-4 are the lowest-priced tests.

Transient elastography (FibroScan) assesses the velocity of a low-frequency (50 Hz) elastic shear wave propagating through the liver. Acoustic vibrations are applied to the abdomen with a probe and how rapidly these are transmitted

Table 8.7 Some biomarker scores for liver fibrosis

| Biomarker score | Components | Sensitivity | Specificity |
|---|---|---|---|
| APRI | AST/platelet count | 41%–91% (in individuals with chronic hepatitis C) | 47%–95% (in individuals with chronic hepatitis C) |
| FIB-4 | AST, ALT, age, platelet count | 65% (in individuals with chronic hepatitis B) | 77% (in individuals with chronic hepatitis B) |
| | | 38%–74% (in individuals with chronic hepatitis C) | 81%–98% (in individuals with chronic hepatitis C) |
| | | 70% (in individuals with chronic hep C + HIV) | 97% (in individuals with chronic hep C + HIV) |
| FibroTest | α2-macroglobulin, haptoglobin, apolipoprotein A1, GGT, bilirubin, age, gender | 75% (in individuals with chronic hepatitis C) | 85% (in individuals with chronic hepatitis C) |
| NFS score | Age, impaired fasting glucose/diabetes, body mass index, platelet count | 43%–77% (in individuals with NAFLD) | 97% (in individuals with NAFLD) |
| ELF score | Age, hyaluronic acid, tissue inhibitor of metalloproteinase 1 (TIMP-1), N-terminal peptide of type 1 collagen | 87% (in a mixed group) | 51% (in a mixed group) |

through liver tissue is measured. This is an indication of how stiff (i.e. fibrosed) the liver is. For stage 2 liver fibrosis the sensitivity has been reported as 86.4% and the specificity 85.3%. Advantages of transient elastography include a short procedure time (<5 min), immediate results and the ability to perform the test at the bedside or in an outpatient clinic. Finally, it is not a difficult procedure to learn and can be performed by a nurse or a technician after minimal training (about 100 examinations).

## 8.6 HEPATOCELLULAR CARCINOMA

### 8.6.1 Importance

Hepatocellular carcinoma, the most common type of primary liver cancer, is, currently, largely a problem of the developing world where 83% (50% in China alone) of the estimated 782,000 new cases occurred in 2012. It is the second most common cause of death from cancer globally.

In men, the regions of high incidence are Eastern and South Eastern Asia. Intermediate rates occur in Southern Europe and Northern America and the lowest rates are in Northern Europe and South-Central Asia. In women, the rates are generally much lower, the highest being in Eastern Asia and Western Africa, the lowest in Northern Europe and Micronesia.

However, the incidence of hepatocellular carcinoma has been rapidly rising in the United States and United Kingdom over the last 20 years. Possible reasons for this include increasing obesity, alcohol misuse and hepatitis C infections.

### 8.6.2 Prevention

As highlighted in relation to liver fibrosis, the prevention of hepatocellular carcinoma depends on forestalling any liver damage in addition to identifying and treating any reversible liver damage early.

### 8.6.3 Earlier recognition

The symptoms of hepatocellular carcinoma are often vague and generally do not appear until the cancer is at an advanced stage. They can include unexplained weight loss, tiredness, loss of appetite, early satiety, nausea and vomiting, abdominal pain and swelling and jaundice.

Screening for hepatocellular carcinoma can identify tumours that are amenable to hepatic resection or liver transplantation. A community-based trial from China examined screening using α-fetoprotein (AFP) plus ultrasound every 6 months. Despite only 60% compliance with the study protocol, fewer deaths from hepatocellular carcinoma were observed in those who underwent screening.

The 2010 Asian Pacific Association for the Study of the Liver guideline recommends screening high-risk patients with AFP and hepatic ultrasound every 6 months. Similarly, the American Association for the Study of Liver Diseases recommends surveillance with non-contrast-enhanced hepatic ultrasound when the hepatocellular carcinoma risk is raised.

The following high-risk groups ought to be considered for case-finding for hepatocellular carcinoma:

- Individuals with established cirrhosis due to hepatitis B, particularly those with ongoing viral replication
- Individuals with established cirrhosis due to hepatitis C
- Individuals with established cirrhosis due to hereditary haemochromatosis
- Males with alcohol-related cirrhosis who are abstinent from alcohol or likely to comply with treatment
- Males with cirrhosis due to primary biliary cirrhosis

The testing should involve 6-monthly hepatic ultrasound assessments in combination with serum AFP estimation.

## FURTHER READING

### Overview

Aertgeerts B, Buntinx F, Ansoms S, Fevery J. Screening properties of questionnaires and laboratory tests for the detection of alcohol abuse or dependence in a general population. *Brit J Gen Pract* 2001;51:206–217.

Gough G, Heathers L, Puckett D et al. The utility of commonly used laboratory tests to screen for excessive alcohol use in clinical practice. *Alcohol Clin Exp Res* 2015;39:1493–1500.

Malet L, Llorca PM, Boussiron D et al. General practitioners and alcohol use disorders. *Alcoholism* 2003;27:61–66.

### Hepatitis B

Kavosi Z, Zare F, Jafari A, Fattahi MR. Economic burden of hepatitis B virus infection in different stages of disease; A report from southern Iran. *Middle East J Dig Dis* 2014;6:156–161.

U.S. Preventive Services Task Force. Screening for Hepatitis B Virus Infection in Nonpregnant Adolescents and Adults: U.S. Preventive Services Task Force recommendation statement. *Ann Intern Med* 2014;161:58–66.

World Health Organization (WHO). *Guidelines for the Prevention, Care and Treatment of Persons with Chronic Hepatitis B Infection*. Geneva: WHO, 2015.

### Hepatitis C

Coward S, Leggett L, Kaplan GG, Clement F. Cost-effectiveness of screening for hepatitis C virus: A systematic review of economic evaluations. *BMJ Open* 2016;6:e011821. doi:10.1136/bmjopen

El Khoury AC, Klimack WK, Wallace C, Razavi H. Economic burden of hepatitis C-associated diseases in the United States. *J Viral Hepat* 2012;19:153–160.
U.S. Preventive Services Task Force. Screening for hepatitis C virus infection in adults: U.S. Preventive Services Task Force recommendation statement. *Ann Intern Med* 2013;159:349–357.
World Health Organization (WHO). Hepatitis C. Fact Sheet 2017. http://www.who.int/mediacentre/factsheets/fs164/en/

## Hereditary haemochromatosis

Bacon BR, Adams PC, Kowdley KV. Diagnosis and Management of Hemochromatosis: 2011 Practice Guideline by the American Association for the Study of Liver Diseases. *Hepatology* 2011;54:328–343.

## Liver fibrosis

Bataller R, Brenner DA. Liver fibrosis. *J Clin Invest* 2005;115:209–218.
European Association for the Study of the Liver. EASL-ALEH Clinical Practice Guidelines: Non-invasive tests for evaluation of liver disease severity and prognosis. *J Hepatol* 2015;63:237–264.
National Institute for Health and Care Excellence (NICE). *Non-alcoholic fatty liver disease (NAFLD): Assessment and management*. London: NICE, 2016.
Oh RC, Hustead TR. Causes and evaluation of mildly elevated liver transaminase levels. *Am Fam Physician* 2011;84:1003–1008.
Vernon G, Baranova A, Younossi ZM. Systematic review: The epidemiology and natural history of non-alcoholic fatty liver disease and non-alcoholic steatohepatitis in adults. *Aliment Pharmacol Ther* 2011;34:274–285.

## Hepatocellular carcinoma

Ryder SD. Guidelines for the diagnosis and treatment of hepatocellular carcinoma (HCC) in adults. *Gut* 2003;52(Suppl III):iii1–iii8.
Zhang BH, Yang BH, Tang ZY. Randomized controlled trial of screening for hepatocellular carcinoma. *J Cancer Res Clin Oncol* 2004;130:417–422.

# 9

# Endocrine and metabolic health

## KEY RECOMMENDATIONS

- For those designing a better value health check incorporating a focus on endocrine and metabolic health it is suggested that the following conditions warrant particular consideration: type 2 diabetes and thyroid dysfunction.
- Encourage weight loss and improvements in physical activity to reduce the risk of developing type 2 diabetes.
- To identify those at risk of developing diabetes, risk scoring should be used in conjunction with glucose and HbA1c testing.
- Case-finding for thyroid dysfunction is recommended for those at elevated risk.

## 9.1 OVERVIEW

In terms of developing a better value health check incorporating a focus on endocrine and metabolic health it is suggested that the following conditions warrant particular consideration: type 2 diabetes and thyroid dysfunction.

There are some other areas that have been considered for inclusion within this chapter but, at present, I felt that the evidence of benefit in terms of delivering value was insufficient. Key amongst these are screening for thyroid cancer and parathyroid disorders. In relation to the latter, it is important to appreciate that 90% of cases of hypercalcaemia are due to primary hyperparathyroidism, cancer or, occasionally, vitamin D intoxication (see Chapter 6). The rational investigation of a raised calcium result discovered at a health check is a better value approach than unrestricted parathyroid hormone screening.

While I would advocate the assessment of bone biochemistry (calcium, phosphate and alkaline phosphatase) as an integral component of the core testing package, the diagnosis of hypercalcaemia is only made when the corrected serum calcium concentration is two standard deviations above the mean. Moreover, to confirm this, a minimum of two samples are required at least 1 week apart over a period of 3 months.

Metabolic syndrome refers to a combination of risk factors (i.e. being overweight, increased waist circumference, having raised blood glucose and triglyceride levels, a low HDL cholesterol, microalbuminuria and hypertension) that, taken together, significantly increase an individual's risk for atherosclerotic cardiovascular disease (see Chapter 4) and type 2 diabetes. However, it remains unclear whether labelling an individual with metabolic syndrome in the context of a health check provides any added value in terms of improving outcomes beyond that to be gained from the appropriate management of the risk factors identified.

Amongst individuals with metabolic syndrome who also have diabetes, the importance and treatment of the diabetes may, on occasions, take a backseat relative to the syndrome. Also, for people who fail to meet the necessary number of criteria to diagnose the syndrome (e.g. only two of the factors are present), the absence of the syndrome may divert attention away from addressing the risk factors that are present.

## 9.2 TYPE 2 DIABETES

### 9.2.1 Importance

Worldwide, an estimated 422 million adults were living with diabetes in 2014, compared to 108 million in 1980. The global prevalence of diabetes has nearly doubled since 1980, rising from 4.7% to 8.5% of the adult population. Over the past decade, diabetes prevalence has also risen faster in low- and middle-income countries than in high-income countries.

In 2010, across England, 7.4% of the population had been diagnosed with diabetes, and this number is expected to rise to 10% by 2030. In addition, one in seven adults may have impaired glucose regulation rather than overt diabetes (defined as HbA1c of 42–47 mmol/mol and/or a fasted plasma glucose between 5.5 and 6.9 mmol/L). The growing burden of type 2 diabetes (and impaired glucose regulation) has been linked to obesity, sedentary lifestyles, dietary trends and aging populations.

The health consequences of diabetes are wide ranging. It is the most common cause of visual impairment and blindness among people of working age and is associated with kidney failure and non-traumatic lower limb amputations. Individuals with diabetes or impaired glucose regulation are also at a significant increased risk for atherosclerotic cardiovascular disease (see Chapter 4). In older people, diabetes has been linked to increased rates of specific cancers in addition to physical and cognitive disability.

Globally, diabetes caused 1.5 million deaths, and impaired glucose regulation caused 2.2 million deaths in 2012. Forty-three percent of these 3.7 million deaths occurred before the age of 70 years particularly in low- and middle-income countries.

Diabetes and its complications result in substantial costs falling on individuals and their families, in addition to healthcare systems and the broader economy. One study estimates that losses in gross domestic product worldwide from

2011 to 2030, including both the direct and indirect costs of diabetes, will total $1.7 trillion, comprising $900 billion for high-income countries and $800 billion for low- and middle-income countries. In the United Kingdom, the total cost of managing type 2 diabetes and its complications is £22 billion per year and this is projected to increase to £35 billion by 2035.

### 9.2.2 Prevention

Excessive weight together with physical inactivity are estimated to cause a large proportion of the global diabetes burden.

Structured lifestyle interventions targeted at increasing physical activity, weight loss and dietary adjustments (i.e. improving fibre intake, lowering total and saturated fat intake plus cutting down refined sugar) including decreasing portion sizes have reduced the incidence of type 2 diabetes by 50% amongst high-risk people. For individuals who are obese, a 7% loss of weight can lead to a 58% reduction in the risk of developing diabetes.

The National Institute for Health and Care Excellence (NICE) guidance suggests that if an individual continues to progress towards diabetes despite participation in an intensive lifestyle programme then treatment with metformin should be offered. NICE also recommends considering orlistat therapy for the prevention of diabetes in people with a body mass index (BMI) of 28 or above who are unable to lose weight through lifestyle change alone.

### 9.2.3 Earlier recognition

Earlier recognition is very important for diabetes and impaired glucose regulation as both are associated with increased morbidity and mortality.

The longer a person lives with undiagnosed and untreated diabetes, the worse their health outcomes are likely to be. In the UK Prospective Diabetes Study, 50% of participants had established diabetes-related end-organ tissue damage at the time of diagnosis: 21% had retinopathy, 23% had evidence of vascular disease and 7% had peripheral neuropathy.

#### 9.2.3.1 RISK ASSESSMENT

Universal screening for type 2 diabetes is not currently recommended but case-finding should be considered for those at heightened risk of developing type 2 diabetes, especially if over the age of 40 years, and based on the following features:

- Overweight (i.e. BMI of 25 or more for most individuals, but 23 or more if from an Asian, African or Chinese background); Central obesity (waist circumference in white Caucasians <102 cm in men and <88 cm in women, and in Asians <90 cm in men and <80 cm in women) is a particular concern.
- Physical inactivity (i.e. less than 30 minutes of physical activity at work or during leisure time each day)
- Current smoker

- First-degree relative with diabetes
- High-risk race/ethnicity (i.e. South Asian, Chinese, African-Caribbean and black African)
- Women who have delivered a baby weighing more than 4 kg or have been diagnosed with gestational diabetes mellitus
- Hypertension (i.e. blood pressure greater than 140/90 or on therapy for hypertension)
- Low HDL levels (less than 0.90 mmol/L)
- Raised triglyceride levels (more than 2.82 mmol/L)
- Women with a history of polycystic ovary syndrome
- HbA1c of 42–47 mmol/mol or fasted plasma glucose between 5.5 and 6.9 mmol/L on previous testing
- Other clinical conditions associated with insulin resistance (e.g. severe obesity and acanthosis nigricans – darkened, thickened patches of skin in the armpit and around the groin and neck)
- History of atherosclerotic cardiovascular disease (see Chapter 4)
- Individuals with mental health problems or physical or learning disabilities
- Individuals taking certain medications such as steroids, anti-retrovirals and some antipsychotic drugs

The following symptoms (especially if present for over 2 months) also point towards the possibility of diabetes mellitus: tiredness, polydipsia, polyuria, recurrent skin infections or rashes, weight loss, blurred vision, slow healing, sensory changes and oral thrush.

A large number of risk scoring tools have also been developed that integrate variables such as age, sex, family history of diabetes, as well as clinical measures of BMI and waist circumference in order to assess the risk of progressing to diabetes. For example,

*FINDRISC* uses age, BMI, waist circumference, family history, history of anti-hypertensive drug treatment or raised blood glucose, physical activity level, and daily consumption of fruits and berries or vegetables to estimate the risk of developing type 2 diabetes over the next 10 years. A score of 9 or more has a sensitivity of 81% and a specificity of 76%.

*AUSDRISK* is a 10-item questionnaire that estimates the risk of progression to type 2 diabetes over 5 years. The score includes questions based on age, sex, ethnicity, family history of diabetes, history of abnormal glucose metabolism, smoking status, current hypertensive treatment, physical activity, fruit and vegetable consumption, and waist circumference. Using a score $\geq$12 the sensitivity is 74% and the specificity 67.7%.

*The Leicester Diabetes Risk Score* has been recommended by NICE for use in the United Kingdom. It consists of seven questions covering age, gender, ethnic background, family history, waist circumference, BMI and hypertension. In a multiethnic population it has been reported as having a sensitivity of 72.1% and a specificity of 54.1% at a cutoff point of 16.

However, it is clear that there are a number of problems with these various risk assessment tools:

- They raise the threshold for blood testing. I would suggest that there is now an argument for testing everyone at heightened risk of diabetes, not simply those with a combination of selected risk factors.
- Although the sensitivities and specificities of the tools might appear reasonable in the populations within which the scores were developed, they generally perform less well elsewhere.
- It can sometimes be challenging to select the appropriate cutoff scores to use in order to determine which individuals are at high risk.

My own view about the various diabetes risk scores is that they are most useful in two specific ways rather than to determine who should or should not progress on to blood testing:

1. As a self-assessment tool for individuals to complete themselves with a view to, perhaps, encouraging those at heightened risk to attend a health check involving a more formal measurement of their blood glucose and HbA1c levels.
2. In the context of a health check during which the glucose and HbA1c have been reported as normal. Here a risk score can add value by ensuring that an individual is kept on the right trajectory by, for example, motivating them to maintain a healthy weight and an appropriate level of exercise.

#### 9.2.3.2 BLOOD TESTING

It is suggested that, at present, both fasting blood glucose and glycated haemoglobin (HbA1c) are measured to check for diabetes in addition to assessing the future risk of diabetes. The recommended intervention levels are as follows:

*Fasted plasma glucose*:

- High risk of developing type 2 diabetes: 5.5–6.9 mmol/L
- Possible type 2 diabetes: $\geq$7 mmol/L

*Glycated haemoglobin (HbA1c)*:

- High risk of developing type 2 diabetes: 42–47 mmol/mol (6%–6.4%)
- Possible type 2 diabetes: $\geq$48 mmol/mol (6.5%)

For those attending a health check the recommended 8-hour fast often presents a challenge. Starvation is not required for HbA1c testing so it has been suggested that this test is used alone in case-finding for diabetes and impaired glucose regulation. However, there are clinical situations where this would be inappropriate:

- Individuals suspected of having type 1 diabetes
- Individuals with symptoms of diabetes for less than 2 months

- Individuals on certain medications (e.g. steroids, anti-psychotics)
- Individuals with acute pancreatic damage

Caution also needs to be exercised in people who are anaemic, have been diagnosed with a haemoglobinopathy or have chronic renal or liver failure.

Another approach to seek to overcome the fasting requirement is to categorise random (non-fasted) plasma glucose levels according to the likely diabetes risk:

Random plasma glucose:

- High risk of developing type 2 diabetes: 7.8–11 mmol/L
- Possible type 2 diabetes: ≥11.1 mmol/L

However, it is important to appreciate that *any results* from a health check suggesting possible diabetes require further confirmatory fasting plasma glucose testing.

Case-finding for type 2 diabetes and diabetes risk appears to be cost effective for those assessed as being at heightened risk. However, to deliver value there is an additional requirement to ensure that appropriate interventions are available for those with impaired glucose regulation.

For those diagnosed with diabetes, aside from ensuring optimal management of the glucose level, ongoing screening and monitoring is needed for the following:

- *Diabetic retinopathy*: Systematic screening for diabetic retinal disease should be provided for all people with diabetes.
- *Diabetes-related kidney disease*: The albumin:creatinine ratio (ACR) should be used to screen for microalbuminuria. An ACR >2.5 mg/mmol in men and >3.5 mg/mmol in women is the earliest sign of diabetic nephropathy.
- *Cardiovascular risk*: Factors such as blood pressure, cholesterol and smoking should be managed aggressively (see Chapter 4).
- *Foot ulcers*: All patients with diabetes should be regularly reviewed to assess their risk of developing a foot ulcer. Risk factors for foot ulceration include peripheral arterial disease and peripheral neuropathy, previous amputation, previous ulceration, the presence of callus, joint deformity and vision or mobility problems.

## 9.3 THYROID DYSFUNCTION

### 9.3.1 Importance

The prevalence of hypothyroidism is between 1% and 2% and it is 10 times more common in women than in men. Rates also rise with age – affecting around 4% of women and 0.8% of men 60 years or older. Subclinical hypothyroidism (with thyroid-stimulating hormone [TSH] levels above the normal range but a normal thyroxine) is found in approximately 10% of individuals over 60 years old.

The prevalence of hyperthyroidism in women is between 0.5% and 2%, and is 10 times more common in women than in men. The reported overall prevalence of subclinical hyperthyroidism (i.e. low TSH but normal thyroxine) ranges from 0.5% to 6.3%, with men and women over 65 years having the highest prevalence.

Globally, too little iodine in the diet is the most common cause of hypothyroidism and almost one-third of the world's population live in areas of iodine deficiency. Populations at particular risk tend to be remote, occupying mountainous areas in South East Asia, Latin America and Central Africa. In iodine-replete areas, most persons with thyroid disorders have autoimmune diseases, for example, primary atrophic hypothyroidism, Hashimoto's thyroiditis or Graves' disease.

## 9.3.2 Prevention

Iodine deficiency remains a major public health problem throughout Africa and is the most common cause of thyroid disorders on this continent. In addition to promoting the consumption of iodine-rich foods such as dairy products and fish, many countries with moderate iodine deficiency have implemented universal salt iodisation.

## 9.3.3 Earlier recognition

It has been suggested that the earlier detection and treatment of thyroid disorders are beneficial by preventing the longer-term morbidity and mortality due to associated conditions such as cardiovascular disease and osteoporosis-related fractures.

### 9.3.3.1 SYMPTOMS

Symptoms that commonly occur in thyroid disorders are often subtle and non-specific. For example, hypothyroidism can present as tiredness, weight gain, constipation, muscle aching, feeling cold, dry skin, lifeless hair, fluid retention, mental slowing and depression. In the case of hyperthyroidism symptoms include restlessness, tremor, weight loss, palpitations, sweating, diarrhoea, shortness of breath, tiredness and muscle weakness, thinning hair and menstrual changes.

### 9.3.3.2 CASE-FINDING

While there is no consensus about population screening for thyroid dysfunction there is compelling evidence to support case-finding in the following circumstances for individuals over the age of 35 years:

- Other autoimmune conditions such as type 1 diabetes, rheumatoid arthritis and vitiligo
- Pernicious anaemia, coeliac disease, osteoporosis or atrial fibrillation
- Family history of thyroid disease in a first-degree relative
- Taking amiodarone, lithium or thyroxine
- Prior history of thyroid surgery or dysfunction

- A history of neck radiation including radioactive iodine therapy for hyperthyroidism and external-beam radiotherapy for head and neck malignancies
- A goitre
- Down syndrome
- Psychiatric disorders or cognitive impairment
- Non-specific and unexplained symptoms such as constipation, fatigue, weight changes, muscle aching or weakness and hair loss (especially women over 50 or men over 60)
- Women planning pregnancy (at any age)

#### 9.3.3.3 BLOOD TESTING

The primary investigation for thyroid dysfunction in those with or without symptoms is TSH testing. Adding in thyroxine testing can help to distinguish subclinical thyroid dysfunction (TSH levels outside the laboratory normal range but thyroxine levels within the laboratory normal range) from overt thyroid dysfunction (both TSH and thyroxine outside the laboratory normal ranges).

A normal serum TSH concentration has a high predictive value in ruling out thyroid disease in healthy subjects. In unselected populations, measurement of serum TSH has a reported sensitivity of 89%–95% and specificity of 90%–96% for overt thyroid dysfunction. However, it is also important to appreciate that there is some continuing disagreement about the normal levels of TSH both in the general population in addition to particular subgroups such as the elderly. Moreover, the accurate interpretation of serum TSH levels is further complicated by the effects of conditions other than thyroid dysfunction on TSH secretion from the pituitary gland.

Aside from measuring TSH and thyroxine levels there is also some evidence in favour of testing for thyroid peroxidase antibodies (TPOAb). In the Whickham survey of thyroid disorders in the community, the annual rate of progression from subclinical to overt hypothyroidism was 3% in women with elevated TSH levels, 2% in women with positive thyroid autoantibodies and 4.3% when both elevated TSH and thyroid autoantibodies were present. Similar findings have been made in the context of the Amsterdam autoimmune thyroid disease cohort study and the Tehran thyroid study. In the latter, it was confirmed that being TPOAb positive was associated with a heightened risk of developing hypothyroidism (8.3%) and hyperthyroidism (2.4%) especially if the antibody concentration is greater than 100 kU/L.

## FURTHER READING

### Overview

Kahn R, Buse J, Ferrannini E, Stern M. The metabolic syndrome: Time for a critical appraisal. Joint statement from the American Diabetes Association and the European Association for the Study of Diabetes. *Diabetes Care* 2005;28:2289–2304.

Minisola S, Pepe J, Piemonte S, Cipriani C. The diagnosis and management of hypercalcaemia. *BMJ* 2015;350:h2723.

## Type 2 diabetes

Buijsse B, Simmons RK, Griffin SJ, Schulze MB. Risk assessment tools for identifying individuals at risk of developing type 2 diabetes. *Epidemiol Rev* 2011;33:46–62.
Chen L, Magliano DJ, Balkau B et al. AUSDRISK: An Australian type 2 diabetes risk assessment tool based on demographic, lifestyle and simple anthropometric measures. *Med J Australia* 2010;192:197–202.
Chowdhury TA, Shah R. Reducing the risk of type 2 diabetes. *BMJ* 2015;351:32–33.
Gillies CL, Lambert PC, Abrams KR et al. Different strategies for screening and prevention of type 2 diabetes in adults: Cost-effectiveness analysis. *BMJ* 2008;336:1180–1184.
John WG. Use of HbA1c in the diagnosis of diabetes mellitus in the UK. The implementation of the World Health Organisation Guidance 2011. *Diabet Med* 2012;29:1350–1357.
Lindstrom J, Tuomilehto J. The diabetes risk score: A practical tool to predict type 2 diabetes risk. *Diabetes Care* 2003;26:725–731.
National Institute for Health and Care Excellence (NICE). *Type 2 Diabetes: Prevention in People at High Risk*. London: NICE, 2012.
Scottish Intercollegiate Guidelines Network (SIGN). *Management of Diabetes*. Edinburgh: SIGN, 2010.
Smetana GW, Abrahamson MJ, Rind DM. Should we screen for type 2 diabetes? *Ann Intern Med* 2016;165:509–516.
U.S. Preventive Services Task Force. Screening for abnormal blood glucose and type 2 diabetes mellitus: U.S. Preventive Services Task Force recommendation statement. *Ann Intern Med* 2015;163:861–868.
World Health Organization. *Global Report on Diabetes*. Geneva: WHO, 2016.

## Thyroid dysfunction

Amouzegar A, Gharibzadeh S, Kazemian E et al. The prevalence, incidence and natural course of positive antithyroperoxidase antibodies in a population-based study: Tehran thyroid study. *PLoS ONE* 2017;12:e0169283. doi:10.1371/journal.pone.0169283
Garber JR, Cobin RH, Gharib H et al. Clinical practice guidelines for hypothyroidism in adults. *Endocr Pract* 2012;18:988–1028.
Ogbera A, Kuku SF. Epidemiology of thyroid diseases in Africa. *Indian J Endocrinol Metab* 2011;15:S82–S88.
Strieder TG, Tijssen JG, Wenzel BE, Endert E, Wiersinga WM. Prediction of progression to overt hypothyroidism or hyperthyroidism in female relatives of patients with autoimmune thyroid disease using the Thyroid Events Amsterdam (THEA) score. *Arch Intern Med* 2008;168:1657–1663.

U.S. Preventive Services Task Force. Screening for thyroid dysfunction: U.S. Preventive Services Task Force recommendation statement. *Ann Intern Med* 2015;162:641–650.

Vanderpump MP, Tunbridge WM, French JM et al. The incidence of thyroid disorders in the community: A twenty-year follow-up of the Whickham Survey. *Clin Endocrinol* 1995;43:55–68.

# 10

# Epithelial health

## KEY RECOMMENDATIONS

- Epithelial health is about the body surface: skin, hair, nails and the oral cavity.
- For those designing a better value health check incorporating a focus on epithelial health, it is suggested that particular consideration is given to skin cancer prevention and the earlier recognition of melanomas.
- Oral cavity health checks are generally undertaken by dentists, but a health check presents an opportunity to highlight the risk factors and the common symptoms of mouth cancer.
- To prevent skin cancers limit exposure to ultraviolet radiation (from sunlight or indoor tanning beds).
- Provide information to those attending health checks concerning the key features of skin cancers.
- Advise individuals to pay particular attention to any atypical moles (dysplastic naevi) in addition to their total body mole count (can be estimated by the number of moles on the right arm).
- Consider a total body skin examination for melanoma case-finding (using the *ABCDE* or the *Weighted 7-Point* checklists) for those at increased risk.

## 10.1 OVERVIEW

In terms of developing a better value health check incorporating a focus on epithelial health, it is suggested that the key priorities are skin cancer prevention and the earlier recognition of melanomas.

It is also necessary to be aware that epithelial changes can suggest other underlying conditions of importance for a health check. For example, thyroid problems are sometimes associated with skin or hair changes, and any rash affecting the breast should always be considered as a possible symptom of breast cancer. Individuals with dermatitis herpetiformis (red, raised skin patches, often with blisters) might turn out to have coeliac disease and those with abnormally thin nails which have lost their convexity, becoming flat or even concave in shape (koilonychia) may have iron-deficiency anaemia. Oral thrush can also sometimes be associated with HIV or diabetes.

Smoking, alcohol misuse and a poor diet are the main risk factors for mouth cancer. It can also be caused by chewing tobacco or betel quid and, in some cases, is associated with human papillomavirus (HPV). Although oral cancer screening is not currently recommended it is suggested that, in the context of a health check, individuals should be made aware that the three most common symptoms of mouth cancer are as follows:

- A sore area in the mouth (ulcer) that will not heal
- Discomfort or pain in the mouth that will not go away
- A persistent white or red patch in the mouth

## 10.2 SKIN CANCER

### 10.2.1 Importance

Currently, between 2 and 3 million non-melanoma skin cancers and 132,000 melanoma skin cancers occur globally each year. Australia and New Zealand have the highest rates of melanoma in the world followed closely by Northern Europe and North America, while it is less common in Asia, Africa and Latin America.

The incidence of both non-melanoma (basal and squamous cell) and melanoma skin cancers has been increasing over the past decades. The 5.4 million new cases of basal (BCC) and squamous cell carcinomas (SCC) in the United States annually and the 76,400 new cases of malignant melanomas each year are a major burden on both individuals and the healthcare services. It has been estimated that skin cancer treatments in the United States now cost more than $8 billion each year and that 10,100 individuals will die from melanomas annually.

### 10.2.2 Prevention

Due to their relative lack of skin pigmentation, Caucasian populations generally have a much higher risk of developing non-melanoma or melanoma skin cancers than dark-skinned populations. People with pale or freckled skin, fair or red hair and blue eyes belong to the highest-risk group. Those with dark hair and eyes who do not normally get sunburnt are at medium risk of developing skin cancer.

Individuals who spend long periods in the sun are also at particular risk such as outdoor workers and those with open air hobbies, for example, sailing or golf. High, but intermittent, exposure to UV radiation (from sunlight or indoor tanning beds) also confers an increased risk of skin cancer.

The evidence suggests that much of the burden of skin cancer could be prevented by:

- Limiting time in the sun especially between the hours of 10 a.m. and 4 p.m.
- Watching for the UV Index, taking particular care to adopt sun safety practices when the UV Index predicts exposure levels of moderate or above.

- Seeking shade when UV rays are the most intense, but being aware that shade structures such as trees, umbrellas or canopies do not offer complete sun protection.
- Wearing protective clothing such as a wide-brimmed hat, sunglasses that provide 99%–100% UVA and UVB protection and lightly woven, loose-fitting clothes.
- Applying a broad-spectrum sunscreen of sun protection factor 15+ liberally and re-applying every 2 hours, or after working, swimming, playing or exercising outdoors.
- Avoiding sunlamps and tanning parlours.

Employers can also assist by providing shaded areas for workers and installing free sunscreen dispensers.

### 10.2.3 Earlier recognition

BCCs and SCCs tend to be locally invasive but can become secondarily infected. Around 5% of SCCs will eventually spread to regional lymph nodes with SCCs of the lip or ear having a higher risk for metastasis. However, in general, if either cancer is detected and treated early the outcomes are excellent, with cure rates above 95%.

The prognosis of a melanoma is affected by a number of factors including the thickness in millimetres (Breslow), the depth related to skin structures (Clark level), the type of melanoma, the presence of ulceration, the location of the lesion and development of regional or distant metastasis. A melanoma with a Breslow thickness of less than 1.5 mm is associated with a 5-year survival of 93%, whereas one with a thickness of more than 3.5 mm only confers a 5-year survival of 37%.

#### 10.2.3.1 RISK ASSESSMENT

Aside from skin type, sun exposure and a history of sunburn there are a number of other risk factors for skin cancer:

- Exposure to ionising radiation (e.g. previous irradiation)
- Family history of melanoma, BCC, SCC or dysplastic naevus syndrome
- Personal history of skin cancer. Importantly, an individual with a previous non-melanoma skin cancer is at increased risk for a melanoma
- Dysplastic naevi and/or multiple naevi (for melanomas)
- Scarred or traumatised skin (e.g. due to chronic varicose ulcers or burns [for SCCs])
- Organ transplant recipients receiving immunosuppressive drugs (for SCCs in particular)

#### 10.2.3.2 VISUAL INSPECTION

In the context of a health check a visual inspection is the main approach to seek to spot skin cancers earlier.

*Basal cell carcinoma*: The typical BCC is in the form of a papule that is elevated from the surrounding skin and has a shiny, pearly quality with overlying telangiectasia. Other presentations include an enlarged flat plaque with a pearly edge, a non-healing scabbing erosion or ulcer, or a pigmented papule.

*Squamous cell carcinoma*: The classical appearance of an SCC is nodular, nodular with central ulceration or ulcerated with a raised everted nodular edge. If the hyperkeratotic scale is removed the tumour will often bleed. Any sore that does not heal after 2–3 months should also be treated with suspicion (predictive value for SCC of 2%–4%).

*Actinic keratoses* (red, scaly patches on chronically sun-exposed skin) and *Bowen's disease* (a red, well-demarcated, thin plaque) also need to be sought as, if left untreated, around 5% will progress to SCCs.

*Melanoma*: The recognition of melanoma, especially early melanoma, can be challenging. In the context of a health check, a useful starting point is to ask individuals about any skin lesions that worry them such as new moles or a change in size, shape or colour of a pre-existing mole. Over half of all melanomas (especially those that involve a change in size or colour) are discovered by patients.

To facilitate earlier diagnosis two checklists have been developed:

1. *ABCDE Checklist*:
   a. **A**symmetrical skin lesion (i.e. if the lesion is bisected, one half is not identical to the other half)
   b. **B**order of the lesion is irregular
   c. **C**olour variegation (i.e. when more than one shade of pigment is present)
   d. **D**iameter: moles greater than 6 mm are more likely to be melanomas than smaller moles
   e. **E**volutionary changes in colour, size, symmetry, surface characteristics (e.g. elevated above skin surface) and symptoms

If a mole exhibits one or more features from this list, then an expert dermatological opinion is warranted.

2. *Weighted Seven-Point Checklist*:
   a. Major features of the lesion (2 points each):
      i. Change in shape
      ii. Irregular shape
      iii. Irregular colour

   b. Minor features of the lesion (1 point each):
      i. Largest diameter 7 mm or more
      ii. Inflammation
      iii. Crusting or bleeding
      iv. Change in sensation

If there is a total score of 3 or more (i.e. at least one major feature plus one minor feature or 3 minor features) then sensitivity and specificity for melanoma diagnosis are 79% and 30%, respectively. In these circumstances referral to a dermatologist is indicated.

In the context of a health check it is important to appreciate that the classical features associated with a BCC or SCC might be absent; also, the checklists for melanoma may prove unhelpful. In these circumstances, a further useful approach is to consider if there has been a new or changing skin lesion which looks unlike anything else on the patient's skin – the 'ugly duckling sign'.

However, early skin cancers continue to be missed and, in cases of doubt, an expert opinion should always be sought from a dermatologist who may assess the lesion by dermatoscopy or biopsy.

#### 10.2.3.3 MELANOMA SCREENING AND CASE-FINDING

Screening for melanoma using visual skin examination and the ABCDE checklist has been advocated by some because the associated morbidity and mortality rates for this type of skin cancer are substantially greater than for others.

However, according to the U.S. Preventive Services Task Force, the evidence in favour of universal screening for melanomas with a clinical visual skin inspection is limited. Moreover, in New Zealand, it has been estimated that an annual full-skin examination of adults aged 35–64 by GPs would occupy up to 5% of a GP's clinical time.

The only direct evidence on the effectiveness of screening in reducing melanoma morbidity and mortality is from the SCREEN (Skin Cancer Research to Provide Evidence for Effectiveness of Screening in Northern Germany) study. In 2003, a skin cancer screening campaign was initiated in the state of Schleswig-Holstein including total-body skin examination being offered to individuals aged 20 and over by dermatologists and non-dermatologists. After 2 years 360,288 individuals (about 19% of the eligible population) had received a single clinical visual skin examination. Subsequently, trends in melanoma death rates were compared with several surrounding regions that had not been subjected to a similar skin cancer campaign. After 10 years, the study found a 48% relative reduction in the risk of dying from melanoma in Schleswig-Holstein compared with the control regions, which translates into an absolute reduction of 1 fewer death from melanoma per 100,000 persons screened.

Unfortunately, in the SCREEN study it is difficult to disentangle the separate effects of the public education element from those of the clinical visual skin examination component. In addition, the melanoma mortality rate in the region receiving the interventions was already declining prior to the introduction of the cancer screening programme. Furthermore, an independent study evaluating an additional 5 years of follow-up in the SCREEN study population found that the observed reduction in melanoma mortality rates did not persist over time but essentially returned to the baseline rates observed before the screening programme was initiated.

The potential harms of skin cancer screening include misdiagnosis, overdiagnosis and the resulting cosmetic and, occasionally, functional adverse effects as a consequence of biopsies and overtreatment. In the SCREEN study, approximately 4.4% of screened individuals (1 for every 23 participants) underwent a skin excision for a suspicious lesion, and the majority of these biopsies did not result in a cancer diagnosis. Overall, for both men and women, 1 case of melanoma was detected per 28 excisions performed.

On balance, the best value approach is to undertake case-finding within specific groups according to their baseline risk such as

- Those with a personal history of skin cancer
- Those with one or more first-degree relatives with a melanoma
- Those with dysplastic naevi or multiple naevi
- Solid-organ transplant recipients

To efficiently assess the requirement to progress to a total-body examination or a specialist referral the following features might also help:

- If an individual has more than 10 dysplastic naevi (i.e. greater than 5 mm in diameter and with irregular edge/pigmentation) they are at high risk for a melanoma.
- If an individual has more than 11 moles on their right arm, then they are highly likely to have more than 100 naevi over their whole body, conferring a significantly increased melanoma risk.

## FURTHER READING

Boniol M, Autier P, Gandini S. Melanoma mortality following skin cancer screening in Germany. *BMJ Open* 2015;5:e008158.

Linos E, Katz KA, Colditz GA. Skin cancer – The importance of prevention. *JAMA Intern Med* 2016;176:1435–1436.

National Institute for Health and Care Excellence (NICE). *Skin Cancer Prevention*. London: NICE, 2016 (Update).

National Institute for Health and Care Excellence (NICE). *Sunlight Exposure: Risks and Benefits*. London: NICE, 2016.

Ribero S, Zugna D, Osella-Abate S et al. Prediction of high naevus count in a healthy UK population to estimate melanoma risk. *Brit J Dermatol* 2016;174:312–318.

Tsao H, Weinstock MA. Visual inspection and the U.S. Preventive Services Task Force Recommendation on skin cancer screening. *JAMA* 2016;316:398–400.

U.S. Preventive Services Task Force. Screening for Skin Cancer: U.S. Preventive Services Task Force recommendation statement. *JAMA* 2016;316:429–435.

# 11

# Mental health

## KEY RECOMMENDATIONS

- For those designing a better value heath check incorporating a focus on mental health it is suggested that the following conditions warrant particular consideration: stress, depression, anxiety disorders and eating disorders.
- Encourage individuals and organisations to manage stress better.
- Preventive strategies to consider for depression and anxiety encompass universal approaches, selective approaches and indicated approaches.
- Universal screening for depression is recommended using the Patient Health Questionnaire (PHQ-9).
- Screening for anxiety is suggested using the Generalised Anxiety Disorder Seven-Item Scale (GAD-7).
- Consideration should be given to case-finding for eating disorders using the SCOFF questionnaire.

## 11.1 OVERVIEW

In terms of developing a better value health check incorporating a focus on mental health it is suggested that the key priorities are stress, depression, anxiety disorders and eating disorders.

There are some other areas that have been considered for inclusion within this chapter but, at present, I felt that the evidence of benefit in terms of delivering value was not sufficiently mature. Key amongst these are the recognition of post-traumatic stress disorder and the prevention and identification of medically unexplained symptoms.

Stress is the feeling of being under too much mental or emotional pressure. In small doses, stress helps individuals to stay focused, energetic and alert. But when stress becomes overwhelming, it can damage a person's health, their mood, their work, their relationships and their quality of life.

Occupational stress is a common and costly problem and is most likely to occur when workplace demands overpower a person's capacity to comfortably handle a situation or when conditions do not meet an individual's needs. Employees who are stressed are more likely to miss work, resign, be involved in an accident and perform worse than their less stressed peers.

Stress is not an illness itself, but it can cause serious illness if it is not addressed. For example, if a person becomes overwhelmed by stress, especially intense or prolonged stress, it can lead to the development of anxiety disorders and depression.

Recognising stress helps individuals to work out better ways to deal with pressure and protects them from adopting unhealthy ways of coping such as smoking, drinking too much, overeating or undereating, or using drugs to relax.

Managing stress is all about encouraging people to take charge of their thoughts, their emotions, their schedule, their environment and the way they deal with problems. Stress management involves an individual changing the stressful situation when they can, changing their reaction when they cannot, taking care of themselves and making time for rest and relaxation. It also helps if they can learn how to manage external pressures better and to develop emotional resilience. Table 11.1 details some specific advice that might be offered to an individual who feels stressed.

Organisations can also help to manage stress by

- Providing access to a stress management programme
- Identifying a dedicated space for employees to relax or a place where they can 'walk away' when angry
- Helping employees build stronger relationships by organising social events
- Encouraging employees to develop a better work-life balance
- Allowing employees time for physical activity during the day
- Providing opportunities for employee input into organisational decisions that impact on stress such as work schedules and management of work demands

## 11.2 DEPRESSION

### 11.2.1 Importance

Depression is a common psychiatric disorder in the general population, with more than 300 million people being affected globally. About 9% of people have major depression in Asian and Middle Eastern countries, such as India and Afghanistan, compared with around 4% in North and South America, Australia, New Zealand and East Asian countries including China, Thailand and Indonesia.

Unrecognised and untreated depression is associated with a decreased quality of life and an increased risk of suicide. Worldwide, around 800,000 people die due to suicide every year, and it remains the second leading cause of death amongst 15 to 29 year olds. Over half of those with depression develop a recurrent or chronic disorder after a first depressive episode and are likely to spend 20% of their lifetime in a depressed condition.

Table 11.1 Advice on dealing with stress

| Intervention | Rationale |
|---|---|
| Keep a stress journal | A stress journal can help to identify the regular stressors in your life and the way you deal with them. Each time you feel stressed, keep track of it in your journal. As you keep a daily log, you will begin to see patterns and common themes. Record what caused your stress; how you felt, both physically and emotionally; how you acted in response; and what you did to make yourself feel better. |
| Avoid unnecessary stress | Not all stress can be avoided – but by learning how to say no, distinguishing between 'shoulds' and 'musts' on your to-do list, and steering clear of people or situations that stress you out – you can eliminate many daily stressors. |
| Alter the situation | If you cannot avoid a stressful situation, try to alter it. Be more assertive and deal with problems head on. Instead of bottling up your feelings and increasing your stress, respectfully let others know about your concerns. Or be more willing to compromise and try meeting others halfway on an issue. |
| Adapt to the stressor | When you cannot change the stressor, try changing yourself. Reframe problems or focus on the positive things in your life. If a task at work has you stressed, think about the aspects of your job you do enjoy. And always look at the big picture: is this really something worth getting upset about? |

Depression also imposes a significant economic burden through direct and indirect costs. In the United States, around $22.8 billion was spent on depression treatment in 2009, and lost productivity (due to both absenteeism and presenteeism) cost an additional estimated $23 billion.

Although there are effective interventions for depression, less than half of those affected across the world – and, in some countries, fewer than 10% – receive such treatments. Barriers to care include inaccurate or inadequate assessment and diagnosis together with the social stigma associated with mental disorders.

### 11.2.2 Prevention

Psychological interventions designed to reduce the incidence of new depressive disorders can be delivered by trained lay people, nurses, psychologists or physicians either to groups of people or for individuals. Another effective mechanism involves signposting to written or online self-help resources. Blended approaches combining, for example, e-health interventions with some therapist input can be particularly effective.

It is also useful to be aware that certain factors protect against depression: social support, personal competencies (e.g. self-understanding) and resilience. Resilience refers to a person's capacity to cope with changes or challenges, especially during difficult times or in the face of adversity.

Preventive interventions for depression can be categorised into selective prevention, indicated prevention and universal prevention.

*Selective prevention* is about identifying and focusing efforts on those at greatest risk for the development of depression due to, for example, illicit drug or alcohol misuse, family history of mental illness, adverse life events (e.g. becoming unemployed, relationship problems or bereavement) and chronic diseases or disorders.

For individuals with long-term health problems such as cardiovascular disease, cancer and diabetes, effective preventive interventions are often based on cognitive behavioural or problem-solving therapeutic principles. There is a particular requirement to promote coping and self-management skills.

*Indicated prevention* is about spotting people who exhibit some depressive symptoms but are sub-threshold to warrant a formal diagnosis. My own approach has been to place individuals scoring between 5 and 9 on the Patient Health Questionnaire (PHQ-9) screening test (see Section 11.2.3) into this group and providing some specific suggestions for them (Table 11.2).

*Universal prevention* is about adopting an approach that involves everyone, such as all the employees in an organisation.

For preventing depression in the workplace, universal programmes can be particularly effective when they incorporate healthy lifestyle change elements plus psychological and motivational approaches to reduce and manage stress.

Mental wellbeing at work is determined by the interaction between the working environment, the nature of the work and the individual. The following suggestions might help to prevent anxiety and depression developing or progressing:

- Review the working environment including workload and work variety; personal relationships, bullying, management processes (e.g. empowerment and giving constructive feedback); and physical factors (noise, dust, dirt).
- Explore opportunities for flexible working (including home working, part-time work, job-shares).
- Promote mental wellbeing within the organisation by improving awareness and understanding about mental illness. Seek to reduce stigma and discrimination.
- Provide good-quality information to all employees on mental health, coping strategies, stress and self-help services.
- Encourage awareness about those most at risk for anxiety and depression (e.g. individuals with long-term health problems, relationship difficulties, recent bereavement, shift workers).

Table 11.2 Depression prevention advice

| | |
|---|---|
| Talk and connect with others | • Talking can help with depression and low mood, and it is extremely important to avoid withdrawing from contact with other people. Socialising can improve your mood.<br>• Self-help groups are another good way of getting in touch with people who have similar problems. They can understand what you are going through. As well as having the chance to talk, you may be able to find out how other people have coped.<br>• Volunteering and learning new skills will also build your confidence and help you to develop new social networks. |
| Keep going and improve your lifestyle | • When people feel down they can get into poor sleep patterns, staying up late and sleeping during the day. Try to get up at your normal time and stick to your routine as much as possible.<br>• Do not avoid things you find difficult. Some people who are low can easily lose their confidence about travelling and working.<br>• A healthy balanced diet combined with regular exercise can help to overcome both anxiety and depression. Reducing alcohol and caffeine intake can also help, as will stopping smoking.<br>• Try to become more aware of the present moment, including your feelings and thoughts, your body and the world around you. Some people call this awareness 'mindfulness' and it can positively change the way you feel about life and how you approach challenges. |
| Go online | • The UK Royal College of Psychiatrists website is a particularly useful source for further information on depression, books/resources, treatment options and self-help organisations: http://www.rcpsych.ac.uk/healthadvice/problemsdisorders/depression.aspx<br>• Cognitive behavioural therapy: Three particularly useful online resources are 'Living Life to the Full': http://www.llttf.com/, MoodGym': https://moodgym.anu.edu.au/welcome, and 'Beating the Blues': http://www.beatingtheblues.co.uk/ |

- Consider mental health problems in an individual if there has been
  - An increase in unexplained absence or sick leave
  - Poor performance/time keeping/decision making
  - Lack of energy and tired all the time; complaining of poor sleeping
  - Uncommunicative/withdrawn/moody behaviour
  - Alcohol or drug problems

- Consider providing appropriate rapid access to cognitive behavioural therapy (CBT) services by accredited therapists (on-line, telephone and face-to-face).
- Keep in touch with employees if away from work with mental health problems and provide ongoing support (that continues when they return to work). Maintaining contact and encouraging return to work is particularly conducive to creating a sense of belonging and reducing the number of sick leave days.

## 11.2.3 Earlier recognition

Depression presents with a wide variety of symptoms such as feeling unhappy most of the time; losing interest in life with an inability to enjoy anything; finding it harder to make decisions; exhaustion; losing appetite and weight; taking 1–2 hours to get off to sleep, and then waking up earlier than usual; loss of self-confidence; and avoiding other people.

However, in the absence of screening, it is estimated that less than 50% of patients with major depression are picked up. Unless directly asked about their mood, people omit information about depressive symptoms for a variety of reasons, including fear of stigmatisation, concerns about medical record confidentiality and worries about being referred to a psychiatrist.

There are two main approaches to seeking to recognise depression earlier in the context of a health check. The first relies on the completion of a questionnaire by every individual attending for a health check – whereas the second is to evaluate individuals for depression if they are assessed as being at higher risk due to having, for example, chronic medical illnesses, chronic pain syndromes, recent life changes or stressors, fair or poor self-rated health and unexplained physical symptoms associated with depression. The likelihood of depressive disorder increases by approximately 1.5–3.5 times if any of these factors are present.

Based on an extensive review of the evidence, the U.S. Preventive Services Task Force (USPSTF) now recommends screening of all adults regardless of risk factors. They concluded that programmes combining depression screening with adequate support systems in place improve clinical outcomes (i.e. the reduction or remission of depression symptoms).

Commonly used depression screening instruments considered by the USPSTF include the PHQ-9, the Hospital Anxiety and Depression Scale and, in older adults, the Geriatric Depression Scale.

The PHQ-9 is a nine-item questionnaire that exhibits validity and reliability in populations similar to those likely to be encountered in health checks. It classifies current symptoms on a scale of 0 (no symptoms) to 3 (daily symptoms). Repeating

Table 11.3 The Patient Health Questionnaire (PHQ-9)

| **Over the last 2 weeks, how often have you been bothered by any of the following problems?** |
| --- |
| • Little interest or pleasure in doing things? |
| • Feeling down, depressed or hopeless? |
| • Trouble falling or staying asleep, or sleeping too much? |
| • Feeling tired or having little energy? |
| • Poor appetite or overeating? |
| • Feeling bad about yourself – or that you are a failure or have let yourself or your family down? |
| • Trouble concentrating on things, such as reading the newspaper or watching television? |
| • Moving or speaking so slowly that other people could have noticed? |
| • Or the opposite – being so fidgety or restless that you have been moving around a lot more than usual? |
| • Thoughts that you would be better off dead, or of hurting yourself in some way? |

the PHQ-9 during treatment allows clinicians to objectively monitor any response to therapy. A PHQ-9 score ≥10 has a sensitivity of 88% and a specificity of 88% for major depression.

The nine questions are detailed in Table 11.3.

Screening should only ever be considered if there are also adequate systems in place to ensure accurate diagnosis, effective treatment and appropriate follow-up.

Following initial screening all individuals scoring more than 10–15 using the PHQ-9 need to be more formally assessed in order to make a definitive diagnosis of depression. Assessing the impact of depressive symptoms on functioning and suicide risk are also critical elements of this more extensive individual evaluation.

Obviously, no questionnaire is 100% accurate and onward referral or assessment might also be warranted for some individuals irrespective of the result from their screening test. Importantly, two-thirds of primary care patients with depression present initially with somatic symptoms (e.g. headache, back problems or chronic pain), making the detection of depression even trickier.

As part of a general health assessment it is also important to consider conditions that might masquerade as depression such as thyroid deficiency (see Chapter 9) in addition to co-existing problems such as diabetes or alcohol misuse.

## 11.3 ANXIETY DISORDERS

### 11.3.1 Importance

Anxiety disorders, including panic disorder (PD), agoraphobia, generalised anxiety disorder (GAD), social anxiety disorder (SAD), specific phobias and separation anxiety disorder, are the most prevalent mental disorders. Clinically significant anxiety is estimated to affect around 10% of people in North America, Western Europe and Australia/New Zealand compared to about 8% in the Middle East and 6% in Asia. It has been calculated that, in 2004, anxiety disorders cost more than €41 billion across the European Union.

However, several studies of anxiety disorders in primary care populations have shown that 20% of individuals suffer from at least one anxiety disorder with 7.6% having GAD, 6.8% PD and 6.2% SAD. One survey of 6370 primary care patients found that 33% of individuals reported anxiety symptoms, and that these symptoms went undiagnosed and untreated in more than half of all cases.

GAD is the most common cause of disability in the workplace in the United States. It is also associated with functional impairment and increased risk of adverse health outcomes, including cardiovascular disease and suicide. It often occurs in conjunction with other psychiatric conditions, including depression, panic disorder, post-traumatic stress disorder and social phobia.

## 11.3.2 Prevention

Psychological prevention programmes have been directed at broad, non-specific anxiety and at more specific anxiety types, such as panic disorder and post-traumatic stress disorder.

Echoing the approaches to depression prevention, both targeted and universal approaches have been advocated but, at present, the research evidence is limited.

## 11.3.3 Earlier recognition

Anxiety is a particular feeling of fear that occurs when faced with a stressful situation. Some individuals might also notice a fast heart rate, a thumping heart, feeling sick, trembling, sweating, dry mouth or fast breathing.

GAD is characterised by excessive, uncontrollable and often irrational worry. It interferes with daily functioning, as individuals with GAD typically anticipate disaster and are overly concerned about everyday matters such as health issues, money, death, family problems, friendship problems, interpersonal relationship problems or work difficulties. Individuals may also exhibit a variety of physical symptoms such as restlessness, fatigue, irritability, problems concentrating, sleep disturbance, headaches, muscle tension, nausea and diarrhoea.

Substantial under-recognition and undertreatment of all anxiety disorders has been demonstrated. It is therefore worth considering universal screening using the Generalised Anxiety Disorder Seven-Item Scale (GAD-7) in conjunction with PHQ-9.

The seven questions within GAD-7 are detailed in Table 11.4.

The total GAD-7 score is calculated by assigning values of 0, 1, 2 or 3 to the response categories of 'not at all', 'several days', 'more than half the days' and 'nearly every day', respectively, and adding together the scores for the seven questions.

Using a threshold score of 10, the GAD-7 has a sensitivity of 89% and a specificity of 82% for GAD. It is also moderately good at recognising three other common anxiety disorders – panic disorder (sensitivity 74%, specificity 81%),

Table 11.4 The Generalised Anxiety Disorder Seven-Item Scale (GAD-7)

| **Over the last 2 weeks, how often have you been bothered by any of the following problems?** |
|---|
| • Feeling nervous, anxious or on edge? |
| • Not being able to stop or control worrying? |
| • Worrying too much about different things? |
| • Trouble relaxing? |
| • Being so restless that it is hard to sit still? |
| • Becoming easily annoyed or irritable? |
| • Feeling afraid as if something awful might happen? |

social anxiety disorder (sensitivity 72%, specificity 80%) and post-traumatic stress disorder (sensitivity 66%, specificity 81%).

As for depression, anxiety screening should only ever be considered if there are also adequate systems in place to ensure accurate diagnosis, effective treatment and appropriate follow-up. When used as a screening tool, further evaluation is recommended when the GAD-7 score is 10 or greater.

As part of a general health assessment it is also important to consider conditions that might masquerade as anxiety such as thyroid problems (see Chapter 9).

## 11.4 EATING DISORDERS

### 11.4.1 Importance

Eating disorders – such as anorexia nervosa and bulimia nervosa – are a group of mental illnesses involving severe disturbances in eating habits and excessive preoccupation about weight and shape. Anorexia nervosa is a serious psychiatric illness characterised by an inability to maintain an adequate, healthy body weight. Bulimia nervosa is marked by recurrent episodes of binge eating in combination with some form of unhealthy compensatory behaviour.

Eating disorders are increasingly recognised as important causes of morbidity and mortality in young individuals. The onset of anorexia nervosa is typically around 15–24 years of age with the highest incidence occurring in adolescent girls between 15 and 19 years.

Prevalence rates in Western countries for anorexia nervosa range from 0.1% to 5.7% in female subjects and, for bulimia nervosa, from 0% to 2.1% in males and from 0.3% to 7.3% in females. The prevalence of eating disorders in non-Western countries is lower than that of the Western countries but appears to be increasing. Eating disorders affect women approximately 7–10 times more often than men, although this ratio is changing.

### 11.4.2 Prevention

Excessive weight and shape concerns have been consistently associated with the onset of eating disorders. Among college-age women with such concerns, an 8-week, Internet-based cognitive-behavioural intervention can significantly reduce weight and shape worries for up to 2 years and, also, decrease the risk for the onset of eating disorders.

Universal efforts to reduce peer, cultural and other sources of thin body preoccupation are also necessary to prevent eating disorders. The increase in the number of subjects with eating disorders or abnormal eating attitudes in non-Western countries has been linked to changing attitudes (the Westernisation hypothesis).

## 11.4.3 Earlier recognition

Early detection and treatment of eating disorders significantly improves outcomes. Raising general awareness about the subtle symptoms and behaviours that can be indicative of an eating disorder is very helpful, for example

- Dieting, missing meals or avoiding food
- Denial of feeling hungry
- Stating a need to eat less than others or eating very small portions
- Eating more slowly
- Playing with and pushing food around the plate
- Avoiding eating with others and opting out of meal times
- Secrecy around food and eating
- Increased interest in preparing food, reading recipes, watching food-based TV programmes
- Wearing baggy clothes or more clothes to conceal weight loss
- Reluctance to participate in activities where the body will be viewed by others (i.e. physical education, swimming)
- Feeling fat and denying they are thin even when people pass comment
- Increased sensitivity about body shape
- Increased interest in weighing and checking in mirrors
- Increased obsessiveness in certain behaviours and perfectionism
- Mood changes – particularly depressive symptoms
- Low self-esteem
- Increase in exercise, both overt and exercising in secret
- Spending increased time in the bathroom after meals
- Use of diuretics, laxatives and self-induced or spontaneous vomiting

Eating disorders can occur at any weight. Obesity is not classified as an eating disorder, since it is defined by a weight metric rather than by thoughts and behaviours. However, obesity is a risk factor for the onset of eating disorders because it is associated with high levels of body image dissatisfaction and dieting behaviour, and can also be a marker of disordered eating, in particular binge eating.

Consideration should be given to sensitively case-finding for eating disorders in the context of a health check using the SCOFF questionnaire – especially amongst those deemed to be at highest risk. Such groups include young women, individuals with low or high body mass index (BMI), those expressing weight or shape concerns, and symptoms such as menstrual disturbances or amenorrhoea, gastrointestinal disorders, hair loss and psychological problems.

The SCOFF questions are as follows:

- Do you make yourself **S**ick because you feel uncomfortably full?
- Do you worry that you have lost **C**ontrol over how much you eat?
- Have you recently lost more than **O**ne stone (14 lb) in a 3-month period?
- Do you believe yourself to be **F**at when others say you are too thin?
- Would you say that **F**ood dominates your life?

Positive responses to at least two of the questions provide a positive likelihood ratio of 6.2 for eating disorders. Positive responses to at least four of the questions gives a positive likelihood ratio of 11.

At a health check, case-finding for eating disorders should only ever be considered if there are also adequate systems in place to ensure accurate diagnosis, effective treatment and appropriate follow-up.

## FURTHER READING

### Overview

Institute for Health and Productivity Studies, Johns Hopkins Bloomberg School of Public Health. *From Evidence to Practice: Workplace Wellness that Works*. Baltimore, MD: Johns Hopkins, 2015.

### Depression

Mihalopoulos C, Vos T. Cost-effectiveness of preventive interventions for depressive disorders: An overview. *Expert Rev Pharmacoecon Outcomes Res* 2013;13:237–242.

National Institute for Health and Clinical Excellence (NICE). *Depression in Adults: Recognition and Management*. London: NICE, 2016 (update).

National Institute for Health and Clinical Excellence (NICE). *Depression in Adults with a Chronic Physical Health Problem: Recognition and Management*. London: NICE, 2009.

National Institute for Health and Clinical Excellence (NICE). *Mental Wellbeing at Work*. London: NICE, 2009.

Smit F, Shields L, Petrea I. *Preventing Depression in the WHO European Region*. Copenhagen: WHO Regional Office for Europe, 2016.

Tan L, Wang MJ, Modini M et al. Preventing the development of depression at work: A systematic review and meta-analysis of universal interventions in the workplace. *BMC Med* 2014;12:74. doi:10.1186/1741-7015-12-74

U.S. Preventive Services Task Force. Screening for depression in adults: U.S. Preventive Services Task Force recommendation statement. *JAMA* 2016;315:380–387.

Williams JW, Noel PH, Cordes JA et al. Is this patient clinically depressed? *JAMA* 2002;287:1160–1170.

## Anxiety

Bandelow B, Michaelis S. Epidemiology of anxiety disorders in the 21st century. *Dialogues Clin Neurosci* 2015;17:327–335.
Baxter AJ, Scott KM, Vos T, Whiteford HA. Global prevalence of anxiety disorders: A systematic review and meta-regression. *Psychol Med* 2013;43:897–910.
Hallgren JD, Morton JR. What's the best way to screen for anxiety and panic disorders? *J Fam Pract* 2007;56:579–580.
Herr NR, Williams JW, Benjamin S, McDuffie J. Does this patient have generalised anxiety or panic disorder? The Rational Clinical Examination Systematic Review. *JAMA* 2014;312:78–84.
Kroenke K, Spitzer RL, Williams JB et al. Anxiety disorders in primary care: Prevalence, impairment, comorbidity, and detection. *Ann Intern Med* 2007;146:317–325.
Lau EX, Rapee RM. Prevention of anxiety disorders. *Curr Psychiatry Rep* 2011;13:258–266.
Seitz DP. Screening mnemonic for generalized anxiety disorder. *Can Fam Physician* 2005;51:1340–1342.
Spitzer RL, Kroenke K, Williams JB et al. A brief measure for assessing generalized anxiety disorder: The GAD-7. *Arch Intern Med* 2006;166:1092–1097.

## Eating disorders

Arcelus J, Mitchell AJ, Wales J, Nielsen S. Mortality rates in patients with anorexia nervosa and other eating disorders. A meta-analysis of 36 studies. *Arch Gen Psychiatry* 2011;68:724–731.
Cotton MA, Ball C, Robinson P. Four simple questions can help screen for eating disorders. *J Gen Intern Med* 2003;18:53–56.
Makino M, Tsuboi K, Dennerstein L. Prevalence of eating disorders: A comparison of Western and Non-Western Countries. *Medscape Gen Med* 2004;6:49–54.
Morgan JF, Reid F, Lacey JH. The SCOFF questionnaire: Assessment of a new screening tool for eating disorders. *BMJ* 1999;319:1467–1468.
Taylor CB, Bryson S, Luce KH et al. Prevention of eating disorders in at-risk college-age women. *Arch Gen Psychiatry* 2006;63:881–888.

# 12

# Men's health

## KEY RECOMMENDATIONS

- For those designing a better value health check incorporating a focus on men's health it is suggested that the following conditions warrant particular consideration: prostate cancer, testicular cancer and erectile dysfunction.
- Support and facilitate smoking cessation using evidence-based interventions with a view to preventing erectile dysfunction.
- Encourage and facilitate weight loss, appropriate dietary modifications and increased exercise using evidence-based interventions to prevent prostate cancer and erectile dysfunction.
- Discuss 5α-reductase inhibitor therapy such as finasteride with a view to reducing prostate cancer risks.
- Offer screening for prostate cancer using prostate-specific antigen after an informed discussion about the pros and cons of such testing.
- Encourage testicular awareness to facilitate the earlier detection of testicular cancer.
- Consider screening for erectile dysfunction (and the possible underlying causes) in men over the age of 40; especially those who smoke, are obese, have diabetes and who undertake little exercise.

## 12.1 OVERVIEW

In terms of developing a better value health check incorporating a focus on men's health it is suggested that the key priorities are prostate cancer, testicular cancer and erectile dysfunction.

There are some other areas that have been considered for inclusion within this chapter but, at present, I felt that the evidence of benefit in terms of delivering value was not sufficiently mature. Key amongst these is looking beyond prostate and testicular cancer to specific screening for other urological cancers such as kidney and bladder by testing for microscopic haematuria. However, not only are bladder and kidney cancers also relevant to women but, as discussed in Chapter 3,

I would argue that urinalysis is one of the core components that should be offered to everyone attending a health check.

Finally, men's health is also, of course, not simply about the conditions focused on in this chapter but also includes all the non-gender-specific diseases and disorders addressed elsewhere.

## 12.2 PROSTATE CANCER

### 12.2.1 Importance

Prostate cancer is the second most common cancer in men globally. An estimated 1.1 million men worldwide were diagnosed with prostate cancer in 2012, accounting for 15% of male cancers, with almost 70% of the cases occurring in the more developed regions.

Prostate cancer incidence varies more than 25-fold across the world; the rates are highest in Australia/New Zealand, the United States and Western and Northern Europe, probably because the practice of prostate-specific antigen (PSA) testing and subsequent biopsy has become widespread in these regions. It is the most common cancer in men in the United States and the United Kingdom (other than skin cancer).

Incidence rates are also relatively high in certain less-developed regions such as the Caribbean, Southern Africa and South America, but remain low in Eastern and South Central Asia.

Treatment options available for prostate cancer include radical prostatectomy (open, laparoscopic or robotically assisted laparoscopic), external-beam radiotherapy, brachytherapy, cryotherapy, focal ablation, androgen deprivation with luteinising hormone-releasing hormone analogues or antiandrogens, intermittent androgen deprivation, cytotoxic agents and active surveillance. However, because of considerable uncertainty regarding the efficacy of treatment and the difficulty with selecting patients for whom there is a known risk of disease progression, opinion remains divided regarding screening for prostate cancer.

### 12.2.2 Prevention

*Lifestyle*: There is evidence that being active helps to lower the risk of prostate cancer. Moreover, being overweight or obese might increase the chances of developing advanced prostate cancer.

Some dietary modifications and supplements have also been suggested as mechanisms to prevent prostate cancer. For example, one study found that the intake of legumes plus yellow-orange and cruciferous vegetables was associated with a lower risk of prostate cancer. However the evidence is inconsistent.

*Chemoprevention*: Based on the Prostate Cancer Prevention Trial, it is suggested that chemoprevention with finasteride reduces the incidence of prostate cancer by 6%. However, no impact has been observed on death rates and any potential benefit must be weighed against sexual side effects such as erectile dysfunction together with the possible increased risk of high-grade prostate cancer.

Based on a comprehensive review of the evidence, the U.S. Food and Drug Administration (FDA) does not, at present, recommend the use of finasteride or other α-reductase inhibitors for the chemoprevention of prostate cancer. However, in Canada it has been suggested that men who are being assessed and monitored for prostate cancer (i.e. are screened regularly – or plan to get yearly PSA tests – and currently have no signs of prostate cancer) might be offered 5α-reductase inhibitor therapy if

- They are ≥50 years of age with a normal PSA level.
- They have an elevated PSA level (2.5–10 ng/mL) and a negative result on prostate biopsy.
- They have moderately symptomatic benign prostatic hyperplasia (BPH).

## 12.2.3 Earlier recognition

### 12.2.3.1 RISK ASSESSMENT

The following features are associated with an increased risk of prostate cancer:

- *Age*: Prostate cancer incidence escalates dramatically with advancing age. Although it is a very unusual disease in men younger than 50 years, rates increase exponentially thereafter.
- *Ethnic origin*: Prostate cancer is more common in black-African men (e.g. African Americans), is of intermediate levels among whites, and is lowest among native Japanese.
- *Family history*: Approximately 15% of men with a diagnosis of prostate cancer will be found to have a first-degree male relative (e.g. brother, father) with prostate cancer.

### 12.2.3.2 SYMPTOMS

Certain symptoms are said to occur more frequently in men with localised prostate cancer (i.e. acute retention, lower urinary tract symptoms [LUTS], haematuria, erectile dysfunction and urinary tract infection). However, none of these symptoms are specific for malignant enlargement of the prostate; LUTS (i.e. nocturia, hesitancy, frequency, urgency) only confers a risk for prostate cancer of 3%.

### 12.2.3.3 SCREENING

In the context of a better value health check the aim of screening for prostate cancer is to identify high-risk, localised prostate cancer that can be successfully treated, thereby preventing the morbidity and mortality associated with advanced or metastatic prostate cancer.

Two screening options are suggested for prostate cancer screening: PSA testing and digital rectal examination (DRE).

*Prostate-specific antigen* (PSA) is a protein made by the prostate gland that naturally leaks into the bloodstream. Sometimes a raised PSA level can be a sign of prostate cancer. However, it can also be caused by an inflamed prostate (prostatitis) or the enlargement of the prostate gland that comes on with ageing (BPH).

There have been at least six trials of prostate cancer screening and most notable amongst these are the Prostate, Lung, Colorectal and Ovarian (PLCO) Cancer Screening Trial and the European Randomized Study of Screening for Prostate Cancer (ERSPC). In the latter study, PSA-based screening was reported to reduce deaths from prostate cancer by about 20% after 13 years of follow-up but was associated with a high risk of overdiagnosis.

A recent systematic review of all the available trial evidence concluded that some evidence from the randomised clinical trials shows that PSA-based screening programmes in men ages 55–69 years may prevent up to 1–2 deaths from prostate cancer per 1000 men screened. Screening programmes might also prevent up to 3 cases of metastatic prostate cancer per 1000 men screened. However, there appeared to be no mortality benefit of PSA-based screening for prostate cancer in men age 70 years and older.

It is also extremely important to be aware of the potential downsides of such screening. Thus, although 1–2 deaths from prostate cancer might be prevented for every 1000 men screened the following consequences need to be considered too:

- Approximately 120 men will have a false-positive result that leads to a biopsy. Importantly, prostatic biopsies are associated with significant complications, including pain, bleeding, infection and rarely sepsis. Approximately 1% of prostate biopsies result in issues requiring hospitalisation. The false-positive and complication rates from biopsy are also higher in older men. In addition, adverse psychological effects can occur in men who have had a prostate biopsy but are not diagnosed with prostate cancer.
- PSA-based screening for prostate cancer leads to the diagnosis of prostate cancer in some men whose cancer would never have become symptomatic during their lifetime. Treatment of these men provides them with no benefit (overdiagnosis). Follow-up of large randomised trials suggests that 20%–50% of men diagnosed with prostate cancer through screening may be overdiagnosed. Due to, in part, reduced life expectancy and delays in treatment benefits, overdiagnosis rates increase with age and are highest in men age 70 years and older.
- Approximately 100 men will be diagnosed with prostate cancer. Of these, 80 will require treatment (either immediately or after a period of active surveillance). Moreover, at least 60 individuals will experience a complication from any surgery or radiotherapy. Harms of prostate cancer treatment include erectile dysfunction, urinary incontinence and bothersome bowel symptoms. About one in five men who undergo a radical prostatectomy develop long-term urinary incontinence and two in three men experience erectile dysfunction. More than half of men who have radiation therapy experience erectile dysfunction and up to one in six men suffer from troublesome bowel symptoms, including bowel urgency and faecal incontinence.

*Digital rectal examination* (DRE) has been advocated for many years by health check organisations. However, the possible contribution of routine annual screening by rectal examination in reducing prostate cancer mortality remains unclear. Part of this problem undoubtedly relates to differences between examiners in relation to their skill and experience with the examination, especially in assessing the consistency and the surface nodularity of the gland. Moreover, a gland that feels normal does not exclude a tumour. In the Prostate Cancer Prevention Trial, the overall sensitivity of rectal examination for prostate cancer was reported as 16.7%. However, some have recommended that a rectal examination should be undertaken in men who elect to have a PSA test to reduce the numbers of false negatives from relying solely on PSA testing (up to 15% of cancers will have a normal PSA).

Based on the recent evidence review for the U.S. Preventive Services Task Force (USPSTF) together with some consensus statements from Prostate Cancer UK and recommendations from the American Cancer Society, the following suggestions are now made in relation to prostate cancer screening:

- Men should have a chance to make an informed decision about whether to be screened for prostate cancer, considering both benefits and risks if they are
  - Aged 50 years or more, are at average risk of prostate cancer and are expected to live at least 10 more years
  - Aged 45 years or more and are assessed as being at increased risk by virtue of a family history (one first-degree relative diagnosed with prostate cancer under the age of 65 years), ethnic origin or having erectile dysfunction
  - Aged 40 years or more and are assessed as being at very high risk by virtue of a particularly strong family history (i.e. more than one first-degree relative diagnosed with prostate cancer under the age of 65 years)

A number of shared decision-making tools are available but I find the following particularly helpful: https://www.asco.org/sites/new-www.asco.org/files/content-files/practice-and-guidelines/documents/2012-psa-pco-decision-aid.pdf

- Asymptomatic men at the appropriate age should consider a single baseline PSA test to help predict their future prostate cancer risk. If the PSA level is found to be above the age-specific median value they can be considered at higher than average risk of prostate cancer and should be encouraged to be re-tested in the future.
- As some men with prostate cancer will not have a raised PSA, a 'normal' PSA reading should also be treated with caution in the presence of symptoms such as
  - Having to rush to the toilet to pass urine
  - Difficulty in passing urine
  - Passing urine more often than usual, especially at night
  - Pain on passing urine
  - Blood in the urine or semen
  - Erectile dysfunction
  - Unexplained back pain

- Offer a rectal examination to all asymptomatic men who have decided to have a PSA test.

Attempts are being made to improve the usefulness of the PSA test and two specific developments are also worth considering:

1. *Free versus total PSA*. The amount of PSA in the blood that is free (i.e. not bound to other proteins) divided by the total amount of PSA (free plus bound) is denoted as the proportion of free PSA. The general opinion seems to be that a higher amount of free PSA is associated with a lower chance of prostate cancer. Some evidence also suggests that a lower proportion of free PSA might also be linked to more aggressive cancers.
2. *PSA velocity and PSA doubling time*. PSA velocity is the rate of change in a man's PSA level over time, expressed as nanogram per millilitre (ng/mL) per year. PSA doubling time is the period of time over which a man's PSA level doubles. Some evidence suggests that the rate of increase in a man's PSA level may be helpful in predicting whether he has prostate cancer. According to Loeb and colleagues, individuals with two successive PSA measurements with a change of more than 0.4 ng/mL/year had an eightfold greater risk of prostate cancer. But undertaking annual testing also needs to be balanced against the increased risks from false-positive results and overdiagnosis. Modelling studies have projected that screening intervals of 2 years will preserve most of the benefits of screening and reduce the harms. Ideally, this repeat testing should be undertaken by the same laboratory – using the same equipment – as there is always some slight variation between laboratories and techniques.

## 12.3 TESTICULAR CANCER

### 12.3.1 Importance

Testicular cancer is the most common cancer amongst males aged 15–34 years. However, with an annual incidence rate of 5.4 cases per 100,000 males it is relatively rare compared to other types of cancer, accounting for just 1% of all cancers in men globally.

The highest rates of testicular cancer are seen in New Zealand, the United Kingdom, Australia, Sweden, the United States, Poland and Spain. India, China and Colombia have the lowest incidences.

In recent decades, the incidence of testicular cancer has been increasing, with a doubling observed since the 1960s in Caucasian populations. However, despite the rise in incidence there has been a dramatic decrease in mortality as a result of effective treatments. Approximately 95% of men with localised testicular cancer (i.e. confined to the testis or only spread to nearby lymph nodes) will survive at least 5 years. Even for cancers that have spread further to distant lymph nodes and the other organs the 5-year survival is 80%.

## 12.3.2 Prevention

Most men with testicular cancer have no known risk factors and, moreover, many of these risk factors cannot be changed. For these reasons, it is not possible to prevent most cases of testicular cancer.

## 12.3.3 Earlier recognition

The low incidence of testicular cancer and the favourable survival outcomes in the absence of screening have led many to conclude that earlier recognition is likely to be of little benefit.

An updated systematic review performed on behalf of the USPSTF, published in 2010, found no randomised trials, cohort studies or case-control studies that examined the benefits of testicular cancer screening (whether by physical examination, self-examination or other screening tests) in an asymptomatic population. Likewise, a Cochrane Collaboration review failed to identify any randomised or quasi-randomised controlled trials that evaluated the effectiveness of screening by a health professional or patient self-examination in reducing mortality from testicular cancer.

However, as a possible component of a better value health check there is also a requirement to consider other outcomes aside from mortality in addition to costs along the subsequent care pathway. Although survival of later-stage testicular cancer has certainly improved dramatically with the advent of new therapies, the heavier burden of treatment required to effect a cure in the context of more advanced disease is associated with higher costs (to health services, individuals and employers) and greater morbidity (e.g. due to treatment side effects such as an increased risk of later cardiovascular disease, lung problems and infertility). Aberger and colleagues showed that treatment of one early testicular cancer is half the cost of an advanced case.

### 12.3.3.1 RISK ASSESSMENT

The following features are associated with an increased risk of testicular cancer:

- *Age*: Testicular tumours are most common in young men aged 18 to 45 years.
- *Ethnicity*: Testicular cancer is most common in Caucasians (it is four times more common amongst white men than black men). With the exception of New Zealand Maoris, the disease is rare in non-Caucasian populations.
- *Cryptorchidism* (testicular maldescent) is associated with a 3- to 17-fold increase in risk. Around 7%–10% of individuals with testicular cancer have a history of cryptorchidism. The risk also applies to the contralateral testis.
- *Inguinal/testicular problems in childhood* that increase risk: Mumps orchitis, inguinal hernia, testicular torsion, hydrocele and testicular atrophy.
- *Other developmental abnormalities*: Gonadal dysgenesis, Klinefelter's syndrome.

- *A family history of testicular cancer, testicular maldescent or cryptorchidism* are risk factors for testicular cancer. It has been estimated that the relative risk for first-degree relatives of a patient with testicular cancer is increased by a factor of 3–10 (at least 2% of patients are in this category).
- *Previous cancer in opposite testis* (4% risk of second cancer).

#### 12.3.3.2 SYMPTOMS AND SIGNS

*Early symptoms*

- Painless mass in testicle (i.e. enlarged testicle or a lump in the testicle) – most common symptom (over 86% of patients)
- Testicular discomfort or pain (31% of patients); a dragging sensation has been reported in 29% of patients
- Newly acquired hydrocele in young males
- 'Epididymitis' that fails to settle completely, 'epididymo-orchitis' not responding to antibiotics or 'recurrent epididymo-orchitis' (15% of patients)

*Later symptoms* include back pain, dyspnoea, abdominal discomfort/swelling and gynaecomastia.

#### 12.3.3.3 TESTICULAR AWARENESS

Most testicular cancers are first detected by men or their partners, either unintentionally or by self-examination. Some are discovered by routine physical examination by a clinician.

Individuals with a family history and those with a history of undescended testes or testicular atrophy should be informed of their potential increased risk for testicular cancer and be 'testes aware.' But there is, at present, no evidence that teaching young men how to examine themselves for testicular cancer would further reduce mortality rates, even amongst those at highest risk.

Clinicians undertaking health checks should also be alert for testicular cancer as a possible diagnosis when young men present with suggestive symptoms and signs. There is some evidence that men who initially present with symptoms of testicular cancer are commonly misdiagnosed with epididymitis, testicular trauma, hydrocele or other benign disorders. In one study 55% of patients eventually found to have cancer were treated initially for epididymitis.

Efforts to promote prompt assessment and better evaluation of testicular problems may be more effective than widespread screening as a means of encouraging earlier detection.

## 12.4 ERECTILE DYSFUNCTION

### 12.4.1 Importance

Erectile dysfunction is defined as the inability to achieve and maintain a penile erection adequate for satisfactory sexual intercourse.

It is estimated that around half of men over the age of 40 suffer from erectile dysfunction. Moreover, it is a worldwide problem and the projections for 2025 suggest a prevalence of approximately 322 million, an increase of nearly 170 million men since 1995. Over the next few years, the largest increases are likely to be in Asia, Africa and South America. The condition has an increasing prevalence with age. However, much of erectile dysfunction is not reported.

Erectile dysfunction matters not only because of the distress it can cause but also because it can be an early sign of underlying health problems such as diabetes, cardiovascular disease and prostate cancer. It can also affect the quality of life for men and their partners and is associated with relationship difficulties.

Erectile dysfunction is linked with an increased risk of cardiovascular disease especially in men with features of metabolic syndrome (i.e. being overweight, increased waist circumference, having raised blood glucose and triglyceride levels, a low HDL cholesterol, microalbuminuria and hypertension). Changes in the small blood vessels supplying the penis are proposed as a sensitive and early indicator of problems that might then arise in the arteries supplying the heart and brain.

### 12.4.2 Prevention

Individuals who smoke, are obese, have diabetes (or impaired glucose regulation) and undertake little exercise are at particular risk of developing erectile dysfunction.

However, in the context of a health check erectile dysfunction should really be viewed more as a risk marker for a variety of other conditions: cardiovascular disease, increased cardiovascular risk, type 2 diabetes (undiagnosed or inadequately controlled), testosterone deficiency, thyroid dysfunction, prostate cancer and anxiety or depression.

### 12.4.3 Earlier recognition

Checking for erectile dysfunction should be considered in all men over the age of 40.

The Sexual Health Inventory for Men (SHIM) is a well-validated five-question screening questionnaire. The sensitivity for erectile dysfunction has been reported as 98% and the specificity as 88% with excellent reliability (kappa 0.82).

The SHIM consists of five questions and, using a scoring system, the erectile dysfunction can also be classified into five severity levels (http://www.fycurology.com/shim-erectile-dysfunction-score-sheet.pdf).

In relation to a health check, individuals identified as having erectile dysfunction should be formally assessed for cardiovascular risk/risk factors, diabetes risk or, in those who already have diabetes, diabetic control and also be offered PSA testing (if over the age of 45 years).

Other causes for erectile dysfunction also need to be borne in mind such as testosterone deficiency and the side effects of a variety of medications, surgery and radiotherapy in addition to neurological or anatomical problems plus underlying anxiety or depression.

Approximately 40% of men aged 45 years or older are affected by testosterone deficiency but less than 5% will have been diagnosed and treated for this condition. In addition to erectile dysfunction, symptoms of low testosterone include mood changes, reduced libido, low energy, decreased muscle bulk and strength, hot flushes and a decreased ability to concentrate.

So, in the context of a health check the following investigations might be considered for an individual with erectile dysfunction: full lipid profile, HbA1c, PSA, testosterone (morning), thyroid function, prolactin, blood pressure, body composition, Patient Health Questionnaire (PHQ-9) (depression) and Generalised Anxiety Disorder Seven-Item Scale (GAD-7).

Stopping smoking, regular exercise, weight loss and improved control of any cardiovascular risk factors such as glucose/diabetes, hypertension and elevated lipids are recommended interventions aside from the actual treatment of the erectile dysfunction.

## FURTHER READING

### Prostate cancer

American Cancer Society Recommendations for Prostate Cancer Early Detection. April 2016. https://www.cancer.org/cancer/prostate-cancer/early-detection/acs-recommendations.html

Andriole GL, Crawford ED, Grubb RL et al. Prostate cancer screening in the randomized Prostate, Lung, Colorectal, and Ovarian Cancer Screening Trial: Mortality results after 13 years of follow-up. *J Natl Cancer Inst* 2012;104:125–132.

Fenton JJ, Werich MS, Durbin S, Liu Y, Bang H, Melnikow J. *Prostate-Specific Antigen–Based Screening for Prostate Cancer: A Systematic Evidence Review for the U.S. Preventive Services Task Force. Evidence Synthesis No. 154. AHRQ Publication No. 17-05229-EF-1.* Rockville, MD: Agency for Healthcare Research and Quality, 2017.

Fleshner N, Ivers N, Lukka H, Shayegan B, Walker-Dilks C, Winquist E, *Genitourinary cancer disease site group. Risk reduction of prostate cancer with drugs or nutritional supplements.* Toronto: Cancer Care Ontario, 2012.

Loeb S, Metter EJ, Kan D et al. Prostate-specific antigen velocity risk count improves the specificity of screening for clinically significant prostate cancer. *BJU Int* 2012;109:508–514.

Prostate Cancer UK. *A Summary of the Prostate Cancer Risk Management Programme and Prostate Cancer UK's Consensus Statements on PSA Testing: Information for GPs in the UK.* London: Prostate Cancer UK, 2016.

Schröder FH, Hugosson J, Roobol MJ et al. Screening and prostate cancer mortality: Results of the European Randomised Study of Screening for Prostate Cancer (ERSPC) at 13 years of follow-up. *Lancet* 2014;384:2027–2035.
Thompson IM, Goodman PJ, Tangen CM et al. The influence of finasteride on the development of prostate cancer. *N Engl J Med* 2003;349:215–224.
Thompson IM, Tangen CM, Goodman PJ et al. Finasteride improves the sensitivity of digital rectal examination for prostate cancer detection. *J Urol* 2007;177:1749–1752.
Wilt TJ, Macdonald R, Hagerty K et al. 5-α-Reductase inhibitors for prostate cancer chemoprevention: An updated Cochrane systematic review. *BJU Int* 2010;106:1444–1451.
U.S. Preventive Services Task Force. Draft Recommendation Statement: Prostate Cancer: Screening. April 2017. https://www.uspreventiveservicestaskforce.org/Page/Document/draft-recommendation-statement/prostate-cancer-screening1

## Testicular cancer

Aberger M, Wilson B, Holzbeierlein JM et al. Testicular self-examination and testicular cancer: A cost-utility analysis. *Cancer Med* 2014;3:1629–1634.
Ilic D, Misso ML. Screening for testicular cancer. *Cochrane Database of Systematic Reviews* 2011;(2):CD007853.
Lin K, Sharangpani R. Screening for testicular cancer: An evidence review for the U.S. Preventive Services Task Force. *Ann Intern Med* 2010;153:396–399.
Shanmugalingam T, Soultati A, Chowdhury S et al. Global incidence and outcome of testicular cancer. *Clin Epidemiol* 2013;5:417–427.
U.S. Preventive Services Task Force. Screening for testicular cancer: U.S. Preventive Services Task Force reaffirmation recommendation statement. *Ann Intern Med* 2011;154:483–486.
U.S. Preventive Services Task Force. Screening for testicular cancer: Recommendation statement. *Am Fam Physician* 2005;72:2069–2070.

## Erectile dysfunction

Ayta IA, McKinlay JB, Krane RJ. The likely worldwide increase in erectile dysfunction between 1995 and 2025 and some possible policy consequences. *BJU Int* 1999;84:50–56.
Cappelleri JC, Rosen RC. The Sexual Health Inventory for Men (SHIM): A five-year review of research and clinical experience. *Int J Impot Res.* 2005;17:307–319.
Heruti RJ, Yossef M, Shochat T. Screening for erectile dysfunction as part of periodic examination programs – Concept and implementation. *Int J Impot Res* 2004;16:341–345.

McKinlay JB. The worldwide prevalence and epidemiology of erectile dysfunction. *Int J Impot Res* 2000;12(Suppl 4):S6–S11.
Muneer A, Kalsi J, Nazareth I, Arya M. Erectile dysfunction. *BMJ* 2014;348:g129. doi:10.1136/bmj.g129
Rew KT, Heidelbaugh JJ. Erectile dysfunction. *Am Fam Physician* 2016;94:820–827.
Rosen RC, Cappelleri JC, Smith MD et al. Development and evaluation of an abridged, 5-item version of the International Index of Erectile Function (IIEF-5) as a diagnostic tool for erectile dysfunction. *Int J Impot Res* 1999;11:319–326.

# 13

# Women's health

## KEY RECOMMENDATIONS

- For those designing a better value health check incorporating a focus on women's health it is suggested that the following conditions warrant particular consideration: breast cancer, ovarian cancer and cervical cancer.
- Identify women at increased risk of breast cancer with a view to discussing chemoprevention.
- Regular breast cancer screening is recommended using mammography.
- Annual cancer antigen 125 (CA-125) testing (and tracking trends) should be considered to improve the earlier recognition of ovarian cancer.
- Do not undertake routine pelvic examination as a screening test for ovarian cancer.
- In assessing hereditary breast or ovarian cancer risk the Familial Risk Assessment – Breast and Ovarian Cancer (FRA-BOC) tool is recommended.
- The Manchester Scoring System is suggested to assist in assessing an individual's likelihood of having a *BRCA* mutation.
- Cervical cancer screening should be undertaken using a combination of liquid-based cytology and human papillomavirus (HPV) testing.

## 13.1 OVERVIEW

In terms of developing a better value health check incorporating a focus on women's health it is suggested that the key priorities are breast cancer, ovarian cancer and cervical cancer. However, it is important to be aware that many countries already have high-quality breast cancer screening, human papillomavirus (HPV) immunisation and cervical cancer screening programmes in place and, therefore, those developing health checks need to carefully consider whether they can enhance value in relation to any current services.

There are some other areas that have been considered for inclusion within this chapter but, at present, I felt that the evidence of benefit in terms of delivering value was not sufficiently mature. Key amongst these is 'pre-pregnancy' screening for younger women; I have certainly developed programmes myself that include both an assessment of ovarian reserve and function (using anti-Müllerian hormone, prolactin and follicle-stimulating hormone) combined with testing for thyroid function, glucose, coeliac disease, folic acid, vitamin $B_{12}$, vitamin D, rubella/chickenpox immunity and anaemia. For those women contemplating embarking on pregnancy it also presents a good opportunity to ensure they are adopting a healthy lifestyle, to review their personal and family medical history, and to start on an appropriate dose of folic acid. However, the other issue that needs to be borne in mind in relation to pre-pregnancy health checks, is that the outcomes are obviously dependent on two people.

I would also recommend that individuals who are pregnant (or think they might be pregnant) ought not to undergo routine health checks but, rather, should remain under regular antenatal surveillance by an appropriately trained clinician incorporating more tailored measurements (e.g. blood pressure, urinalysis, weight and foetal assessments) together with testing for anaemia, glucose and certain sexually transmitted conditions. It also presents an opportunity to promote breastfeeding.

Finally, women's health is also, of course, not simply about the conditions focused on in this chapter but also includes all the gender-non-specific diseases and disorders addressed elsewhere.

## 13.2 BREAST CANCER

### 13.2.1 Importance

Breast cancer is the most common cancer among women globally with an estimated 1.67 million new cancer cases diagnosed in 2012 (25% of all cancers). Incidence rates vary nearly fourfold across the world's regions, with rates ranging from 27 per 100,000 in Middle Africa and Eastern Asia to 92 in Northern America. The number of cases worldwide has significantly increased since the 1970s, a phenomenon partly attributed to the adoption of Western lifestyles. Each year in the United States, there are around 250,000 cases of invasive breast cancer and 40,000 deaths.

Breast cancer is now the most frequent cause of cancer death in women in less-developed regions. The low survival rates in these countries can be explained mainly by the lack of early detection programmes, resulting in a high proportion of women presenting with late-stage disease, as well as by the lack of adequate diagnosis and treatment facilities.

### 13.2.2 Prevention

In the context of health check individuals should be made aware that the following factors might increase the risk of breast cancer: obesity, lack of exercise and alcohol intake. Serious consideration should be given to reducing excessive alcohol intake (associated with breast cancer in a dose-dependent fashion), maintaining a healthy weight and exercising for 30 minutes most days of the week.

The U.S. Preventive Services Task Force (USPSTF) recommends that clinicians engage in shared, informed decision making with women who are at increased risk for breast cancer about medications to reduce their risk. For women who are at increased risk for breast cancer and at low risk for adverse medication effects, clinicians should offer to prescribe risk-reducing medications, such as tamoxifen or raloxifene. More specifically, the UK National Institute for Health and Care Excellence has recommended offering the following:

- Tamoxifen for 5 years to pre-menopausal women at high risk of breast cancer unless they have a history or may be at increased risk of thromboembolic disease or endometrial cancer
- Anastrozole for 5 years to post-menopausal women at high risk of breast cancer unless they have severe osteoporosis

## 13.2.3 Earlier recognition

### 13.2.3.1 RISK ASSESSMENT

In relation to assessing an individual's baseline breast cancer risk, it is suggested that particular attention is paid to the following:

*Age*: The risk of breast cancer rises rapidly after the age of 40–50 years.

*Hormone replacement therapy (HRT)*: Use of combined hormone therapy after menopause increases the risk of breast cancer. This enhanced risk can be seen with as little as 2 years of use but disappears within about 5 years of stopping.

*Ionising radiation*: Exposure of the breast to ionising radiation (e.g. after treatment for Hodgkin's lymphoma) is associated with an increased risk of developing breast cancer, starting 10 years after exposure and persisting lifelong. Risk depends on dose and age of exposure, with the highest risk occurring after irradiation during puberty.

*Personal history of breast cancer*: Women who develop breast cancer are more likely to develop a second breast cancer.

*Certain benign breast conditions*:

a. *Proliferative lesions without atypia* seem to raise a woman's risk of breast cancer slightly. They include ductal hyperplasia (without atypia), fibroadenoma, sclerosing adenosis, papillomatosis and radial scar.
b. *Proliferative lesions with atypia* include atypical ductal hyperplasia and atypical lobular hyperplasia. Breast cancer risk is raised three and a half to five times higher than normal in women with these changes.
c. *Lobular carcinoma in situ* confers a much higher risk of developing cancer in either breast.

*Reproductive/menstrual history*: The following are associated with an increased risk of breast cancer: nulliparity, late pregnancy (i.e. first child born after the age of 30 years), early menarche (under age 12 years) and late menopause (after age 55 years). However, breastfeeding (linked to the *cumulative* period of breastfeeding for all children) reduces the risk of developing breast cancer.

*Family history*: Breast cancer has a large (and complex) familial component. It has been estimated that over a quarter of younger patients with breast cancer have a strong family history.

In the context of a health check, it is suggested that particular attention is paid to attempting to identify those with the following family histories:

1. At least one first-degree female relative with breast cancer diagnosed under the age of 40 years
2. At least one second-degree paternal or maternal female relative with breast cancer diagnosed under the age of 40 years
3. Two first- or second-degree relatives diagnosed with breast cancer (or two first- or second-degree relatives with either breast cancer or ovarian cancer) at any age
4. A first-degree relative with bilateral breast cancer at any age (especially if first primary was diagnosed at younger than 50 years of age)
5. Male breast cancer in a first-degree relative at any age
6. Complicated cancer family histories (i.e. multiple cancers, sarcoma, glioma especially if at ages under 50 years)

(*NB*: Ashkenazi Jewish heritage also confers an increased risk for hereditary breast cancer.)

In assessing hereditary breast cancer risk, the Familial Risk Assessment – Breast and Ovarian Cancer (FRA-BOC) tool is helpful: https://canceraustralia.gov.au/clinical-best-practice/gynaecological-cancers/familial-risk-assessment-fra-boc

In assessing general breast cancer risk, the following tool is useful: http://www.cancer.gov/bcrisktool/.

#### 13.2.3.2 SYMPTOMS AND SIGNS

In the context of a health check, it is suggested that particular attention is paid to the presence of new breast lumps or masses, nipple discharge, nipple distortion/retraction, eczema-like skin rashes, breast contour change or intractable or unilateral breast pain.

It is also important to be aware that around a quarter of individuals with breast cancer may present with symptoms other than lumps. These women unfortunately often suffer the longest delays and the worst outcomes.

#### 13.2.3.3 SCREENING

A number of screening modalities have been suggested for breast cancer: clinical breast examination, breast self-examination, screening mammography or magnetic resonance imaging of the breast.

*Clinical breast examination* is often undertaken in individuals attending for health checks. However, there is a need to be aware of the limitations (in terms of reliability and accuracy) of the clinical examination and that negative findings (e.g. in the context of some specific symptoms or medical history) might still warrant further investigation.

The accuracy of breast examination varies with the size of the tumour and the age of the patient. The sensitivity is about 88% for lumps larger than 1 cm but only 34%–55% for lumps smaller than 1 cm. The examination is also less accurate for younger women and the sensitivity may be as low as 37% in women under the age of 35. Moreover, there is no evidence for any impact of clinical breast examination on mortality rates.

Some have advocated undertaking both clinical breast examination *and* mammography in the context of a health check. However, there is also no evidence for any additional mortality benefit gained by combining the two modalities and might simply increase false-positive findings from 0.89% to 3% resulting in more unnecessary biopsies.

*Breast self-examination* is not recommended as a screening test as the sensitivity is approximately 26% with no evidence for any impact on death rates. The health check should be used as an opportunity to encourage women to become 'breast aware' by

- Knowing what is normal for them
- Encouraging them to look at their breasts and feel them
- Knowing what changes to look for
- Reporting any changes to a doctor without delay
- Attending routine breast screening with mammography

*Mammography* is 68%–88% sensitive and 95%–98% specific (based on data from trials that used mammography alone). The sensitivity appears to be lower for women under the age of 50 years, possibly related to breast density or to the more rapid growth of cancers in younger women.

Several trials have reported that screening mammography reduces the risk of death from breast cancer. In a pooled analysis of all these studies, it was concluded that screening was associated with a reduction in breast cancer mortality of around 20% for all women at average risk. Average risk is defined as those *without*

- A personal history of breast cancer, and/or
- A confirmed or suspected genetic mutation in a breast cancer susceptibility gene known to increase risk of breast cancer (e.g. *BRCA1*, *BRCA2*), and/or
- A history of previous radiotherapy to the chest at a young age

Providing biennial screening mammography for women aged 50–74 years at average risk has been categorised as high-value care. Over the age of 75 years, it is suggested that screening should only be offered to those in good health with a life expectancy of at least 10 years. Although the sensitivity and specificity of mammography increase with age, overdiagnosis also rises because of reduced life expectancy and a greater proportion of slower-growing cancers.

At a health check it is always important that those undergoing mammography are informed about the benefits and harms of breast screening. Potential risks of mammography include false-positive results, overdiagnosis, false-negative results, false reassurance and procedure-associated pain. However, there is no direct evidence that ionising radiation from mammography causes breast cancer. In facilitating informed choice, the following link to a 16-page leaflet, available in 18 languages, is extremely helpful (https://www.gov.uk/government/publications/breast-screening-helping-women-decide).

For those involved in a health check it is also recommended that the radiologist is informed about any symptoms, past medical history, current treatments (especially hormone replacement therapy), family history and findings from the clinical examination. This additional information always adds value to their interpretation of the mammogram.

Routine breast screening for women under the age of 50 years remains an area of controversy. However, in considering an individual's baseline risk it is clear that younger women with, for example, a breast cancer family history, may benefit from mammography as much as older women with fewer risk factors. Attention needs to be given to the benefits and harms of screening, as well as to a woman's preferences and breast cancer risk profile. For many women, the potential reduction in breast cancer mortality rate associated with screening mammography will outweigh all other considerations.

The decision to start screening mammography in women prior to age 50 years at average risk should be an individual one after discussion of the following issues:

- While screening mammography in women aged 40–49 years may reduce the risk of breast cancer death, the number of deaths averted is smaller than that in older women and the number of false-positive results and unnecessary biopsies is greater.
- In addition to false-positive results and unnecessary biopsies, all women undergoing regular screening mammography are at risk for the diagnosis and treatment of non-invasive and invasive breast cancer that would otherwise not have become a threat to their health, or even apparent, during their lifetime. Beginning mammography screening at a younger age and screening more frequently may increase the risk for such overdiagnosis and subsequent overtreatment.

It is also important to be aware that annual mammography screening provides significant additional benefit over biennial screening in pre-menopausal women.

*Magnetic resonance imaging of the breast* is not currently recommended for breast cancer screening in the general population. However, it might be appropriate for certain groups; for example

- Women with a known *BRCA* mutation
- Women who are untested but have a first-degree relative with a *BRCA* mutation
- Women who were treated for Hodgkin disease with radiation to the chest at a young age

#### 13.2.3.4 GENETIC TESTING FOR *BRCA*-RELATED BREAST AND OVARIAN CANCERS

A *BRCA* mutation can affect either *BRCA1* or *BRCA2* tumour suppressor genes.

On average, around 12.3% of women will develop breast cancer during their lifetime and 1.4% of women will develop ovarian cancer. However, the cumulative breast cancer risk to age 80 years is 72% for *BRCA1* and 69% for *BRCA2* mutation carriers. Moreover, the cumulative ovarian cancer risk to age 80 years is 44% for *BRCA1* and 17% for *BRCA2* mutation carriers.

In the general population, these mutations occur in an estimated 0.2%–0.3% of women but the prevalence is around 2.1% amongst Ashkenazi Jewish women.

Family history factors associated with increased likelihood of potentially harmful *BRCA* mutations include

- Breast cancer diagnoses before age 50 years in blood relatives
- Bilateral breast cancer in a female relative
- Family history of breast *and* ovarian cancer
- Presence of breast cancer in a male family member
- Multiple cases of breast cancer in the family
- Family history of pancreatic, colon or prostate cancer

Several familial risk stratification tools are available to assist in assessing an individual's likelihood of a *BRCA* mutation such as the Ontario Family History Assessment Tool, the Manchester Scoring System and FHS-7. The Manchester Scoring System is straightforward to use and focuses on the following factors:

- Age at onset of female breast cancer
- Age at onset of male breast cancer
- Age at onset of ovarian cancer
- Pancreatic cancer at any age
- Age at onset of prostate cancer

The overall score is calculated by adding up the values for each cancer in a direct blood lineage (all individual cancers must be on the same side of the family).

Tests for *BRCA* mutations are highly sensitive and specific for known mutations, but the interpretation of results is complex and generally requires post-test counselling. Test results for genetic mutations are reported as positive (that is, potentially harmful mutation detected), variants of uncertain clinical significance, uninformative-negative or true-negative. Women who have relatives with known *BRCA* mutations can be reassured about their inherited risk for a potentially harmful mutation if the results are negative (that is, a true-negative). An uninformative-negative result occurs when a woman's test does not detect a potentially harmful mutation but no relatives have been tested or no mutations have been detected in tested relatives.

Interventions in women who are *BRCA* mutation carriers include earlier, more frequent or intensive cancer screening; risk-reducing medications (e.g. tamoxifen or raloxifene); and risk-reducing surgery (e.g. mastectomy or salpingo-oophorectomy).

## 13.3 OVARIAN CANCER

### 13.3.1 Importance

Ovarian cancer accounts for 4% of all cancers in women, with over 200,000 diagnoses each year worldwide. It is the fourth most common cause of death from cancer amongst women in the developed world and, despite advances in treatment, there has been little change in the mortality rate with an average 5-year survival of about 35%.

Earlier stage ovarian cancer is associated with improved outcomes: in the United Kingdom, survival for cancers at stage 1 is 80%–90% compared with 20% for stage 3. Moreover, there is also a significant impact on total healthcare expenditure as it is clear that picking up an early stage ovarian cancer is cheaper both in relation to the initial treatment and also the costs linked to recurrence (Table 13.1).

These health costs will be mirrored by the costs for individuals and organisations. However, currently only 30% of individuals are diagnosed at an early stage so there is a clear opportunity to deliver much better value care. It takes several years for a new ovarian cancer to progress to an advanced stage, providing an estimated window of opportunity for early detection of 4.3 years.

### 13.3.2 Prevention

There is no known way to prevent ovarian cancer, but some factors seem to be associated with a lower chance of getting ovarian cancer:

- Combined oral contraceptive use for at least 5 years
- Increasing parity
- Gynaecological surgery (i.e. tubal ligation and simple hysterectomy)
- Bilateral oophorectomy
- Breastfeeding for a year or more

Table 13.1 Ovarian cancer treatment costs by disease stage

| Ovarian cancer stage | Treatment costs per person (United Kingdom) | Treatment costs per person if any recurrence (United Kingdom) |
|---|---|---|
| 1 | £5328 | £1504 |
| 2 | £10,217 | £8623 |
| 3 | £11,207 | £12,276 |
| 4 | £15,081 | N/A |

## 13.3.3 Earlier recognition

### 13.3.3.1 RISK ASSESSMENT

The following features seem to be associated with an increased risk for ovarian cancer:

*Age*: Most ovarian cancers occur in women over the age of 45 years (majority post-menopausal, with the peak at age 65–75 years).
*Obesity*: There is some evidence that women with a body mass index greater than 30 have a higher risk of developing ovarian cancer.
*Breast cancer*: A personal history of breast cancer might confer an increased risk for developing ovarian cancer.
*Family history*: Ovarian cancer has a large (and complex) familial component; it has been estimated that a family history is present in between 5% and 10% of women with ovarian cancer. A family history of ovarian cancer in a first- or second-degree relative is one of the strongest risk factors for ovarian cancer. In the context of a health check it is suggested that particular attention is paid to identifying the following:

1. One or more first- or second-degree relatives affected with probable ovarian cancer at any age. A reported history of, for example, 'stomach' or 'womb' cancer in a family with a history of breast and ovarian cancer should always raise the suspicion that this could have been ovarian.
2. Breast cancer-ovarian cancer syndrome (e.g. due to *BRCA1 or BRCA2* mutations). In addition to cases of ovarian cancer, particular attention should also be directed towards identifying breast cancer cases diagnosed under the age of 60 years and male breast cancer at any age.
3. Cancer family syndromes. It is important to seek to identify other cancers in the family aside from ovarian and breast (i.e. colorectal, gastric, small bowel and endometrial). Lifetime risks of ovarian cancer associated with hereditary nonpolyposis colon cancer vary between 9% and 12%.

In assessing hereditary ovarian cancer risk, the FRA-BOC risk assessment tool is helpful (https://canceraustralia.gov.au/clinical-best-practice/gynaecological-cancers/familial-risk-assessment-fra-boc).

Also, please see Section 13.2.3.4 on *BRCA* testing.

### 13.3.3.2 SYMPTOMS

Ovarian cancer is challenging to detect as the symptoms are often vague and non-specific. Certain symptoms are said to occur more frequently in women with ovarian cancer (i.e. abdominal bloating; unexplained pelvic/abdominal pain; unexplained loss of appetite, weight loss or feeling full quickly; urinary symptoms (urgency or frequency); and persistent changes to bowel habits such as unexplained constipation or more frequent or loose motions).

However, such symptoms are common and therefore in the context of a health check it is suggested that particular attention is paid to presence of the following:

- The combination of bloating, increased abdominal size and urinary symptoms. According to Goff and colleagues, this cluster was found in 43% of those with cancer but in only 8% of those presenting to primary care clinics without cancer.
- The frequency at which individuals experience bloating, increased abdominal size, pelvic or abdominal pain, difficulty eating or feeling full quickly and urinary symptoms (urgency or frequency) in addition to the speed of onset and severity of these symptoms. For example,
    - Any of the following symptoms at least 12 times per month (but present for less than 1 year): pelvic or abdominal pain, urinary urgency or frequency, increased abdominal size/bloating; difficulty eating or feeling full
    - Any of the following symptoms for at least a week during the previous year: urinary frequency or urgency, abdominal distension or bloating, pelvic or abdominal pain, loss of appetite

- A history of unsuccessful treatments for irritable bowel syndrome or urine infections.
- In 15% of women there is post-menopausal bleeding or, in younger women, menstrual irregularity.

The UK National Institute for Health and Care Excellence (NICE) recommended that women with symptoms that might be caused by ovarian cancer should be offered a cancer antigen 125 (CA-125) blood test.

#### 13.3.3.3 PELVIC EXAMINATION

Traditionally, pelvic examinations have been included within health checks with a view to detecting ovarian cancer. However, based on a comprehensive review of the research evidence by the American College of Physicians it has been concluded that there are no data supporting the use of the pelvic examination in asymptomatic women. Moreover, they can cause pain, discomfort, fear, anxiety or embarrassment in around 30% of women.

Even in individuals with symptoms, the bimanual pelvic examination exhibits low sensitivity and specificity and poor reliability.

#### 13.3.3.4 SCREENING

In 2011, the Prostate, Lung, Colorectal and Ovarian (PLCO) randomised controlled trial of ovarian cancer screening with CA-125 and transvaginal ultrasound (TVUS) concluded that, after 13 years of follow-up, simultaneous screening with these modalities did not reduce ovarian cancer mortality. Moreover, the screening caused significant harms, most notably from the further diagnostic evaluation (mainly surgery-related complications) in the 5% of individuals with false-positive results.

However, modelling studies that used data from the PLCO trial suggested that up to a third of the ovarian cancer cases could have been detected earlier if the trends in CA-125 values had been used instead of a fixed cutoff.

In the UK Collaborative Trial of Ovarian Cancer Screening, 202,638 women aged 50–74 years were randomly allocated into three groups. One group had no screening, the second group annual screening with TVUS and the third group multimodal screening (MMS). MMS involved measuring CA-125 each year and then using an algorithm (Risk of Ovarian Cancer Algorithm [ROCA]) to stratify an individual as normal, intermediate or elevated risk. Importantly, ROCA looks at changes in CA-125 over time after a baseline measure rather than relying on a single cutoff point.

Each of these three risk levels was then associated with a specific management approach:

- *Normal risk*: Annual screening path
- *Intermediate risk*: Repeat CA-125 in 12 weeks path
- *Elevated risk*: Ultrasound path

After 14 years of overall follow-up, the relative reduction in ovarian cancer mortality compared to no screening in the TVUS arm was 11% and in the MMS group 14%. Although these results were not statistically significant it was found that excluding the cancers likely to be present at the start of the study gave a relative mortality reduction in the MMS group of 28%.

Based on this trial it would seem more sensible to consider annual CA-125 testing in women over the age of 50 (and from age 40/45 if at increased baseline risk). Attention should be focused on both the absolute CA-125 level in addition to the trends from year to year. However, it is also important to ensure individuals are aware that CA-125 can be high in many normal or benign conditions, such as pregnancy, menstruation, endometriosis and pelvic inflammatory disease, in addition to understanding the consequences of any false positives in terms of further investigations. Also, around 15% of women with ovarian cancer will not have a raised CA-125 result.

Although ovarian cancer screening using annual CA-125 testing remains controversial, this seems likely to be a much better value option in terms of outcomes and costs. The alternative is to simply continue to rely on the vagaries of clinicians actually considering CA-125 testing when faced with yet another individual with a vague or unexplained abdominal, pelvic or urinary symptom.

## 13.4 CERVICAL CANCER

### 13.4.1 Importance

Cervical cancer is the fourth most common cancer in women with over 500,000 new cases each year worldwide. In the United Kingdom, 2900 women are diagnosed with cervical cancer with just under 1000 dying of the condition annually.

A large majority (around 85%) of the global burden occurs in the less-developed regions, where it accounts for almost 12% of all female cancers. Cervical cancer remains the most common cancer in women in eastern and middle Africa.

Almost all types of cervical cancer are now thought to be associated with HPV infection, most particularly HPV type 16 and HPV type 18. The prevalence of

HPV also varies geographically with the highest rates in sub-Saharan Africa, Latin America and India.

## 13.4.2 Prevention

There are three main approaches to preventing cervical cancer:

- Avoid contact with the HPV by adopting safe sexual practices such as the use of condoms and restricting the number of sexual partners.
- HPV immunisation. In the United Kingdom, all girls aged 12–13 are offered HPV immunisation as part of the National Health Service childhood vaccination programme. Ideally, women should get the vaccine before they become sexually active and exposed to HPV. Females who are sexually active may also benefit from immunisation, but they might get less benefit because they may have already been exposed to one or more of the HPV types targeted by the vaccines. However, few sexually active young women are infected with all HPV types prevented by the vaccines, so most young women could still get protection by getting vaccinated. It is also very important to appreciate that no vaccine provides complete protection against all cancer-causing types of HPV, so routine cervical cancer screening is still necessary.
- Cigarette smoking doubles the risk of cervical cancer. Therefore, serious consideration should be given to stopping smoking.

## 13.4.3 Earlier recognition

### 13.4.3.1 RISK ASSESSMENT

About 95% of women with invasive cervical cancer have evidence of HPV infection. However, many women with HPV infection never develop cervical cancer and it is therefore considered that HPV infection is *necessary* but not *sufficient* for development of cancer. Aside from smoking, other factors that increase the risk of cervical cancer in HPV-infected women include the following:

*Immune deficiency.* This may be caused by, for example, HIV infection, organ transplant or long-term immunosuppressant use.

*High parity.* The odds ratio for women with seven or more full-term pregnancies is 3.8 compared to nulliparous women.

*Long-term use of oral contraceptives.* The odds ratio for women who used oral contraceptives for 5–9 years is 2.8, and for 10 or more years the odds ratio is 4.

*Family history.* If an individual's mother or sister had cervical cancer the chances of developing the disease are increased two- to threefold.

### 13.4.3.2 SYMPTOMS

In the context of a health check it is important to appreciate that certain symptoms occur more frequently in women with cervical cancer (i.e. inter-menstrual bleeding, post-coital bleeding, post-menopausal bleeding, vaginal discharge [blood stained] and pelvic pain).

#### 13.4.3.3 SCREENING

The Papanicolaou (Pap) cervical cytology smear has been the mainstay of cervical cancer screening for 60 years. An abnormal cytologic report then requires biopsy and confirmation by histology. The sensitivity of cytology has been reported as 78% with a specificity of 62%, but it is important to appreciate that there are significant variations between cytology laboratories and countries, with some reporting sensitivities as low as 30%. In recent years, there has been a shift from cervical cytology smears to liquid-based cytology.

The evidence indicates that regular Pap screening decreases cervical cancer incidence and mortality by at least 80%. However, it also leads to additional diagnostic procedures (e.g. colposcopy) and treatment for low-grade squamous intra-epithelial lesions, that often regress without treatment.

HPV testing was originally used as reflex testing (after the cytologic diagnosis of atypical squamous cells) to help to triage atypical Pap smears to colposcopy or close follow-up.

Nowadays, HPV testing is increasingly being applied in two ways:

1. *Combination testing using HPV plus cytology.* For example, based on a careful review of the available evidence, the USPSTF recommends screening women aged 21–65 with cytology every 3 years or, for women aged 30–65 years who want to lengthen the screening interval, using a combination of cytology and HPV testing every 5 years. However, although co-testing is more sensitive in detecting cervical abnormalities, it is associated with more false positives than the Pap test alone. Abnormal test results can lead to more frequent re-testing and invasive diagnostic procedures.
2. *Primary HPV testing with cytology or colposcopy triage.* In the United Kingdom, the NHS approach is currently shifting towards using high-risk HPV testing as the first-line screening test with cytology being undertaken on those samples testing positive for HPV amongst women aged 25–64. The high-risk HPV test can specifically identify the key HPV types HPV-16 and HPV-18 in addition to testing for 12 other high-risk types, such as HPV-31 and HPV-45.

The view from an expert panel in the United States is now also that primary high-risk HPV screening can be considered as an alternative to current U.S. cytology-based cervical cancer screening approaches including cytology alone and co-testing. HPV testing and reflex cytology represent good value by achieving a reasonable balance of disease detection in relation to the number of screening tests and the subsequent colposcopies required. However, primary screening for high-risk HPV should not be used for women younger than 25 as HPV infections are common in this age group and often resolve without treatment.

Other key recommendations on cervical screening for average-risk women are as follows:

- Screening should commence at age 21.
- Women over 65 years of age who have had regular screening in the previous 10 years (i.e. three consecutive negative cytology tests or two consecutive negative co-test results with the most recent test occurring within the last 5 years) should stop cervical cancer screening as long as they have not had any serious pre-cancers (like CIN2 or CIN3) found in the last 20 years. Women with a history of CIN2 or CIN3 should continue to have testing for at least 20 years after the abnormality was found.
- Women who have had a total hysterectomy should stop screening unless the hysterectomy was done as a treatment for cervical pre-cancer (or cancer). Women who have had a hysterectomy without removal of the cervix (called a supra-cervical hysterectomy) should also continue cervical cancer screening.

Women who are at high risk of cervical cancer because of a suppressed immune system may need to be screened more often. For example, the above guidance does not apply to women who have been diagnosed with HIV infection. These women should have follow-up testing and cervical cancer screening as recommended by their own healthcare team.

In the context of a health check it is also important to appreciate that taking a sample from the cervix incorporates visualising the cervix. On speculum examination, invasive cervical cancer may appear necrotic, ulcerated or as a protuberant 'cauliflower' lesion. It is therefore recommended that any lesion on the cervix that bleeds easily on gentle examination should be regarded with suspicion even if a recent smear has been reported as normal.

One of the remaining issues about cervical screening is to improve coverage. More than 90% of women in low- and middle-income countries have never had a Pap smear because of a lack of infrastructure and the need for skilled cytotechnologists. Even in the developed world around 20% of women do not attend cervical screening for a number of reasons including difficulties relating to travel, childcare, work commitments and problems in accessing screening at an appropriate time and place. Others are put off by the potential embarrassment and discomfort of the whole process.

Clearly, clinician testing and using cytology or high-risk HPV testing remain the aspiration but, if this is not possible, then there are now two alternatives:

- *HPV self-testing using a vaginal swab.* In a study of 100,242 Mexican women aged 25–75 and from low-income backgrounds, 11% of women self-tested positive for HPV. Within the United Kingdom, HPV self-testing has been assessed as being a cost-effective use of NHS resources.
- *Urine testing for HPV.* Based on a systematic review it was concluded that the identification of HPV in urine has good accuracy for the detection of cervical HPV and is an acceptable alternative to cervical testing.

# FURTHER READING

## Breast cancer

Kuchenbaecker KB, Hopper JL, Barnes DR et al. Risks of breast, ovarian, and contralateral breast cancer for BRCA1 and BRCA2 mutation carriers. *JAMA* 2017;317:2402–2416.

Miglioretti DL, Zhu W, Kerlikowske K et al. Breast tumor prognostic characteristics and biennial vs annual mammography, age, and menopausal status. *JAMA Oncol* 2015;1:1069–1077.

Myers ER, Moorman P, Gierisch JM et al. Benefits and harms of breast cancer screening: A systematic review. *JAMA* 2015;314:1615–1634.

National Institute for Health and Care Excellence (NICE). *Familial Breast Cancer: Classification, Care and Managing Breast Cancer and Related Risks in People with a Family History of Breast Cancer*. London: NICE, 2017 (update).

Smith RA, Andrews KS, Brooks D et al. Cancer screening in the United States, 2017: A review of current American Cancer Society Guidelines and current issues in cancer screening. *CA Cancer J Clin* 2017;67:100–112.

U.S. Preventive Services Task Force. Medications for risk reduction of primary breast cancer in women: U.S. Preventive Services Task Force recommendation statement. *Ann Intern Med* 2013;159:698–708.

U.S. Preventive Services Task Force. Risk assessment, genetic counseling, and genetic testing for BRCA-related cancer in women: U.S. Preventive Services Task Force recommendation statement. *Ann Intern Med* 2014;160:271–281.

U.S. Preventive Services Task Force. Screening for breast cancer: U.S. Preventive Services Task Force recommendation statement. *Ann Intern Med* 2016;164:279–296.

## Ovarian cancer

Bloomfield HE, Olson A, Greer N et al. Screening pelvic examinations in asymptomatic, average-risk adult women: An evidence report for a clinical practice guideline form the American College of Physicians. *Ann Intern Med* 2014;161:46–53.

Buys SS, Partridge E, Black A et al. Effect of screening on ovarian cancer mortality. The Prostate, Lung, Colorectal and Ovarian (PLCO) cancer screening randomized controlled trial. *JAMA* 2011;305:2295–2303.

Close RJH, Sachs CJ, Dyne PL. Reliability of bimanual pelvic examinations performed in emergency departments. *West J Med* 2001;175:240–244.

Drescher CW, Shah C, Thorpe J et al. Longitudinal screening algorithm that incorporates change over time in CA125 levels identifies ovarian cancer earlier than a single-threshold rule. *J Clin Oncol* 2013;31:387–392.

Goff BA, Mandel LS, Melancon CH, Muntz HG. Frequency of symptoms of ovarian cancer in women presenting to primary care clinics. *JAMA* 2004;291:2705–2712.

Hamilton W, Peters TJ, Bankhead C, Sharp D. Risk of ovarian cancer in women with symptoms in primary care: Population based case-control study. *BMJ* 2009;339:b2998.

Incisive Health. Saving lives, averting costs. *An Analysis of the Financial Implications of Achieving Earlier Diagnosis of Colorectal, Lung and Ovarian Cancer.* London: Cancer Research UK, 2014.

Jacobs IJ, Menon U, Ryan A et al. Ovarian cancer screening and mortality in the UK Collaborative Trial of Ovarian Cancer Screening (UKCTOCS): A randomised controlled trial. *Lancet* 2016;387:945–956.

Lu KH, Skates S, Hernandez MA et al. A two stage ovarian cancer screening strategy using the Risk of Ovarian Cancer Algorithm (ROCA) identifies early stage incident cancers and demonstrates high positive predictive value. *Cancer* 2013;119:3454–3461.

Menon U, Ryan A, Kalsi J et al. Risk algorithm using serial biomarker measurements doubles the number of screen-detected cancers compared with a single-threshold rule in the United Kingdom Collaborative Trial of Ovarian Cancer Screening. *J Clin Oncol* 2015;33:2062–2071.

National Institute for Health and Care Excellence (NICE). *Ovarian Cancer: Recognition and Initial Management.* London: NICE, 2011.

## Cervical cancer

Goodman A. HPV testing as a screen for cervical cancer. *BMJ* 2015;350:31–35.

Huh WK, Ault KA, Chelmow D et al. Use of primary high-risk human papillomavirus testing for cervical cancer screening: Interim clinical guidance. *Gynecol Oncol* 2015;136:178–182.

Kitchener HC, Denton K, Soldan K, Crosbie EJ. Developing role of HPV in cervical cancer prevention. *BMJ* 2013;347:26–31.

Kitchener HC, Gittins M, Rivero-Arias O et al. A cluster randomised trial of strategies to increase cervical screening uptake at first invitation (STRATEGIC). *Health Technol Assess* 2016;20:1–138.

Lazcano-Ponce E, Lőrincz AT, Torres L et al. Specimen self-collection and HPV DNA screening in a pilot study of 100,242 women. *Int J Cancer* 2014;135:109–116.

Pathak N, Dodds J, Zamora J, Khan K. Accuracy of urinary human papillomavirus testing for presence of cervical HPV: Systematic review and meta-analysis. *BMJ* 2014;349:g5264.

Smith RA, Andrews KS, Brooks D et al. Cancer screening in the United States, 2017: A review of current American Cancer Society Guidelines and current issues in cancer screening. *CA Cancer J Clin* 2017;67:100–112.

U.S. Preventive Services Task Force. Screening for cervical cancer: U.S. Preventive Services Task Force recommendation statement. *Ann Intern Med* 2012;156:880–891.

# 14

# Sexual health

## KEY RECOMMENDATIONS

- For those designing a better value health check incorporating a focus on sexual health it is suggested that consideration is given to human immunodeficiency virus (HIV), gonorrhoea/chlamydia and syphilis.
- HIV testing should take into account the local prevalence but, in most settings, universal HIV screening ought to be considered for all adults (up to age 65).
- For those at increased risk of any age, annual HIV testing should be undertaken.
- After carefully considering the local context and existing sexual health services it may be appropriate to undertake case-finding for gonorrhoea/chlamydia and syphilis.

## 14.1 OVERVIEW

In terms of developing a better value health check incorporating a focus on sexual health it is suggested that the key priorities are human immunodeficiency virus (HIV), gonorrhoea/chlamydia and syphilis. Sexual health also links to men's and women's health, and the prevention of hepatitis B and C.

There are some other areas that have been considered for inclusion within this chapter but, at present, I felt that the evidence of benefit in terms of delivering value was insufficient. Key amongst these are routine serological screening for herpes simplex virus in asymptomatic adults.

Intensive behavioural counselling is also recommended for all sexually active adults who are at increased risk for sexually transmitted infections. According to the U.S. Preventive Services Task Force (USPSTF), specific target groups include adults with current sexually transmitted infections or other such infections within the past year, adults who have multiple sexual partners and adults who do not consistently use condoms. Behavioural interventions provide basic information about sexually transmitted infections together with skills training (e.g. condom use) and communication about safe sex.

Table 14.1 Case-finding for chlamydia, gonorrhoea and syphilis

| | Chlamydia and gonorrhoea | Syphilis |
|---|---|---|
| Risk assessment | Age is a risk factor for chlamydial and gonococcal infections, with the highest infection rates occurring in women aged 20–24. Other risk factors include new or multiple sex partners, a sex partner with concurrent partners or a sex partner with a sexually transmitted infection; inconsistent condom use among persons who are not in mutually monogamous relationships; previous or concurrent sexually transmitted infection; and exchanging sex for money or drugs. | Men who have sex with men and persons living with HIV have the highest risk for syphilis infection. Other factors that are also associated with increased prevalence rates include a history of incarceration or commercial sex work, geography, race/ethnicity and being a male younger than 29 years. |
| Approaches to testing | Chlamydial and gonococcal infections are diagnosed by using nucleic acid amplification tests from<br>• Male and female urine<br>• Clinician-collected endocervical, vaginal, and male urethral specimens<br>• Self-collected vaginal specimens<br>The same specimen can be used to test for chlamydia and gonorrhoea. | There are numerous screening tests for syphilis. The most common is a combination of non-treponemal and treponemal antibody tests. |
| Recommendations | • The USPSTF recommends screening for chlamydia and gonorrhoea in sexually active women age 24 years and younger and in older women who are at increased risk for infection.<br>• Canadian guidelines recommend screening for chlamydia in all sexually active males and females younger than 25 years and re-testing at 6 months after treatment in infected patients. | • The USPSTF recommends screening for syphilis infection in persons who are at increased risk for infection.<br>• The Centers for Disease Control and Prevention recommend that individuals living with HIV should be screened at least annually; more frequent screening may be appropriate based on individual risk behaviours and local epidemiology. |

There is also research evidence in support of chlamydia, gonorrhoea and syphilis case-finding (Table 14.1). However, careful consideration needs to be given to whether it is appropriate to offer such tests as part of a general health check in appreciation of the additional requirements to undertake contract tracing, to provide treatments and to provide post-test counselling. The final decision will need to take into account the local circumstances and the existing provision.

## 14.2 HUMAN IMMUNODEFICIENCY VIRUS (HIV)

### 14.2.1 Importance

Human immunodeficiency virus infection and acquired immune deficiency syndrome (HIV/AIDS) is a spectrum of conditions caused by infection with the human immunodeficiency virus (HIV). Following initial infection, a person might not notice any symptoms or may experience a brief period of influenza-like illness followed by a time with no symptoms. As the infection progresses, it interferes more with the immune system, increasing the risk of common infections like tuberculosis, as well as other opportunistic infections, and malignancies.

Approximately 36.7 million people have HIV worldwide, with the number of new infections in 2016 being about 1.8 million. Sub-Saharan Africa is the region most affected. In 2010, an estimated 68% of all HIV cases and 66% of all deaths (1.2 million) occurred in this region. South Africa has the largest population of people with HIV of any country in the world at 5.9 million. South and South-East Asia is the second most affected area with an estimated 4 million cases; 2.4 million of these being in India.

Many HIV-positive people are unaware that they are infected with the virus. For example, in 2001 less than 1% of the sexually active urban population in Africa had been tested. Of the approximately 2.3 million HIV-infected individuals living in Europe, it is estimated that only one in three are aware of their HIV status. In the United States, it has been calculated that 20% of infected Americans do not know they have HIV.

Currently, in Western Europe, as a result of late diagnosis 45%–50% of newly recognised HIV-positive individuals enter care late. This is associated with increased HIV-related morbidity and mortality, poorer response to treatment, greater healthcare costs and enhanced transmission rates.

### 14.2.2 Prevention

Only certain body fluids – blood, semen, rectal fluids, vaginal fluids, and breast milk – from a person who has HIV can transmit HIV. These fluids must come in contact with a mucous membrane or damaged tissue or be directly injected into the bloodstream (from a needle or syringe) for transmission to occur. Mucous membranes are found inside the rectum, vagina, penis and mouth.

HIV can be spread by

- Having anal or vaginal sex with someone who has HIV without using a condom or taking medicines to prevent or treat HIV.
- Sharing needles or syringes, rinse water or other equipment used to prepare drugs for injection with someone who has HIV. HIV can survive in a used needle up to 42 days depending on temperature and other factors.
- From mother to child during pregnancy, birth or breastfeeding.
- A needle injury with an HIV-contaminated needle or other sharp object. This is a risk mainly for healthcare workers.
- Receiving blood transfusions, blood products or organ/tissue transplants that are contaminated with HIV.
- Contact between broken skin, wounds or mucous membranes and HIV-infected blood or blood-contaminated body fluids.

According to the World Health Organization (WHO), the following HIV prevention strategies are recommended:

- Correct and consistent use of condoms with condom-compatible lubricants.
- Oral pre-exposure prophylaxis containing tenofovir disoproxil fumarate should be offered as an additional prevention choice for individuals at substantial risk of HIV infection.
- Post-exposure prophylaxis should be available after possible exposure to HIV.
- Circumcision is suggested for the prevention of heterosexually acquired HIV infection in men.
- All people who inject drugs should have access to sterile injecting equipment through needle and syringe programmes.

To prevent transmission of HIV to healthcare workers in the workplace, such individuals must assume that blood and other body fluids from all patients are potentially infectious. They should:

- Routinely use barriers (such as gloves and goggles) when anticipating contact with blood or body fluids.
- Immediately wash hands and other skin surfaces after contact with blood or body fluids.
- Carefully handle and dispose of sharp instruments during and after use.

## 14.2.3 Earlier recognition

### 14.2.3.1 SCREENING AND CASE-FINDING

Over recent years, the USPSTF has shifted its position to recommend screening for HIV infection for all U.S. adults up to the age of 65 and for older adults at increased risk. This universal recommendation is based on estimates that 20% of individuals in the United States with HIV infection are unaware of their condition.

For the UK population, HIV testing is recommended for individuals at increased risk:

- Those with symptoms or signs that may indicate a recent HIV infection such as sore throat, rash or fever.
- Those with symptoms or signs that might indicate a previous HIV infection such as unexplained weight loss, oral candidiasis, chronic diarrhoea and lymphadenopathy.
- Those reporting a medical history of, for example, lymphoma, cervical cancer or dysplasia, Kaposi sarcoma, tuberculosis, candidiasis, herpes zoster or community-acquired pneumonia. See the following link for the complete list of significant conditions: http://hiveurope.eu/Portals/0/Indicator%20diseases/CHIP_Guidance%20in%20short_UK_updated%20JUN2016_mlj.pdf.
- Leucopenia or thrombocytopenia on blood testing.
- Recent travel from a country or community with a high rate of HIV infection.
- If male, discloses that they have sex with men, or is known to have sex with men, and has not had an HIV test in the previous year.
- Is a trans woman who has sex with men and has not had an HIV test in the previous year.
- Reports sexual contact (either abroad or in the United Kingdom) with someone from a country with a high rate of HIV.
- Discloses high-risk sexual practices such as having multiple sexual partners.
- Is diagnosed with, or requests testing for, a possible sexually transmitted infection including hepatitis B or C.
- Reports a history of injecting drug use.
- Discloses that they are the sexual partner of someone known to be HIV positive, or of someone at high risk of HIV (e.g. female sexual contacts of men who have sex with men).

Linking these two recommendations together in the context of a health check I would suggest the following:

1. HIV testing should take into account the local prevalence but, in most settings, universal HIV screening should be considered for in all adults (up to age 65).
2. For those at increased risk of any age, annual HIV testing should be offered.

#### 14.2.3.2 HIV TESTING

There are three types of HIV diagnostic tests: nucleic acid tests, antigen/antibody tests and antibody tests. Moreover, in relation to delivery there are a growing number of rapid point-of-care HIV tests that allow individuals to be tested for HIV antibodies using fingerprick blood samples or saliva and to receive their results during the same visit.

However, the results from such point-of-care HIV antibody tests cannot be considered definitive. For example, if a test is negative, also called non-reactive, and the individual is potentially in the window period, another blood-based test will be needed to confirm the result 3 months later. The window period (lasting several weeks to months) is the time between a person becoming infected and the time when enough antibodies have been generated to be detectable by testing. In addition, if the rapid test is positive, called a preliminary positive or reactive result, the individual should be encouraged to get confirmatory testing.

A recent review of HIV testing concluded that

- Commercial, over-the-counter HIV tests performed least well overall, not only in terms of detecting acute infection but, also, in returning a false-negative rate of 7%.
- Combination HIV antigen/antibody tests are far more accurate than antibody-based assays, particularly during the acute stage of infection.
- Laboratory-based tests still outperform at-site, point-of-care HIV tests, most especially in cases of recent HIV exposure.

A suggested approach to HIV testing in laboratories is as follows:

- Laboratories should conduct initial testing for HIV with an antigen/antibody combination immunoassay that detects HIV-1 and HIV-2 antibodies and HIV-1 p24 antigen to screen for established infection with HIV-1 or HIV-2 and for acute HIV-1 infection. No further testing is required for specimens that are non-reactive on the initial immunoassay.
- Specimens with a reactive antigen/antibody combination immunoassay result (or repeatedly reactive, if repeat testing is recommended by the manufacturer or required by regulatory authorities) should be tested with an antibody immunoassay that differentiates HIV-1 antibodies from HIV-2 antibodies. Reactive results on the initial antigen/antibody combination immunoassay and the HIV-1/HIV-2 antibody differentiation immunoassay should be interpreted as positive for HIV-1 antibodies, HIV-2 antibodies or HIV antibodies, undifferentiated.
- Specimens that are reactive on the initial antigen/antibody combination immunoassay and non-reactive or indeterminate on the HIV-1/HIV-2 antibody differentiation immunoassay should be tested with an HIV-1 nucleic acid test.
- Laboratories should use this same testing algorithm, beginning with an antigen/antibody combination immunoassay, with serum or plasma specimens submitted for testing after a reactive (preliminary positive) result from any rapid point-of-care HIV test.

# FURTHER READING

## Overview

Public Health Agency of Canada. *Canadian Guidelines on Sexually Transmitted Infections*. Ottawa: Public Health Agency of Canada, 2008.

U.S. Preventive Services Task Force. Behavioral counselling to prevent sexually transmitted infections: U.S. Preventive Services Task Force recommendation statement. *Ann Intern Med* 2014;161:894–901.

U.S. Preventive Services Task Force. Screening for chlamydia and gonorrhea: U.S. Preventive Services Task Force recommendation statement. *Ann Intern Med* 2014;161:902–910.

U.S. Preventive Services Task Force. Screening for syphilis infection in nonpregnant adults and adolescents: U.S. Preventive Services Task Force recommendation statement. *JAMA* 2016;315:2321–2327.

Workowski KA, Bolan GA, Centers for Disease Control and Prevention. Sexually transmitted diseases treatment guidelines, 2015. *MMWR Recomm Rep* 2015;64:1–137.

## HIV

Centers for Disease Control and Prevention (CDC). *Quick Reference Guide – Laboratory Testing for the Diagnosis of HIV Infection: Updated Recommendations*. Atlanta, GA: CDC, 2014.

National Institute for Health and Care Excellence (NICE). *HIV Testing: Increasing Uptake among People Who May Have Undiagnosed HIV*. London: NICE, 2016.

Pilcher CD, Louie B, Facente S et al. Performance of rapid point-of-care and laboratory tests for acute and established HIV infection in San Francisco. *PLoS ONE* 2013;8:e80629. doi:10.1371/journal.pone.0080629

U.S. Preventive Services Task Force. Screening for HIV: U.S. Preventive Services Task Force recommendation statement. *Ann Intern Med* 2013;159:51–60.

World Health Organization (WHO). *Consolidated Guidelines on HIV Prevention, Diagnosis, Treatment and Care for Key Populations*. Geneva: WHO, 2016.

# 15

# Older people's health

## KEY RECOMMENDATIONS

- For those designing a better value health check incorporating a focus on older people's health it is suggested that the following conditions warrant particular consideration: cognitive impairment, sensory disorders and frailty.
- Focus on the prevention of vascular dementia.
- Undertake case-finding for dementia and test for possible underlying causes of cognitive impairment.
- Consider approaches to prevent age-related macular degeneration.
- Routine eye and hearing checks should be undertaken by those with appropriate expertise.
- Undertake comprehensive assessments of older people with a view to identifying those at particular risk of frailty.
- The personalised health plan is an important element in the assessment and management of individuals with frailty.

## 15.1 OVERVIEW

In terms of developing a better value health check incorporating a focus on older people's health it is suggested that the key issues are cognitive impairment, sensory disorders and frailty. These priorities reflect an increasing emphasis on the preservation of functionality and quality of life with these taking precedence over simple extended biologic longevity as individuals get older.

To complement the areas covered in this chapter, it is important to be aware that many countries already have immunisation programmes in place targeted at older people and covering influenza, pneumococcal disease and herpes zoster. However, checking an older person's tetanus status should also be considered as the majority of tetanus cases in the United States occur in under-immunised adults over the age of 60.

Older people's health is also, of course, not simply about the conditions focused on in this chapter but includes many of the diseases, disorders and risk factors addressed elsewhere. More specifically it remains important to consider the earlier recognition of breast cancer, colorectal cancer, ovarian cancer, cervical cancer, type 2 diabetes, atherosclerotic cardiovascular disease, atrial fibrillation, osteoporosis and depression in addition to continuing to address lifestyle issues such as smoking, obesity, exercise and alcohol misuse.

For example, in relation to colorectal cancer, the U.S. Preventive Services Task Force (USPSTF) recommends that the decision to screen for colorectal cancer in adults aged 76–85 years should be an individual one, taking into account the patient's overall health and prior screening history. More specifically:

- Adults in this age group who have never been screened for colorectal cancer are more likely to benefit.
- Screening would be most appropriate among adults who (1) are healthy enough to undergo treatment if colorectal cancer is detected and (2) do not have co-morbid conditions that would significantly limit their life expectancy.

However, currently it is not recommended to undertake routine screening for colorectal cancer in adults aged 86 years and older. In this age group, competing causes of survival preclude a mortality benefit that would outweigh the harms.

Unfortunately, many older adults are not receiving appropriate preventative and screening services. For example, in the United States, according to the Centers for Disease Control and Prevention:

- More than 31% of adults aged 65 and older reported not receiving influenza immunisation in the past year.
- Nearly 17% of women aged 65–74 reported not receiving a mammogram within the past 2 years.
- More than 36% of adults aged 65–74 reported not receiving colorectal cancer screening.
- Thirty-one percent of adults aged 65 and older without diagnosed diabetes reported not receiving a test for high blood sugar or diabetes within the past 3 years.
- Sixty-two percent of black women and 54% of American Indian/Alaska Native women reported never receiving osteoporosis screening compared to 33% of white women aged 65 and older.
- Five percent of adults aged 65 and older reported not receiving blood cholesterol screening within the past 5 years.
- Thirty percent of women aged 65 and older reported not receiving advice to quit smoking during their annual checkup, compared to 24% of older men.

## 15.2 COGNITIVE IMPAIRMENT

### 15.2.1 Importance

Dementia is a decline in cognitive function severe enough to affect social or occupational wellbeing. Other common symptoms include emotional problems, problems with language and a decrease in motivation.

The most common type of dementia is Alzheimer's disease, which makes up 50%–70% of cases. Other types include vascular dementia (25%) and Lewy body dementia (15%).

Globally, dementia afflicts over 35 million people with a projected growth to over 155 million people by 2050. Most of the increase will take place in the developing South-East Asian countries such as China and India as their populations age.

Dementia places a considerable burden on individuals plus their families and also on health and social care provision. Of all chronic diseases, dementia is one of the most important contributors to dependence and disability. In the United States, dementia affects 5.4 million individuals at an estimated annual cost of $157 billion to $215 billion.

### 15.2.2 Prevention

Efforts to prevent vascular dementia in the context of a health check are about both identifying and reducing risk factors for atherosclerotic cardiovascular disease (see Chapter 4) and diabetes (see Chapter 9) including addressing the adverse lifestyle issues of obesity, smoking, alcohol excess and physical inactivity.

Intellectual activities such as reading, learning a new language, playing cards and board games plus playing a musical instrument can postpone the onset and slow the progression of both Alzheimer's and vascular dementia.

According to a recent review, it seems that high homocysteine levels, low educational attainment and decreased physical activity are particularly strong predictors of incident Alzheimer's disease. Moreover, individuals with mild cognitive impairment may benefit from screening for homocysteine levels; treating those with elevated levels using vitamin B supplementation.

### 15.2.3 Earlier recognition

Although the USPSTF does not recommend routine screening for cognitive impairment in older adults, there is some evidence that, once recognised, pharmacological and non-pharmacological interventions can be used to improve the quality of life both for affected individuals and importantly, also, for their carers.

Therefore, in the context of a health check it is suggested that case-finding for dementia should be considered in the following groups, especially if aged over 75 years:

- Individuals at elevated atherosclerotic cardiovascular risk (see Chapter 4)
- Individuals with type 2 diabetes
- Individuals with Parkinson's disease
- Individuals with learning disabilities
- Those with possible early signs and symptoms of dementia such as
    - Forgetfulness
    - Disorientation

- Impaired performance of daily tasks
- Impaired language
- Impaired abstract thinking
- Impaired judgement
- Changes in mood
- Changes in personality

If in doubt, the following question can be useful in identifying those who might have a cognitive impairment: 'Has your memory been poor in the last 12 months and is it affecting your life?' In addition, a close relative or friend might have expressed a concern about an individual's memory.

There are a number of brief instruments that can be used at a health check to test for cognitive impairment. Of these, the General Practitioner Assessment of Cognition (GPCOG) tool is a valid, efficient and well-accepted instrument applicable to the population attending for a health check. It generally takes less than 5 minutes to complete. The sensitivity is 85% and the specificity 86%.

The GPCOG comprises two components: a six-item cognitive assessment of the individual attending the health check and, if appropriate, an informant interview. A GPCOG score of 9 indicates no significant cognitive impairment, whereas a score of 4 or less indicates a probable cognitive impairment requiring expert referral and review. The informant interview is only required if the initial score falls in the intermediate range of 5–8.

It is also always useful to both consider and test for possible underlying causes of cognitive impairment by checking an individual's full blood count, biochemistry (liver, renal and bone), thyroid function, vitamin $B_{12}$/folate, homocysteine level, glucose/HbA1c and urinalysis.

## 15.3 SENSORY DISORDERS

### 15.3.1 Importance

Deteriorating vison and hearing are important issues for older people. There is evidence that various eye diseases are associated with declines in mobility, loss of physical strength, falls, hospitalisations and reduced quality of life.

Age-related macular degeneration (AMD), glaucoma, diabetic retinopathy and cataracts are the most common causes of visual problems in those aged over 50.

Hearing loss can lead to poorer quality of life and social isolation (possibly also linked to depression and cognitive impairment). In the United Kingdom, it is estimated that over half of those more than 60 have some form of hearing loss and this increases to 80% of 80 year olds.

### 15.3.2 Prevention

Smoking, sunlight and poor diet are probable risk factors for both the development of cataracts and AMD. Therefore, it is recommended to stop smoking and to wear sunglasses in strong sunshine. Research has also suggested that some supplements (i.e. zinc, lutein, zeaxanthin, vitamin C, vitamin A and vitamin E) can protect against AMD.

There is little that can be done to prevent age-related hearing loss. It is likely that being exposed to a lot of loud noise over long periods may make hearing loss worse when individuals are older. For example, those working in noisy environments should wear ear protection. It is also advisable to avoid excessive noise during leisure time.

A healthy lifestyle may help to reduce the likelihood of hearing loss later by decreasing the risk of problems such as diabetes, heart disease, high blood pressure and diseases of the blood vessels. These conditions in turn seem to increase the chances of developing hearing loss.

## 15.3.3 Earlier recognition

It has been argued that resolving visual limitations early is beneficial and maintains health-related quality of life. However, based on a comprehensive review of the evidence, the USPSTF were unable to recommend routine screening for glaucoma. But, importantly, their analysis only concerned the evidence applicable to screening offered by clinical individuals not trained as opticians or ophthalmologists.

This has implications for health checks as some continue to include vision and glaucoma screening undertaken by, for example, nurses or physiologists. The USPSTF expressed concerns about the accuracy of such assessments.

In terms of delivering a better value health check, it is recommended that routine eye checks are no longer undertaken in the context of a health check but, those undertaking health checks become more aware of the earlier symptoms of AMD and cataracts with a view to signposting individuals to an optician or an ophthalmologist. Moreover, everyone over the age of 40 should have a regular eye assessment by an optician especially if there is a personal history of diabetes or eye problems (e.g. AMD in one eye) or a family history of AMD or glaucoma.

In the early stages of glaucoma there are often no symptoms. The loss of vision occurs gradually and might only be recognised when at an advanced stage. The initial loss in the field of vision is usually in the shape of an arc a little above or below the centre when looking straight ahead. Eventually, the blank area spreads leading to tunnel vision.

Most importantly, detecting glaucoma is *not* simply about measuring the eye pressures but also about carefully examining both eyes in addition to checking the visual fields.

The most typical symptom for AMD is a gradual loss – or blurring – of central (but not peripheral) vision. Central vision is needed for detailed work and for things like reading and driving.

Other symptoms include the following:

- Visual distortion (for example, straight lines – such as between the tiles in a bathroom – can appear wavy or crooked)

- Blank patch or dark spot in the middle of the vision
- Colours appearing less bright
- Difficulty recognising faces
- Words in a book or newspaper becoming blurred

The first visual symptom of a cataract might be noticing that vision has become a little blurred with reduced ability to see blue colours.

Other symptoms include the following:

- Noticing halos around bright lights
- Becoming easily dazzled by bright lights such as the headlights of an oncoming car

At present, the evidence does not support routine screening for hearing loss (by questioning, whispering or using a hand-held audiometer) in the context of a health check. However, individuals expressing concerns about a possible hearing problem, or experiencing cognitive or depressive symptoms that might be related to a hearing loss, should be passed onto an audiologist for a formal assessment.

It is recommended that routine hearing checks are no longer undertaken by physiologists or nurses in the context of a routine health check.

## 15.4 FRAILTY

### 15.4.1 Importance

Frailty has been defined as a state of increased vulnerability resulting from aging-associated decline in reserve and function across multiple physiologic systems, such that the ability to cope with everyday or acute stressors is compromised.

Frailty is a common clinical syndrome in older adults that carries an increased risk for poor health outcomes including falls, disability, hospitalisation and mortality. Around 10% of people aged over 65 years have frailty, rising to between a quarter and a half of those aged over 85 years.

### 15.4.2 Prevention

There is evidence that both exercise and diet can help to prevent frailty and the effects of frailty. For exercise, the following suggestions are made for older people (if possible):

- Spending 5 hours each week engaged in moderate-intensity activity
- Undertaking muscle strengthening activities on 2 or more days a week that work all major muscle groups (i.e. legs, hips, back, abdomen, chest, shoulders and arms)
- Joining a strength and balance training programme tailored to the individual and monitored by an appropriately trained professional

- Considering taking part in regular tai chi sessions to reduce the risk of falls as this approach places particular emphasis on balance, co-ordination and movement

The evidence for diet is less extensive but a suboptimal protein or total calorie intake and vitamin D insufficiency have all been implicated. There is also emerging evidence that frailty increases in the presence of obesity particularly in the context of other unhealthy behaviours such as inactivity, a poor diet and smoking. In overweight older people, a combination of weight loss and exercise is more effective at improving physical function than either intervention alone.

Vitamin D deficiency is common among older people (see Chapter 6) and can impair muscle strength and, possibly, neuromuscular function. In addition, the use of combined calcium and vitamin D supplementation has been found to reduce fracture rates. The USPSTF recommends vitamin D supplementation to prevent falls in community-dwelling adults aged 65 years or older who are at increased risk for falls.

The personalised health plan (see Chapter 3) is also a very important approach in the assessment of older people in the context of a health check with a view to helping to prevent frailty. More specifically, it has particular value in identifying and addressing issues in relation to

- The appropriate use of medications (considering effectiveness, safety, side effects and interactions)
- The management of ongoing conditions (especially in the context of multimorbidity)

### 15.4.3 Earlier recognition

A number of approaches can be used to identify frail individuals who might benefit from more specific advice in relation to their ongoing health conditions (and medications), diet, exercise and, perhaps, vitamin D supplementation.

1. *Frailty measures*

   In a recent review, the PRISMA-7 questionnaire was found to have particularly good accuracy. This tool consists of seven questions:

   a. Is the individual more than 85 years old?
   b. Is the individual male?
   c. In general, does the individual have health problems that require them to limit their activities?
   d. Does the individual need someone to help them on a regular basis?
   e. In general, does the individual have any health problems that require them to stay at home?
   f. In case of need, can the individual count on someone close to them?
   g. Does the individual regularly use a stick, walker or wheelchair to get about?

   Answering in the affirmative to three of more questions suggests frailty.

2. *Falls history/risk*
   The National Institute for Health and Care Excellence (NICE) recommends that older people should be asked routinely whether they have fallen in the past year in addition to enquiring about the frequency, context and characteristics of any falls. In identifying those at risk of falling, the following questions based on the Falls Risk Assessment Tool (FRAT) can also be helpful:
   a. Is there any history of a fall in the previous 12 months?
   b. Is the individual on four or more medications per day?
   c. Has the individual had a stroke or been diagnosed with Parkinson's disease?
   d. Do they report any problems with balance or unsteadiness?
   e. Are they unable to rise from a chair of knee height without using their arms?

   The presence of three or more of these risk factors confers a specificity of 92% in relation to future falls risk. However, the sensitivity is only 42%, so a negative result needs to be reviewed in relation to the additional information obtained from the assessment of physical performance together with the measurement of grip strength.
3. *Physical performance*
   There are a variety of physical performance measures currently available for assessing functional states in older adults. Many of these could be undertaken in the context of a health check without the requirement for extensive equipment.

   A particularly simple test of performance is to assess gait speed. Individuals are instructed to walk 3 metres at their own pace and the time taken to complete the distance is measured with a stopwatch. Gait speed is also strongly correlated with longevity, overall function and wellbeing.

   The Short Physical Performance Battery is a tool designed to quantify physical performance and decline over time. The test focuses primarily on lower extremity function and includes a 4-metre walk to measure gait speed, one chair stand (followed by five timed chair stands, if the first is successfully completed), and balance stands with the feet held in different positions for 10 seconds each. The test is designed to be easily administered in a variety of contexts or settings, and takes about 10 minutes to complete.

   The Timed Up and Go test is recommended by both the USPSTF and NICE to assess performance. It measures the time that a person takes to rise from a chair, walk 3 metres, turn around, walk back to the chair and sit down. During the test, the person is expected to wear their regular footwear and use any mobility aids that they would normally require.

   Provided that there are no safety concerns (especially with the balance test), direct assessment of physical performance is preferred as it is more accurate than relying on reports by individuals or their relatives or friends.
4. *Grip strength*
   Hand grip strength can be quantified by measuring the amount of static force that the hand can squeeze around a dynamometer. Among healthy men in

late middle age and early older age, hand grip strength has been found to be highly predictive of functional limitations and disability 25 years later. It has been suggested that hand grip is a good marker of overall muscle strength and the ability to tolerate the effects of loss of muscle power with ageing.

As an indicator of resilience, it is interesting to note that a poor grip strength also appears to be related to a variety of other health conditions and outcomes including premature mortality, cardiovascular disease and an increased risk of complications or a prolonged length of stay in a hospital after illness or surgery.

5. *Body composition*

   Age-related sarcopenia refers to the reduction of lean mass (including muscles and bones) that is associated with ageing and is linked with frailty. In the context of a health check, bioelectrical impedance analysis (see Chapter 16) can be helpful in determining the balance between an individual's fat mass and lean mass.

## FURTHER READING

### Overview

Benson WF, Aldrich N. *CDC Focuses on Need for Older Adults to Receive Clinical Preventive Services, Critical Issue Brief.* Centers for Disease Control and Prevention, 2012, http://www.chronicdisease.org/nacdd-initiatives/healthy-aging/meeting-records.

U.S. Preventive Services Task Force. Screening for colorectal cancer: U.S. Preventive Services Task Force recommendation statement. *JAMA* 2016;315:2564–2575.

### Cognitive impairment

Agronin ME. *Alzheimer's Disease and Other Dementias. A Practical Guide.* New York, NY: Routledge, 2014.

Beydoun MA, Beydoun HA, Gamaldo AA et al. Epidemiologic studies of modifiable factors associated with cognition and dementia: Systematic review and *meta-analysis. BMC Public Health* 2014;14:643. doi:10.1186/1471-2458-14-643

Brodaty H, Pond D, Kemp NM et al. The GPCOG: A new screening test for dementia designed for general practice. *J Am Geriatr Soc* 2002;50:530–534.

Robinson L, Tang E, Taylor JP. Dementia: Timely diagnosis and early intervention. *BMJ* 2015;350:h3029.

Smith AD, Refsum H. Dementia prevention by disease-modification through nutrition. *J Prev Alz Dis* 2017;4:138–139.

Tsiachristas A, Smith AD. B-vitamins are potentially a cost-effective population health strategy to tackle dementia: Too good to be true? *Alzheimers Dement* 2016;2:156–161.

U.S. Preventive Services Task Force. Screening for cognitive impairment in older adults: U.S. Preventive Services Task Force recommendation statement. *Ann Intern Med* 2014;160:791–797.

## Sensory disorders

Parke DW, Repka MX, Lum F. The U.S. Preventive Services Task Force recommendation on vision screening in older adults. A narrow view. *JAMA Ophthalmol* 2016;134:485–486.
U.S. Preventive Services Task Force. Screening for glaucoma: U.S. Preventive Services Task Force recommendation statement. *Ann Intern Med* 2013;159:484–489.
U.S. Preventive Services Task Force. Screening for hearing loss in older adults: U.S. Preventive Services Task Force recommendation statement. *Ann Intern Med* 2012;157:655–661.
Wong IYH, Koo SCY, Chan CWN. Prevention of age-related macular degeneration. *Intern Opthal* 2011;31:73–82.

## Frailty

Bohannon RW. Hand-grip dynomometry predicts future outcomes in aging adults. *J Ger Phys Therapy* 2008;31:3–10.
Guralnik JM, Ferrucci L, Pieper CF et al. Lower extremity function and subsequent disability: Consistency across studies, predictive models, and value of gait speed alone compared with the short physical performance battery. *J Gerontol A Biol Sci Med Sci* 2000;55:M221–M231.
Hoogendijk EO, van der Horst HE, Deeg DJ et al. The identification of frail older adults in primary care: Comparing the accuracy of five simple instruments. *Age Ageing* 2013;42:262–265.
Nandy S, Parsons S, Cryer C et al. Development and preliminary examination of the predictive validity of the Falls Risk Assessment Tool (FRAT) for use in primary care. *J Public Health* 2004;26:138–143.
National Institute for Health and Care Excellence (NICE). *Falls in Older People: Assessing Risk and Prevention.* London: NICE, 2013.
Nicholas JA, Hall WJ. Screening and preventive services for older adults. *Mt Sinai J Med* 2011;78:498–508.
Rantanen T, Guralnik JM, Foley D et al. Midlife hand grip strength as a predictor of old age disability. *JAMA* 1999;281:558–560.
Ribeiro SML, Kehayias JJ. Sarcopenia and the analysis of body composition. *Adv Nutr* 2014;5:260–267.
U.S. Preventive Services Task Force. Prevention of falls in community-dwelling older adults: U.S. Preventive Services Task Force recommendation statement. *Ann Intern Med* 2012;157:197–204.
Xue QL. The frailty syndrome: Definition and natural history. *Clin Geriatr Med* 2011;27:1–15.

# 16

# Organisational health

## KEY RECOMMENDATIONS

- For those designing a better value health check incorporating a focus on organisational health it is suggested that particular consideration is given to the following issues: excessive weight, poor diet, physical inactivity, cigarette smoking, alcohol misuse, low back pain and stress.
- Careful baseline assessments of body size and composition, fitness and physical activity, smoking status, alcohol misuse and the extent of any anxiety or depression should be undertaken for all members of an organisation prior to designing a workplace wellness improvement programme.
- To be effective a workplace wellness improvement programme requires organisational commitment together with an integrated and balanced approach.
- Evidence-based interventions should be harnessed in order to facilitate appropriate changes in risk factors and to improve both individual and organisational outcomes.
- Follow-up health checks are suggested as a key mechanism to chart progress.

## 16.1 OVERVIEW

In terms of developing a better value health check incorporating a focus on organisational health, it is suggested that the key priorities are excessive weight, poor diet, physical inactivity, cigarette smoking, alcohol misuse, low back pain and stress. Stress is addressed in Chapter 11, alcohol misuse in Chapter 8 and low back pain is covered within Chapter 6.

Research from various work sites in the United States has indicated that the prevalence of some key risk factors for poor health are as presented in Table 16.1.

Linked to these factors it is also important to appreciate that 37.5% of workers have raised cholesterol, 28.7% hypertension and 8.3% diabetes.

There are associations between all these issues and organisational performance as a consequence of absenteeism and presenteeism. Presenteeism is about being at work but, due to illness or other health conditions, not fully functioning.

Taking Tables 16.1 and 16.2 together, it is important to appreciate that the greatest adverse impacts on productivity are correlated with excessive weight

Table 16.1 Selected risk factors and their prevalence

| Risk factor | Percentage of workers (%) |
|---|---|
| Excessive weight | 63.1 |
| Low intake of fruit and vegetables | 76.6 |
| Physical inactivity | 49.0 |
| Smoking | 20.6 |
| Alcohol misuse | 5.0 |
| High stress | 43.0 |

(6.1%), high stress (3.2%) and inactivity (2.4%). Although smoking (1.6%) and alcohol (0.5%) are important risk factors it is pertinent to note that the magnitude of their effect on productivity is considerably less than obesity.

This chapter focuses on health checks as a mechanism to provide information to organisations on the health of their employees and to identify key risk factors that require consideration. However, in the context of developing such a 'public health plan' (see Chapter 3) this information might be supplemented by other sources of data, for example

- The overall profile of the company in relation to demographics, divisions and working practices (e.g. shift workers)
- Aggregated information derived from employee health records (e.g. common employee health risks and conditions)
- Environmental audit to identify potential physical hazards (air, water, chemical, electrical and mechanical)
- Culture audit to assess employees' perceptions of healthy and unhealthy work site norms
- Employee focus groups to ascertain preferences for work site programmes, policies and incentives
- Surveys of employees' perceived productivity can be used to investigate the possible impact of health risks on absenteeism and presenteeism
- Medical claims data analysis

Table 16.2 Approximate percentage of annual workload loss by health issues

| Health issue | Absenteeism (%) | Presenteeism (%) | Total (%) |
|---|---|---|---|
| Excessive weight | 1.40 | 8.30 | 9.70 |
| Physical inactivity | 0.28 | 4.59 | 4.87 |
| Smoking | 2.84 | 4.78 | 7.62 |
| Alcohol misuse | 5.00 | 4.78 | 9.78 |
| High stress | 3.08 | 4.45 | 7.53 |
| Raised cholesterol | 3.14 | 4.91 | 8.05 |
| Hypertension | 0.37 | 5.70 | 6.07 |
| Diabetes | 4.94 | 18.26 | 23.20 |

Until relatively recently, there was a widely held view that an individual had a disorder such as hypertension or raised cholesterol or they did not. This led to the view that those with, for example, 'normal' blood pressure or 'normal' cholesterol were not at risk of having a stroke or a heart attack. But it has now been recognised that there is a continuous relationship between blood pressure or cholesterol and the risk of atherosclerotic cardiovascular disease with no one being at zero risk.

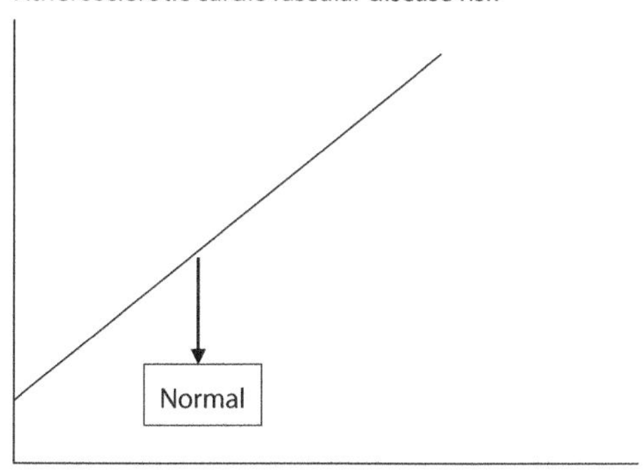


As can been seen from the above figure, a cholesterol result greater than the 'normal' cutoff point generates a high risk. However, for an individual with a result below the 'normal' cutoff point their risk is simply lower. In some ways the public have been sold the story that, for example, having a blood pressure or a cholesterol level below a certain level is safe whereas in reality those developing guidelines have simply decided that the risk is acceptable.

Being aware about the continuum of risk emphasises that a large number of people exposed to a small risk might result in more disease than a small number of people exposed to a high risk. Thus, for those seeking to design health checks for a population – such as a large organisation – the question is 'should the purpose be to identify and intervene in those with the highest risk of developing heart disease (e.g. due to a LDL cholesterol of, for example, 5 mmol/L or greater) or to seek to focus efforts across a much broader swathe of individuals at a much lower level of risk'? The dilemma is that a health check that brings large benefits to an organisation might offer little to each participating individual.

Going for those at highest risk has, in general, been the favoured approach as any advice given or interventions recommended make more sense to the individual and to their doctor. It is certainly a lot more straightforward to suggest to a person who is sedentary and obese that they should eat less and exercise more. However, it is also important to appreciate that eating, smoking, drinking, exercising and other lifestyle characteristics are all substantially shaped and constrained by the norms of a society and the behaviour of the members of an organisation. For example, if a working environment encourages binge drinking then investing in health checks that simply seek to identify the heaviest drinkers or those with liver damage due to fibrosis might be seen as insufficient – or behaviourally inadequate – in improving the overall wellbeing of all the employees.

Therefore, my suggestion is that a balanced approach ought to be considered by those responsible for workplace wellness improvement programmes. High-risk individuals must be identified and supported but, in addition, as everyone will also face a small and potentially avoidable risk (especially due to excessive weight, inactivity and stress) their level of exposure should be reduced too.

A useful study from Sweden examined the high-risk individual approach (i.e. systematic risk factor screening and counselling) nested within the broader framework of a population-based strategy (i.e. dietary, activity, alcohol-related and psychosocial advice carried out by community organisations, sports clubs, media, employers and food retailers together with food labelling). Over a 5-year period, significant changes occurred in both cholesterol and blood pressure levels with an estimated overall 19% reduction in cardiovascular risk.

It is important that those developing workplace wellness programmes do not target too many issues simultaneously. Based on a recent systematic review, it was found that interventions comprising education (e.g. providing information about behaviours associated with health risks) and skills training (e.g. teaching skills that equip participants to engage in less risky behaviours) targeting multiple risk behaviours concurrently are associated with alterations in diet and physical activity. However, changes in smoking were negatively associated with modifications to other behaviours, suggesting it may not be sensible to address smoking cessation at the same time as seeking to facilitate adjustments to dietary intake and activity levels.

There is also some evidence that specific initiatives that integrate injury and illness prevention efforts with work-related safety and health hazard initiatives (referred to as 'Total Worker Health Interventions') might be particularly effective in improving some adverse health behaviours by concentrating the wellbeing focus.

In summary, in order to deliver better value organisational health, there is a requirement for careful baseline assessments to be undertaken of body size and composition, fitness and physical activity, smoking status, alcohol misuse and the extent of any anxiety or depression. Moreover, this information needs to be assembled *prior to* designing a workplace wellness improvement programme and supplemented with other relevant organisational data.

The subsequent programme should then seek to strike an appropriate balance between individuals at elevated risk and the rest of the workforce. In addition, occupational health and safety functions need to become better integrated with health promotion activities across all organisations.

Finally, underpinning everything, is a requirement for all elements of an organisation to be committed to health and wellbeing.

## 16.2 EXCESSIVE WEIGHT

### 16.2.1 Importance

Excessive weight increases the risk of developing a range of conditions including cardiovascular diseases, diabetes, some cancers and disability. Overweight and obese workers are also likely to be absent more frequently and are less productive at work.

Between 2006 and 2008, in the United States it was calculated that normal weight employees cost, on average, $3830 per annum in terms of medical, sickness, disability and compensation claims, whereas morbidly obese employees cost $8067 per year.

A recent review of all available studies found that the cost-effectiveness of workplace weight loss programmes ranged from $1.44 to $4.16 per pound of lost weight.

### 16.2.2 Identification and assessment

*Measurement.* Body mass index (BMI), calculated from accurate measurements of height and weight, is traditionally recommended as the primary screening test for obesity. However, it has some limitations in assessing obesity-related diseases in persons with low muscle and high body fat as well as in individuals with increased body fat and normal BMI. Moreover, athletic adults with a high muscle mass might be wrongly classified as obese. Therefore, it is suggested that the BMI is always supplemented, if possible, with the assessment of body fat by the measurement of waist circumference and the use of bioelectric impedance analysis.

Bioelectric impedance analysis works on the theory that lean mass contains ions in water solution, which are able to conduct electricity better than fat mass. A harmless electrical current is passed through the body via a two- or four-electrode device in either a standing or a lying position. The method is simple, quick and painless but the cost of the device may vary, and the equipment requires controlled conditions to attain accurate and reliable measurements, as body water content, body temperature and time of the day may affect the results.

*Questionnaire.* In collecting information on an individual's dietary practices many instruments are available – some of which are extremely extensive. However, in the context of a health check for organisations I would suggest the following six questions:

- Do you eat foods high in fibre every day (e.g. wholemeal bread, high fibre cereals, wholemeal foods such as brown rice and brown pasta)?
- Do you try to limit your intake of saturated fat (e.g. butter, full-fat milk, cream, cakes and fatty meats)?
- Do you eat five or more portions of fruit and/or vegetables every day?
- Do you eat more poultry than red meat?
- Do you eat fish at least once a week?
- Do you drink eight or more glasses of fluid per day including water and soft drinks?

All of these questions simply require Yes/No responses which makes the aggregation and presentation of the data extremely straightforward.

### 16.2.3 Interventions

There is evidence in support of a number of interventions that employers can undertake to facilitate weight loss. Some examples are as follows:

1. Review policies and working practices
   a. Establish policies that support dietary changes (e.g. healthy vending machines, healthy foods in cafeterias, required nutrition labelling).
   b. Consider a travel expenses policy that encourages walking and cycling.
2. Workplace food provision
   a. Increase the number of healthy choices available and reduce the price of healthy choices relative to unhealthy choices.
   b. Organise vending machine advertising and placement to make healthy options the most attractive.
   c. Provide healthy food at workplace events such as fresh fruits.
   d. Make water available, and promote its consumption. Careful placement of drinking fountains, water coolers, or bottled water in vending machines can make water more readily accessible. Replacing sugary beverages with water makes a significant difference in weight loss.
3. Weight management programmes
   a. Provide free or low-cost self-management programmes for healthy eating and weight loss. Programmes can be in-person or online, in group or individual settings, or provided by dieticians or other healthcare practitioners.
   b. Physical activity is a critical component of any weight loss programme.
4. Information, advice and signposting
   a. Brochures, videos, posters, classes and other written or online information can all be used to address the benefits of healthy eating.
   b. Educational programmes are most effective when dieticians provide tailored nutrition education to participants.
   c. Provide nutrition information on restaurant menus and cafeteria signboards. Promotional messages used in conjunction with calorie labels may also increase their effectiveness, and calorie labels that include a symbol (e.g. a traffic light image, or a 'heart' symbol next to healthy items) can further reduce the calories ordered.
   d. Signpost towards other services (e.g. multicomponent weight management programmes) to assist with weight loss.
5. Self-monitoring
   a. Food diaries and advanced meal planning can help to facilitate weight loss.
   b. Individuals who include mobile technology in a comprehensive lifestyle programme for weight loss are more successful in short-term weight loss compared to those who try to lose weight on their own.

## 16.2.4 Impact

A follow-up health check after a year can be helpful in assessing any impact on employees' weights. This might be supplemented by also collecting data on participation rates and progress toward health targets (e.g. number of educational classes attended by employees, number of healthy items available at cafeterias and snack bars, results from a questionnaire on employees' nutrition knowledge).

# 16.3 PHYSICAL ACTIVITY

## 16.3.1 Importance

There is good evidence for the effectiveness of regular physical activity in the prevention of several chronic diseases (e.g. cardiovascular disease, diabetes, cancer, hypertension, obesity, depression and osteoporosis) in addition to premature death.

Encouraging employees to become more physically active can create a healthier workforce, increase employee productivity and decrease absenteeism. Studies show that physically fit employees are absent less frequently than their inactive counterparts, and employees who get at least 75 minutes of vigorous physical exercise per week miss on average 4.1 fewer days of work per year.

Systematic reviews of the effectiveness of workplace wellness programmes at increasing physical activity for employees have identified significant impacts on exercise levels. These improvements included increased hours of weekend activity and total minutes walked per week; habits that were sustained for at least 4 years.

## 16.3.2 Identification and assessment

*Measurement.* In the context of a health check, a step test might be undertaken to assess levels of fitness. It involves stepping up onto and down from a 12-inch-high step at a specific rate. Individuals are usually requested to step on and off the step in time with a metronome beat – that is, up (right), up (left), down (right), down (left) at a rate of 24 completed steps per minute.

Three items are generally measured: the resting heart rate; the heart rate after exercise and the oxygen level in the blood. A VO2 Max cardiovascular fitness score might also be calculated. Importantly, a fitness assessment can also motivate some people to maintain or to increase their exercise levels over the subsequent 12 months.

However, a step test should *not* be undertaken if any individual has raised blood pressure or answers in the affirmative to any of the following questions:

- Have you ever been diagnosed with any heart condition?
- Do you feel pain in your chest or become very short of breath when you do physical activity (such that you have difficulty speaking)?
- In the past month have you had any chest pain, when you are not doing physical activity, that lasted for more than 30 minutes?
- Do you lose your balance because of dizziness or do you ever lose consciousness?
- Do you have a bone or joint problem (e.g. back, knee or hip) that could be made worse by participating in physical activity?
- Are you currently taking medicines for high blood pressure, or diabetes, or for any heart condition?
- Have you been told you are currently anaemic or have any kidney problems?
- Has any doctor ever told you that you should not do physical activity or are you aware of any reason why you should not do physical activity?

*Questionnaire*. It is very useful to collect some information on an individual's activity levels. Many instruments are available – some of which are extremely extensive – but in the context of a health check for organisations I would suggest the following six questions:

- Does your work involve exercise that causes you to notice increases in your breathing or heart rate?
- In a typical week how many days do you walk or cycle for at least 30 minutes (as a total over the course of a day) to get to and from places?
- In your leisure time do you do any aerobic exercise (such as swimming, cycling, jogging, brisk walking, aerobics or dancing) that causes you to notice increases in your breathing or heart rate?
- In your leisure time do you undertake any strength activity (such as weight training in the gym or using your own body weight)?
- In your leisure time do you undertake any flexibility activities (such as stretching, yoga or tai chi)?
- Aside from sleeping how many hours do you spend sitting or lying down in a typical day?

### 16.3.3 Interventions

There is evidence in support of a number of interventions that employers can undertake to facilitate improvements in activity levels. Some examples are as follows:

1. Review policies and working practices
   a. Consider a travel expenses policy that encourages walking/cycling.
   b. Allow for flexible work schedules or breaks during the day for physical activity.
2. Focus on the buildings
   a. Post prompts at key locations to encourage physical activity. A sign that says, 'Take a Few Steps to Better Health' in a stairwell can encourage stair climbing instead of taking the elevator. 'StairWELL to Better Health' was a low-cost intervention conducted by the Centers for Disease Control and Prevention, and they demonstrated that physical improvements, motivational signs and music increased stairwell use.
   b. Develop safe routes near the work site and encourage employees to walk or jog during lunch and break times.
   c. Set up active work stations, such as standing desks or treadmill desks to help reduce sedentary time.
   d. Provide showers and changing facilities for people who exercise at work.
3. Encourage physical activity
   a. Offer gentle fitness classes that combine yoga, low-impact aerobics and relaxation techniques. These may appeal particularly to those who are new to exercise or have special physical needs or limitations.
   b. Provide selected pieces of exercise equipment in suitable locations for use during breaks and lunchtime.

   c. Where feasible, equip a designated break area with basketball hoops, table-tennis equipment and other recreational equipment.
   d. Offer discounts or subsidies for fitness-club memberships for those who meet minimum guidelines for use and adherence.
   e. Suggest pedometer programmes or Internet-based approaches (e.g. online walking or cycling challenges).
4. Information, advice and signposting
   a. Increase employee awareness of the importance of physical activity by providing or signposting to physical activity education programmes.
   b. Education programmes can also help employees set personalised goals and monitor progress towards achieving them, reinforce behaviour change and provide employees with tools to overcome obstacles.
   c. Other educational opportunities include individual coaching sessions, personalised programmes for behaviour change and group support.

### 16.3.4 Impact

A follow-up health check after a year can be helpful in assessing any impact on employees' fitness levels. This might be supplemented by also collecting data on participation rates and progress toward health targets (e.g. number of minutes of physical activity per week per employee).

## 16.4 SMOKING

### 16.4.1 Importance

Smoking is linked to numerous types of cancer in addition to chronic lung diseases and atherosclerotic cardiovascular diseases. It is also estimated that around 49,000 deaths each year in the United States are due to secondhand (passive) smoke, and non-smokers who are regularly exposed to secondhand smoke face a 60% increased risk of heart disease.

The financial impact of tobacco use on productivity is significant. In the United States, $150.7 billion of lost productivity per year is attributed to smoking, with an additional $5.7 billion per year lost due to premature deaths caused by smoking. Secondhand smoke also causes massive losses, with research estimating $5.6 billion per year in lost productivity due to secondhand smoke. On top of this, employers may face a host of additional problems from employees who smoke. For example, smokers drive up maintenance costs (via litter and tobacco smoke pollution), and increase the risk of accidents and fires. Smokers might also put employers at risk of legal liability if non-smokers are exposed to secondhand smoke.

### 16.4.2 Identification and assessment

In order to ascertain smoking status (i.e. current or former smokers, the type of smoking and the amount smoked) most health checks rely on direct questioning of individuals.

However, estimates based on self-reporting, particularly of socially undesirable behaviours, are subject to bias. The widespread implementation of legislation prohibiting smoking in workplaces and public areas together with prominent health warnings on cigarette packages may reinforce the perception of smoking as socially undesirable, and thereby increased the tendency to downplay or deny smoking.

To validate self-reported smoking status, urine, blood and saliva testing for cotinine can be used. Cotinine is the major metabolite of nicotine and an individual's levels are proportional to the magnitude of their exposure to tobacco smoke. However, when measuring cotinine a number of caveats need to be borne in mind:

- African American smokers generally have higher plasma cotinine levels than Caucasian smokers. Males will also have higher plasma cotinine levels than females. Therefore, cutoff levels need to be individually tailored.
- The half-life of cotinine is around 20 hours but is typically detectable for up to 1 week after stopping smoking.
- The use of nicotine replacement therapies (i.e. gum, lozenge, patch, inhaler and nasal spray) in addition to e-cigarettes will result in a positive test for cotinine.

Compared with estimates based on cotinine concentration, smoking prevalence based on self-reporting is generally lower, although the extent of the difference varies by country. Self-reports are more likely to be inaccurate in low- and middle-income countries, particularly amongst women. For example, the prevalence of self-reported smoking among Iranian men and women aged 19 years and above was 18.7% and 1.3%, respectively, compared to 21.2% and 6.7%, respectively, based on serum cotinine level.

In the context of a health check, it is suggested that the 5 A's framework is applied:

- Asking every individual about smoking
- Advising all smokers to quit
- Assessing the willingness of all smokers to make an attempt to quit
- Assisting smokers with their attempt to quit
- Arranging follow-up

### 16.4.3 Interventions

There is evidence in support of a variety of interventions that employers can undertake to assist with smoking cessation. Some examples are as follows:

1. Review policies and working practices
   a. Create a rule banning smoking on organisation property together with a tobacco use policy.
   b. Stop any sales of tobacco products on organisation property in addition to curtailing smoking breaks for staff.

2. Focus on the buildings
    a. Eliminate ashtrays and any previously designated smoking areas.
    b. Post signs (e.g. 'No Smoking') with information about the tobacco use policy.
3. Facilitate smoking cessation
    a. Offer brief behavioural interventions (e.g. individual, group or telephone counselling).
    b. Encourage individuals to seek pharmacotherapy (e.g. nicotine replacement therapy, varenicline) and address any barriers – for example, by funding the costs of such medications.
    c. Permit staff to attend smoking cessation services during working hours without loss of pay.
4. Information, advice and signposting
    a. Provide self-help materials in written and electronic formats.
    b. Signpost smokers to cessation telephone counselling and quit lines.
    c. Encourage tobacco users to sign-up for tobacco cessation text messaging programmes. There is also evidence that phone apps using text messaging to help quit smoking can almost double the chances of success.

### 16.4.4 Impact

A follow-up health check after a year can be helpful in assessing any impact on employees' smoking status levels. This might be supplemented by also collecting data on participation rates in any workplace smoking cessation support programmes.

## FURTHER READING

### Overview

Chenoweth D. *Promoting Employee Well-Being. Wellness Strategies to Improve Health, Performance and the Bottom Line*. Alexandria, VA: SHRM Foundation, 2011.

Feltner C, Peterson K, Weber RP et al. The effectiveness of total worker health interventions: A systematic review for a National Institutes of Health pathways to prevention workshop. *Ann Intern Med* 2016;165:262–269.

Institute for Health and Productivity Studies, Johns Hopkins Bloomberg School of Public Health. *From Evidence to Practice: Workplace Wellness that Works*. Baltimore, MD: Johns Hopkins, 2015.

Meader N, King K, Wright K et al. Multiple risk behavior interventions: Meta-analyses of RCTs. *Am J Prev Med* 2017;53:19–30.

Rose G. *The Strategy of Preventive Medicine*. Oxford: Oxford University Press, 1992.

Weinehall L, Westman G, Hellsten G et al. Shifting the distribution of risk: Results of a community intervention in a Swedish programme for the prevention of cardiovascular disease. *J Epidemiol Community Health* 1999;53:243–250.

## Excessive weight

Burke LE, Ma J, Azar KMJ et al. Current science on consumer use of mobile health for cardiovascular disease prevention. *Circulation* 2015;132:1157–1213.

Gates DM, Succop P, Brehm BJ, Gillespie GL, Sommers BD. Obesity and presenteeism: The impact of body mass index on workplace productivity. *J Occup Environ Med* 2008;50:39–45.

Mialich MS, Sicchieri JMF, Junior AAJ. Analysis of body composition: A critical review of the use of bioelectrical impedance analysis. *Int J Clin Nut* 2014;2:1–10.

National Institute for Health and Care Excellence (NICE). *Identification, Assessment, and Management of Overweight and Obesity in Children, Young People and Adults*. London: NICE, 2014.

U.S. Preventive Services Task Force. Screening for and management of obesity in adults: U.S. Preventive Services Task Force recommendation statement. *Ann Intern Med* 2012;157:373–378.

Van Nuys K, Globe D, Ng-Mak D et al. The association between employee obesity and employer costs: Evidence from a panel of U.S. employers. *Am J Health Promot* 2014;28:277–285.

## Physical activity

Centers for Disease Control and Prevention. StairWELL to Better Health. Healthier Worksite Initiative. www.cdc.gov/nccdphp/dnpao/hwi/toolkits/stairwell/index.htm

Institute for Health and Productivity Studies, Johns Hopkins Bloomberg School of Public Health. *From Evidence to Practice: Workplace Wellness that Works*. Baltimore, MD: Johns Hopkins, 2015.

National Institute for Health and Care Excellence (NICE). *Physical Activity in the Workplace*. London: NICE, 2008.

## Smoking

National Institute for Health and Care Excellence (NICE). *Smoking: Workplace Interventions*. London: NICE, 2007.

Sarraf-Zadegan N, Boshtam M, Shahrokhi S et al. Tobacco use among Iranian men women and adolescents. *Eur J Public Health* 2004;14:76–78.

U.S. Preventive Services Task Force. Behavioral and pharmacotherapy interventions for tobacco smoking cessation in adults, including pregnant women: U.S. Preventive Services Task Force recommendation statement. *Ann Intern Med* 2015;163:622–634.

Wong SL, Shields M, Leatherdale S et al. Assessment of validity of self-reported smoking status. *Health Rep* 2012;23:47–53.

# 17

# Conclusion

Within this book I have sought to set out a new approach to health checks based on value. I have outlined six architectural features for a better value health check in addition to suggesting some key operational issues that ought to be addressed before, during and after a health check.

Building on a careful assessment of a wealth of research evidence and guidance, I have also highlighted some conditions that might be included in a health check focused on adults and appropriate for particular population groups. In making these recommendations, I have considered how best to improve health outcomes while, at the same time, also keeping an eye on the overall costs that might fall on health services, individuals, families and organisations. However, these chapters are offered up as a basis for an informed discussion with those undergoing, purchasing or procuring health checks, as opposed to a proscriptive list.

One further issue that needs to be addressed is the obvious tension at the interface between those delivering health checks and those with longer-term responsibilities for an individual's continuing healthcare. Within the National Health Service (NHS), my hope is that an emphasis on value will engender an improved dialogue between NHS GPs, such as myself, and those with an interest in health checks.

Ideally, an individual attending a health check ought to be able to request information from their regular physician detailing their past medical history, risk profile and recent investigations. Inevitably, in many circumstances, it will then be discovered that some of the core tests will already have been undertaken, saving costs by avoiding unnecessary duplication and, possibly, also unwarranted anxiety. Moreover, it might be that a health check can then build on this information by

- Providing better access to high-value tests such as FIT or CA-125
- Improving accessibility and acceptability; for example, self-testing for human papillomavirus
- Enhancing precision in relation to, for example, cardiovascular risk and liver fibrosis assessments
- Identifying significant changes in any test results or measurements over time
- Facilitating access to specialist test interpretation services, for example, electrocardiograms

- Ensuring that any new components introduced in a health check, such as genetic testing, are firmly based on value
- Communicating back to the individual's regular physician with more helpful information and suggestions

As discussed in Chapter 3, the personalised health plan is about allowing individuals sufficient time to have a conversation with an experienced doctor following a health check in order to enhance the value of any testing. In the context of a time-pressured healthcare service – such as the UK NHS – a health check might therefore provide people with an opportunity – and the implied permission – to raise other health-related concerns (especially those of a sensitive or embarrassing nature). For the clinician delivering a health check, they can also inform individuals about health risks, emerging health information and the appropriate utilisation of healthcare.

# Appendix: Quality criteria

## A.1 WILSON AND JUNGNER CLASSIC SCREENING CRITERIA (1)

1. The condition sought should be an important health problem.
2. There should be an accepted treatment for patients with recognised disease.
3. Facilities for diagnosis and treatment should be available.
4. There should be a recognisable latent or early symptomatic stage.
5. There should be a suitable test or examination.
6. The test should be acceptable to the population.
7. The natural history of the condition, including development from latent to declared disease, should be adequately understood.
8. There should be an agreed policy on whom to treat as patients.
9. The cost of case-finding (including diagnosis and treatment of patients diagnosed) should be economically balanced in relation to possible expenditure on medical care as a whole.
10. Case-finding should be a continuing process and not a 'once and for all' project.

## A.2 SUGGESTED MODIFICATIONS TO WILSON AND JUNGNER CRITERIA (2)

1. The screening programme should respond to a recognised need.
2. The objectives of screening should be defined at the outset.
3. There should be a defined target population.
4. There should be scientific evidence of screening programme effectiveness.
5. The programme should integrate education, testing, clinical services and programme management.
6. There should be quality assurance, with mechanisms to minimize potential risks of screening.
7. The programme should ensure informed choice, confidentiality and respect for autonomy.
8. The programme should promote equity and access to screening for the entire target population.

9. Programme evaluation should be planned from the outset.
10. The overall benefits of screening should outweigh the harm.

## A.3 CRITERIA FOR APPRAISING THE VIABILITY, EFFECTIVENESS AND APPROPRIATENESS OF A SCREENING PROGRAMME (3)

1. The condition should be an important health problem as judged by its frequency and severity. The epidemiology, incidence, prevalence and natural history of the condition should be understood, including development from latent to declared disease, and there should be robust evidence about the association between the risk or disease marker and serious or treatable disease.
2. All the cost-effective primary prevention interventions should have been implemented as far as practicable.
3. If the carriers of a mutation are identified as a result of screening the natural history of people with this status should be understood, including the psychological implications.
4. There should be a simple, safe, precise and validated screening test.
5. The distribution of test values in the target population should be known and a suitable cutoff level defined and agreed.
6. The test, from sample collection to delivery of results, should be acceptable to the target population.
7. There should be an agreed policy on the further diagnostic investigation of individuals with a positive test result and on the choices available to those individuals.
8. If the test is for a particular mutation or set of genetic variants the method for their selection and the means through which these will be kept under review in the programme should be clearly set out.
9. There should be an effective intervention for patients identified through screening, with evidence that intervention at a pre-symptomatic phase leads to better outcomes for the screened individual compared with usual care. Evidence relating to wider benefits of screening, for example, those relating to family members, should be taken into account where available. However, where there is no prospect of benefit for the individual screened then the screening programme should not be further considered.
10. There should be agreed evidence-based policies covering which individuals should be offered interventions and the appropriate intervention to be offered.
11. There should be evidence from high-quality randomised controlled trials that the screening programme is effective in reducing mortality or morbidity. Where screening is aimed solely at providing information to allow the person being screened to make an 'informed choice' (such as Down's syndrome or cystic fibrosis carrier screening), there must be evidence from high-quality trials that the test accurately measures risk. The information that is provided about the test and its outcome must be of value and readily understood by the individual being screened.

12. There should be evidence that the complete screening programme (test, diagnostic procedures, treatment and intervention) is clinically, socially and ethically acceptable to health professionals and the public.
13. The benefit gained by individuals from the screening programme should outweigh any harms, for example, from overdiagnosis, overtreatment, false positives, false reassurance, uncertain findings and complications.
14. The opportunity cost of the screening programme (including testing, diagnosis and treatment, administration, training and quality assurance) should be economically balanced in relation to expenditure on medical care as a whole (value for money). Assessment against this criterion should have regard to evidence from cost-benefit or cost-effectiveness analyses and have regard to the effective use of available resources.
15. Clinical management of the condition and patient outcomes should be optimised in all healthcare providers prior to participation in a screening programme.
16. All other options for managing the condition should have been considered (such as improving treatment or providing other services), to ensure that no more cost-effective intervention could be introduced or current interventions increased within the resources available.
17. There should be a plan for managing and monitoring the screening programme and an agreed set of quality assurance standards.
18. Adequate staffing and facilities for testing, diagnosis, treatment and programme management should be available prior to commencement of the screening programme.
19. Evidence-based information, explaining the purpose and potential consequences of screening, investigation and preventative intervention or treatment, should be made available to potential participants to assist them in making an informed choice.
20. Public pressure for widening the eligibility criteria for reducing the screening interval, and for increasing the sensitivity of the testing process, should be anticipated. Decisions about these parameters should be scientifically justifiable to the public.

## A.4 EUROPEAN CONSENSUS AGREEMENT (4)

1. The provider shall provide information that is understandable, timely, verifiable, accurate, complete, truthful and not misleading.
2. The provider shall provide information on the aim, benefits and harms and potential adverse consequences of the health check, the prevalence and incidence of the condition or risk factor searched for, the target population for the health check, the potential positive and negative results and options, costs and consequences of follow-up of the health check offered.
3. The provider shall provide information on any (clusters of) parallel findings that might occur as a (direct or indirect) result of the health check, including their benefits and harms, prevalence and incidence.

4. The information should enable the client to ascertain the presence or absence of balance between benefits and harms of the health check for target or age group and make an informed choice about the personal usefulness of the health check.
5. The provider shall inform the client on what will happen with the residual material from the test and get informed consent if this material and data are used for other purposes than the test only.
6. The provider shall explain the complaints procedure to the client, including available insurance coverage.
7. The provider shall ensure that the client has given explicit informed consent before performing a health check.
8. The provider shall specify for what findings the client gives consent and will respect the right not to know (clusters of) incidental or parallel findings that might occur as a (direct or indirect) result of the health check.
9. The provider shall provide sufficient time and opportunity to the client to reconsider performing the health check, proportional to the condition the health check aims for (either directly or indirectly via risk factor).
10. The provider shall specify what is addressed by the health check, including the following:
    a. Which condition is it aimed for (either directly or indirectly)?
    b. What is the natural course and seriousness of the condition?
    c. Which are the known risk factors for acquiring the condition?
    d. What are the symptoms at different stages of the condition?
    e. What treatment or follow-up is available for the condition or risk factor?
    f. How can or cannot the health check and follow-up alter the natural course of the condition or risk factor?
11. The provider shall define the purpose of the health check.
12. The provider shall define the inclusion and exclusion criteria of the target population for the health check.
13. The provider shall provide a personalised risk assessment and ascertain whether the client meets the inclusion criteria and does not meet the exclusion criteria of the target population.
14. The provider shall provide sufficient rationale and documentation in case the use of the test deviates from the standard use or the intended population.
15. The provider shall specify
    a. The test and test procedure
    b. The purpose (analytic assessment and clinical purpose)
    c. Available alternatives to the test
    d. The burden and harms of the test and test procedure
    e. The analytic sensitivity, specificity and reliability
16. When specifying alternatives, the alternative of not doing the health check should be included.
17. The provider shall define and implement the clinical practice guidelines and protocols to carry out the tests.
18. The provider shall analyse the test results in accordance with available and established protocols and motivate and document when and why established

protocols are not used. The provider shall explain and document possible benefits and harms of any deviations from established protocols.

19. The provider shall specify
    a. The cutoff value that defines positive and negative test results
    b. The clinical sensitivity and specificity
    c. The positive and negative predictive value
    d. The positivity rate
20. The provider shall specify the test results, including
    a. The interpretation of the result
    b. The associated uncertainties of the test and followed protocols
    c. Any parallel findings, if consented beforehand
21. The provider shall provide a written report of results, interpretation and uncertainties and possibilities for follow-up.
22. The provider shall advise the client on strategies the client can follow to reduce any further risk of acquiring a condition or its negative consequences.
23. The provider shall follow established protocols and professional standards used in the healthcare system for follow-up.
24. The provider shall motivate and document when recommendations do not follow established protocols and professional standards. Recommendations shall be safe and realistic. The provider shall explain and document benefits, harms and costs of these recommendations.
25. The provider shall establish, implement, maintain and continually improve management systems, according to recognized national/European or international standards, for
    a. Quality management
    b. Client/patient safety management
    c. Information security management

## REFERENCES


1. Wilson JMG, Jungner G. *Principles and Practice of Screening for Disease.* Geneva: World Health Organization, 1968.
2. Andermann A, Blancquaert I, Beauchamp S et al. Revisiting Wilson and Jungner in the genomic age: A review of screening criteria over the past 40 years. *Bull World Health Organ* 2008;86:317–319.
3. Criteria for appraising the viability, effectiveness and appropriateness of a screening programme. October 2015. https://www.gov.uk/government/publications/evidence-review-criteria-national-screening-programmes/criteria-for-appraising-the-viability-effectiveness-and-appropriateness-of-a-screening-programme
4. Bijlsma M, Rendering A, Chin-On N et al. Quality criteria for health checks: Development of a European consensus agreement. *Prev Med* 2014;67:238–241.

# Glossary

**Case-finding** This seeks to target individuals or groups for testing that are considered to be at increased risk for a particular disease or disorder by virtue of, for example, age, gender, personal medical history, family medical history, lifestyle factors or symptoms.

**Diagnosis** The collection and use of clinical data in the context of a known abnormality (e.g. symptom, sign or test finding) with the intention of

- Detecting or excluding disorders by increasing the certainty as to their presence or absence, *and*
- Contributing to the decision-making process with regard to further diagnostic or therapeutic management, *and*
- Impacting on patient and health service outcomes

**Disease** A pathophysiological response to external or internal factors.

**Disorder** A disturbance or derangement that affects the function of mind or body, such as an anxiety disorder.

**Iatrotropic symptoms** These are symptoms that lead an individual to seek advice from a doctor. They need to be distinguished from the non-iatrotropic symptoms that are only disclosed during the course of a clinical interview.

**Lead-time bias** This is the potential overestimation of survival time due to the backward shift in the starting point for measuring survival that arises when diseases such as cancer are detected early (i.e. the interval between the detection of a disease by screening and its diagnosis by traditional criteria such as symptoms). But if the earlier diagnosis has no impact on outcomes then all that will have been achieved is giving some individuals added months of anxiety rather than added months of life.

**Likelihood ratio** The likelihood that a given result in relation to the clinical data would be expected in an individual with the disease or disorder compared to the likelihood that the same result would be expected in an individual without the disease or disorder. Likelihood ratios indicate how many times more (or less) likely a result is in an individual with the disease or disorder compared to an individual free of the disease or disorder.

**Positive predictive value** The probability that the disease or disorder is present if the clinical data result is positive [present] (the negative predictive value is the probability that the disease or disorder is absent if the clinical data result is negative [absent]).

**Receiver operator characteristic (ROC) curve** A graphic representation of the relationship between the true-positive rate of clinical data and the false-positive rate of the same clinical data as the criterion (cutoff point) of a positive result is changed.

**Reliability/reproducibility** The extent to which repeated measurements of a stable phenomenon produce similar results.

**Screening** The presumptive identification of unrecognised disease or disorders in asymptomatic people by the application of tests, examinations or other procedures that can be applied rapidly.

**Sensitivity** The probability of a positive result in relation to the clinical data if the disease or disorder is present (the 'true-positive' rate).

**Specificity** The probability of a negative result in relation to the clinical data if the disease or disorder is absent (the 'true-negative' rate)

**Utility** The ability of tests, examinations or other procedures to bring about improvements in outcomes relative to the current best alternative.

**Value** The health outcomes achieved relative to the costs of care. Therefore, value increases when better outcomes are achieved at comparable (or lower) cost, or when equivalent outcomes are achieved at lower cost.

# Index

## B

## I

## P



## Q



## R

## S

## T



## U



## V

## W